# KENNETH COPELAND

# THE BLESSING OF THE LORD

## MAKES RICH AND HE ADDS NO SORROW WITH IT

### PROVERBS 10:22

KENNETH
COPELAND
PUBLICATIONS

**THE BLESSING of The LORD Makes Rich and He Adds No Sorrow With It**
**Proverbs 10:22**

ISBN-13 978-1-60463-114-2                                    30-0072

16 15 14 13 12 11                                             8 7 6 5 4 3

© 2011 Kenneth Copeland

Kenneth Copeland Publications
Fort Worth, TX  76192-0001

For more information about Kenneth Copeland Ministries, call 800-600-7395 or visit www.kcm.org.

# Table of Contents

# Preface

When The LORD first revealed to me the magnitude of THE BLESSING, He instructed me to mark my thinking by writing it in capital letters whenever I referred to it in print. I am following that instruction throughout this book. I believe it will have the effect on you that it has had on me, and will help renew your mind to the full power and scope of THE BLESSING.

# Prologue

Someone asked me, "Why did you title this book, *THE BLESSING of The LORD Makes Rich"?*

Well, the whole book is about THE BLESSING that began in Genesis 1-2. God's last work of Creation was to bless man. *Genesis 1:1 says,* "In the beginning God...."

You can't get any closer to the beginning than that.

THE BLESSING is the very creative force of God. It created all we see. We've lost the power of the word *blessing,* which means "to empower." It's God's empowerment, His power that established the universe. He put the same creative power and anointing on Adam and his wife—mankind—who were created in His image, and told them to replenish the earth, be fruitful and dominate it in love.

God rested the seventh day after He finished His work of Creation. His last work was not the creation of man—it was THE BLESSING of man. Then, He sat down. After man sinned, however, God had to go back to work, and that's what this book is about: God's restoration of THE BLESSING on mankind, where it belonged, through His blood covenant with Abraham, Isaac and Jacob, passing it down the line, until Jesus was born out of that covenant.

Even when sin erupted and the earth was destroyed in the Flood, God continued THE BLESSING through covenant with Noah: "And God BLESSED Noah and his sons" (Genesis 9:1). God started it all again. How did He do it? The first thing He *said* was, "Be fruitful and multiply," which is exactly what He said to Adam.

Centuries later, when Jesus was crucified and made a curse for us (Galatians 3:13), God made the way for THE BLESSING of

Abraham to come, not only on the natural descendants of Abraham, but also on the gentiles. Because of Jesus' redemptive work on the cross, *we* also can walk in THE BLESSING. It is now back on the sons of Noah—Ham, Japheth and Shem. Ham and Japheth followed Adam's lead, which resulted in the creation of the Babylonian system—men trying to meet their own needs without THE BLESSING of God. But, Abraham came out of Shem, and Jesus out of Abraham. Now, through Christ Jesus, we who were once known as *gentiles*—which means "outside the covenant of God"—are grafted in (Romans 11:17). He has, once again, provided for us a Source!

If you want to see THE BLESSING at work, look at Job. Take a look at what had Satan so upset. He said to God: "Does he [Job] serve You for nothing? You have BLESSED him and all that he has, and You've built a wall around him. And look how rich he is!" (Job 1:9-10, paraphrase, *King James Version, New Living Translation*)

Well, doesn't Proverbs 10:22 say, "THE BLESSING of The LORD, it maketh rich, and he addeth no sorrow with it"? The word *sorrow* is translated "toil." THE BLESSING cancels out toiling for a living. You don't have to toil in exchange for THE BLESSING of God. He didn't put a price on it. Whether you're working for minimum wage or God has called you to manage a bank, you're a citizen of the kingdom of God, and the Bible, the constitution of His kingdom, says THE BLESSING will work in your behalf.

Notice that the important part of Proverbs 10:22 is, "THE BLESSING of The LORD, *it* makes...." The world tries to meet its own needs without THE BLESSING. They say, "We've got to make a living," "I make deals," "We make appointments." But God's constitution, The WORD of God, says, *"THE BLESSING makes...."*

When we seek and live in THE BLESSING by faith in God's WORD, then *it* makes all these things to be added to us. If God assigns you to be a janitor in a church, for example, or an apostle, or a car dealer, or whatever it is, He needs you there.

And every workman is worthy of his hire (Luke 10:7)—but you're not limited to that hire, because of THE BLESSING. The employer may be a channel God uses, but he's not your source. Only God, through THE BLESSING of Abraham that came on us through Christ Jesus, is our Source.

When you look to that Source, you become a joint-owner of the kingdom of God. When God says, "I want you to go over there," don't expect those people to pay you anything. God's going to pay you. Do you remember what He told His disciples? "Don't bring any money. Don't bring any clothes." He wasn't telling them to be poor. He was telling them, "Quit bringing your stuff. You're working for Me. I'll take care of you."

This is a timely message to a hurting world. THE BLESSING is the answer.

I want to share something The LORD said to me in October 2008. All this economy mess was just at the beginning of its crash. The Babylonian system has been attacking, particularly, the United States for the last 110-115 years, although it attacked the whole world within that time frame in some respects, erupting into the Bolshevik Revolution in Eastern Europe in 1917. Though the Babylonian system has been operating since the tower of Babel, this was the time it began to be called "socialism," "communism," "Nazism," and all the "isms" that government, attempting to meet man's needs without God, were coined. Those systems have always failed because only God gives increase. But men continually want to create systems with rules to keep God out because they want to be in control. Their lord, the devil, is the one who's behind their attempts. He's after that BLESSING any way he can get it. Jesus said of him, "The thief cometh not, but for to steal, and to kill, and to destroy" (John 10:10).

The WORD of God is the *source* of THE BLESSING because The WORD is the source of faith (Romans 10:17). And, "They which be of *faith* are blessed with faithful Abraham" (Galatians 3:9). It is still the connection for THE BLESSING in our lives today, and brings into manifestation from the spiritual world, material goods, healing—whatever needs to be changed in the natural world, and it destroys the curse. The anointing is part of THE BLESSING, and the power of the anointing is what strips out the curse. It removes burdens and destroys yokes (Isaiah 10:27).

The LORD said to me that day in October 2008:

> Don't pay attention to or make any plans based on what the media says or what [politicians] say. Stand on My WORD in John 16. Pay attention to Me. I [the Holy Spirit] *will* obey verses 13-15. I will show you things to come. I will lead you through troubled times. I already have THE plan for you, and it's very good. Follow it. It will not only get you through, it will place you in a very high place—a rich place—a strong place of victory.

See what God is saying? We're in this world but we're not of it. We're citizens of the kingdom of God. Jesus said if you will seek this kingdom first, inquiring of God and His kingdom about every word, deed and plan, all the things you need will be added to you. They come out of the Kingdom, not the government, not your job.

God has a plan. He'll place you, and when you obey and follow Him, you don't need to pay attention to what it looks like. Just go on and do what He said to do because He has a plan, and your provision is part of it. Don't pay any attention to what the world has or doesn't have for you. Let God take care of that.

The LORD said:

> You will have to discipline yourself and be diligent to listen to Me. *All* the other voices will have a plan....

My goodness! I've never heard so many political plans in all my life, particularly during elections, when all the politicians have their plans. And almost all of it has a cap that limits its success because the Babylonian system is limited, and no one has the guts to say what God has already said in *His* plan.

So listen to this:

[They all have] a word, an idea for your future and security. Don't listen to Babylon's system. It has fallen apart.

Notice that America isn't falling apart. The Babylonian system we've allowed to come in and bungle things up for the past hundred-plus years is falling apart.

My system is stronger than ever. My kingdom is flourishing, and THE BLESSING is the place to be.

That's what this book is about—to teach you how to get into that place of THE BLESSING. How do you get there from where you are now? How do you get out of that dark kingdom and over into the kingdom of God? You were born into it! Colossians 1:13 says very plainly that He has *already* delivered you from the authority of darkness—that's the Babylonian system—and translated you into the kingdom of His dear Son. So you don't need to be living as a natural-born citizen of God's kingdom and trying to live by the rules of the kingdom of darkness. Those rules produce fear, and fear is a serious, damaging, polluting agent to faith, which is the power of THE BLESSING kingdom. THE BLESSING is the place to be!

Keep your eyes on My WORD. Listen to it. It will guide you and I will perform it. Love Me. Love My people as I have loved you. Walk in it. Love *never* fails, and neither does My plan.

This word has changed Gloria's and my life personally. We've been walking this out and learning about THE BLESSING since I was a student at Oral Roberts University in Tulsa, Oklahoma, many years ago. While there, I heard Kenneth E. Hagin say we've been redeemed from the curse, and THE BLESSING of Abraham is ours. At that time, "blessing" didn't mean much more to me except something one said after a sneeze.

So when Kenneth E. Hagin said that, I thought, *Well, it would probably be good to find out what THE BLESSING of Abraham is.* So, I began reading how God blessed Abraham, saying, "I will make of thee a great nation, and I will bless thee, and make thy name great; and thou shalt be a blessing: And I will bless them that bless thee, and curse him that curseth thee: and in thee shall all families of the earth be BLESSED…. And Abram was very rich…" (Genesis 12:2-3, 13:2).

I was stunned. I already knew that God wanted us to prosper, but I never heard of *very* rich "…in cattle, silver, and in gold." I kept going back and seeing, "That THE BLESSING of Abraham might come on the Gentiles…" (Galatians 3:14). And it was talking about the seed of Abraham.

I continued reading in Galatians 3:29, which says, "And if ye be Christ's, then are ye Abraham's seed, and heirs according to the promise." I began digging into that promise and seeing it was all the way through the New Testament!

As I studied the promise year after year, it kept growing bigger inside me. I began to see that THE BLESSING was at the very beginning, too, when the BLESSED One BLESSED Adam.

I found that THE BLESSING spans the whole Bible!

Much of why the Spirit of God had me write this book, and why I had such a desire to get this information on paper and into people's hands, is found in Isaiah 51:1. But it needs to be understood from Galatians 3:7-9:

> Know ye therefore that they which are of faith, the same are the children of Abraham. And the scripture, foreseeing that God would justify the heathen through faith, preached before the gospel unto Abraham, saying, In thee shall all nations be BLESSED. So then they which be of faith are BLESSED with faithful Abraham.

THE BLESSING, then, is the gospel—the good news! Now read verses 13-14:

> Christ hath redeemed us from the curse of the law, being made a curse for us: for it is written, Cursed is every one

that hangeth on a tree: that THE BLESSING of Abraham might come on the Gentiles through Jesus Christ; that we might receive the promise of the Spirit through faith."

Look at verses 26, 29:

For ye are all the children of God by faith in Christ Jesus.... And if ye be Christ's, then are ye Abraham's seed, and heirs according to the promise.

Now, come back over to Isaiah 51:1-2:

Hearken to me, ye that follow after righteousness, ye that seek The LORD: look unto the rock whence ye are hewn, and to the hole of the pit whence ye are digged. Look unto Abraham your father, and unto Sarah that bare you [Or, Look unto Abraham your father, and unto Jesus who gave you the new birth.]: for I called him alone, and blessed him, and increased him.

We're the seed of that BLESSING! The promise is on us. Verse 3 goes on to say, "For The LORD shall comfort Zion: he will comfort all her waste places; and he will make her wilderness like Eden, and her desert like the garden of The LORD; joy and gladness shall be found therein, thanksgiving, and the voice of melody."

Hebrews 12:18-24 calls the Body of Christ "Mount Zion," but that is not a proof text for "replacement theology." The Body of Christ doesn't replace Israel as Zion. We are *in* Christ Jesus. We don't take anything away from Israel. We are the continuation of God's promise to Abraham.

Isaiah 51:3 is the Eden Covenant! It was the covenant between God and Adam *before* he sinned. God wants His Garden back. He intended for that Garden to be spread all over this planet until the earth became the garden spot of the universe.

Your place can be the garden spot of your universe. That was God's plan, and He never changes. He made man to live in a garden. And that should have been the worst environment man ever experienced because, "Eye hath not seen, nor ear heard, neither have entered into the heart of man, the things which God hath prepared for them that love him" (1 Corinthians 2:9). The Garden of Eden was just the starting point. It should have been expanded by Adam and Eve and their descendants into a greater and greater area, while God just observed His children at work because He had handed over the *power* and authority to continue to create that Garden all over the earth.

I'm convinced that God's plan was for us to finish expanding the Garden of Eden all over the earth, then take care of the other planets, and continue on and on. It's still His plan, but He had to start over again because sin got into the universe all the way up to and touching heaven. It didn't get into heaven, but the heavenly utensils of worship had to be re-sanctified by the blood of Jesus (Hebrews 9:21-23).

THE BLESSING, then, is the key issue to creating the Garden of Eden in your life and influencing the world around you. It was Jesus' key issue, too. The reason the Pharisees and religious people got so mad at Him was because He was preaching THE BLESSING of Abraham. They'd never heard that. They had heard the law and its curse. The people got so excited, they said, "You mean we're BLESSED?" THE BLESSING was healing and raising people from the dead. It was the power of the BLESSED One, Jesus, God's BLESSED Son. And THE BLESSING will do the same thing in your life!

The Bible is THE BLESSING Book. This book you're reading is simply a help to get you into the true BLESSING Book to bring its blessings into your life.

God's WORD will take you from living *outside* that BLESSING— where storms, disasters and hard times tear up and destroy things, to living inside it, appropriating THE BLESSING in your own life and replenishing the earth around you with it.

In a short time, you will learn how to use the power and authority God gave you to release THE BLESSING into your life.

Father, I pray for my Partners, and for those who will read
this book. According to Ephesians 1:16-23, open the eyes of
their understanding. You begin the book of Ephesians (1:3)
with the word *BLESSED:* "BLESSED…with all spiritual
blessings in heavenly places." All THE BLESSING is ours,
throughout eternity, before the foundation of the world. Oh
God, fill our spirits with light and understanding about what
You did for us through Jesus on the cross, and His power
toward us through the resurrection. Thank You, LORD. In
Jesus' Name. Amen.

# THE
# BLESSING
## OF
## THE LORD

MAKES RICH AND HE ADDS NO SORROW WITH IT

PROVERBS 10:22

# Chapter One

# THE BLESSING: Love's Ultimate Gift

### Get Ready to Fly

I first caught sight of the power of THE BLESSING back in 1967. My initial revelation of it included only a fraction of what I now know, yet it hit me with such power that it transformed my thinking and changed my life almost overnight.

And, I don't mind telling you, I was desperate for change.

I'd been born again only a few years at the time. I'd come out of a lifestyle so steeped in sin that everything I enjoyed before I was saved was either illegal, immoral or fattening. Because I knew next to nothing of what the Bible says about how to live in victory, even after I made Jesus The LORD of my life, I continued to stumble from one failure to another.

In most ways, my life was a mess. A failed business venture had left me broke and unemployed. A lifetime of borrowing money (Gloria is convinced that as a child I borrowed money on my tricycle!) had buried me under a mountain of debt that I had no way to repay. I knew I was called to preach. I also knew The LORD was leading me to go to Oral Roberts University, but I wouldn't do it because I couldn't see how I could possibly afford it. How could I go to school full time when I had a wife and family to support?

Even if I did, where would I get the tuition money?

Gloria, on the other hand, was in favor of obeying God, regardless of the cost. She wanted to pack up what little we had, put the kids in the car, point it toward Tulsa and head for ORU.

"If we did that, we'd starve," I told her.

"Kenneth, we're starving now," she answered. "We might as well starve in the will of God as starve outside of it."

She was right, and I knew it. So in 1966 we moved to Tulsa. For the first time in my adult life, I found myself in the perfect will of God, and I was thrilled about it. But even so, as a 30-year-old student making only a part-time income, I had no idea how I was going to make it financially. The only thing I knew for sure was: *If there were a way, I would find it in The WORD of God.* So, I threw myself into The WORD night and day.

In addition to reading and studying my Bible, I lugged a reel-to-reel tape recorder with me everywhere I went. I set it next to my bed at night so I could go to sleep listening to the word of faith being preached. I got up in the morning, turned the recorder back on and listened to the tapes again. I shaved, ate and drove with The WORD being preached to me the whole time.

It was then that the reality of what God has done for us through the plan of redemption began to dawn on me. As I listened to messages about the new covenant, and pored over scriptures like Galatians 3:9 that tell how we, by faith, are "BLESSED with faithful Abraham," I got my first glimpse of THE BLESSING and it sent shock waves through my spirit. For the first time ever, I realized that truly:

> Christ hath redeemed us from the curse of the law, being made a curse for us: for it is written, Cursed is every one that hangeth on a tree: that the BLESSING of Abraham might come on the Gentiles through Jesus Christ; that we might receive the promise of the Spirit through faith.... And if ye be Christ's, then are ye Abraham's seed, and heirs according to the promise (verses 13-14, 29).

The day I actually grasped what those verses were saying, it hit me like a freight train coming through a tunnel: *I am the seed of Abraham! I am the product of a blood-sworn oath, a covenant cut between God and His firstborn Son. The LORD Jesus Christ is my blood Brother!*

Because of my American Indian background, I knew something about blood covenants. I knew how real and serious they are, so it didn't take me long to realize that as a blood-covenant heir of Abraham, everything God promised him belonged to me. I didn't know for sure all that included, but I was smart enough to know that he and his family prospered everywhere they went. There wasn't a poor man among them. Every one of them was rich.

Even my lightning-fast mind could figure out what that meant. *Glory to God, I'm not poor anymore!*

I went to bed that night a wealthy man. It didn't matter to me that I was still in debt. I didn't care that on the outside my circumstances hadn't yet changed. What mattered was the change that had taken place on the inside. Finally, after years of thinking like a poor man, the spirit of adoption was crying out within me: *I have a blood covenant with Almighty God! I have a heavenly Father and He's rich and He's powerful, and He is backing me as surely as He backed Abraham—as surely as He backed Jesus Himself! I'm not under a financial curse anymore. I'm BLESSED with every spiritual BLESS-ING in heavenly places. Because I'm the righteousness of God in Christ, THE BLESSING of Abraham is mine!*

I no longer had the mentality of a poor man. In a matter of days, that mindset was gone. In its place was the realization that I am BLESSED!

Eleven months later, the mountain of debt that once towered over us was gone. Every cent of it was paid, and Gloria and I promised The LORD we'd never borrow money again. That wasn't always an easy promise to keep. A few years later, The LORD told me to begin a radio broadcast. Over the next 12 months, we went on 700 stations in the continental United States. Our ministry budget went from

$300,000 the year before, to $400,000 *per month* for the radio bill alone! THE BLESSING was working!

By then, The LORD had made it clear to me that in addition to operating debt free, I was never to ask anyone for money. *You receive offerings according to the Scripture,* He said, *but don't ever put pressure on people. Put pressure on My WORD instead. Put pressure on THE BLESSING of Abraham that's yours in Christ and it will bring in what you need.*

I knew very little about what that meant back then, but I acted on the part I did understand. Sure enough, the bills got paid and the ministry kept growing. As a result, through the past 40-plus years, we've been able to preach the uncompromised WORD just like God told us to, "on every available voice, from the top of the world to the bottom and all the way around." It has cost more than a billion dollars to do it, but that's OK because THE BLESSING of God has provided every cent.

### Just the Beginning

I make no apologies for preaching about the prosperity that's included in THE BLESSING. I was overjoyed back in 1967 to find out that, as a believer, I've been set free from lack, and I'm still elated about it today. But I also realize that being BLESSED includes far more than having money. Financial prosperity is only one small portion of THE BLESSING. It's one of the first parts God revealed to me, but it wasn't the only part. In fact, The LORD has been expanding my understanding of what it means to be BLESSED, for decades now.

During that time, He's taught me more about different parts of His BLESSING. He's increased my revelation of the new birth and the salvation part of it. He's opened my eyes more and more to the healing part of it, the peace that passes understanding part, and the gifts of the Spirit part. He's shown me how His BLESSING can affect not only our own lives, our families and the Church, but also our government and nation.

He has put the pieces together for me, one at a time.

That's how we develop and grow, you know—a little at a time. No one has ever learned anything advanced or complex all at once. It's a process. In spiritual things, just as in natural things, we must build one revelation on another. We move forward in our understanding, step by step, if we're going to get very far.

If you doubt that, look at the history of the Church. Ever since the Dark Ages, when the devil tried to strip the Church of her power and rob her of revelation by convincing ungodly leaders to lock up The WORD in monasteries away from God's people, The LORD has been restoring lost truths to us little by little. He started in Martin Luther's day by restoring the foundational truth of the new birth, "The just shall live by faith" (Romans 1:17). That truth came as a shock to people back in the 1500s. Religious leaders were enraged by it. Multitudes puzzled over whether or not to believe it. Yet today, the entire evangelical Church takes that revelation for granted. We don't argue about it anymore. We know we're saved, not by our own works, but by simple faith in Jesus.

After that revelation was restored, God began adding others. Through the Pentecostal movement that emerged in the early 1900s, for example, He took us on from the new birth and reintroduced the scriptural truth about the Baptism in the Holy Spirit (Matthew 3:11). Forty years later, during the great healing revival, He restored the revelation of divine healing (1 Peter 2:24). During the charismatic movement in the 1960s, He added revelation about the gifts of the Spirit (1 Corinthians 12:4-10). At the end of that decade, He taught us about the power and integrity of His written WORD and how to operate by faith in that WORD (Hebrews 4:12; Mark 11:23-24).

Here's my point: God didn't pour out those revelations on the Church all at once. They were always there, but He restored them one by one. That's the way He always works, both with His Body as a whole, and with us as individual believers. He develops us a little at a time. He takes us, as the Bible says, "from faith to faith" and "from glory to glory" (Romans 1:17; 2 Corinthians 3:18).

We must never forget that. While we guard as precious, the

things God has already revealed to us in His WORD, we must always remember there are things in The WORD we have not yet seen. There are scriptural truths we have not yet learned. There are biblical revelations we have not yet received.

God isn't finished with us yet.

When we forget this fact, we get stuck. We start thinking our group (or denomination) knows all there is to know. We set up camp around the last revelation we received and refuse to go any further. Believers have done that again and again. Years ago, some groups grabbed hold of the truth about the new birth and blessed multitudes of people by teaching them how to get saved by faith. But when anyone tried to tell them about the Baptism in the Holy Spirit and speaking in tongues, they slammed their doors on that revelation. "No, we're not having any of that around here!" they said. "We have the new birth, and that's all we need."

Some of the Holy Spirit-baptized believers made the same mistake. When God sent someone to teach them about receiving healing and financial provision by faith, they would have none of it. They closed their minds to scriptural truth and said, "Bible or no Bible, that's not what Grandma taught, and I'm not going to believe it."

Don't get me wrong. I'm not picking on those groups of believers. I love them and believe we all owe them a debt of gratitude for the truths they've helped restore to the Body of Christ. But, I also realize we should learn from each other's mistakes. We must recognize and overcome our carnal tendency to resist new revelation. We must see that what we have learned is not a campground. It's a building base. We must understand this if we want to go on and grow up, as the Bible says, into "the measure of the stature of the *fulness* of Christ" (Ephesians 4:13).

### Get a Drink From the Fire Hose

I've been reminded of that again and again as God has expanded my understanding of THE BLESSING. Every time He has shown me something new about it in The WORD, I'd think,

*This is it! Now, I have the whole picture.* Then He'd teach me something else, and I'd find myself saying, "I'm surprised I never saw this before!"

The process has been much like the flight training I've received as a pilot. When I first began to fly airplanes, the instructor didn't tell me everything at once. I've spent thousands of hours through the years, learning different aspects of flying. I started by learning the basic skills, one at a time, and practicing them with an instructor in a little, two-seater, single-engine Cessna.

I'll never forget the first time I finally got to fly that plane solo. I was so excited I could hardly stand it. I figured I knew everything I needed to know, and I was ready to go. But there was one thing I hadn't considered. I'd done all my training flights in the early morning. At that time of day, there was very little air traffic, so coming in for a landing was simple. I'd radio the tower and they'd clear me to land right away.

I took off on my first solo flight, however, at 4 o'clock in the afternoon, a much busier time of day. So, when I got ready to land and radioed the tower for clearance, I didn't get the response I expected. I didn't hear, "Roger, Cessna 55 X-ray. You're clear for touch-and-go, land on runway 17."

Instead, I heard this. "Cessna 55 X-ray, you're No. 8 to follow a DC-3 just outside the outer marker. Call when you get him in sight."

*What?! No. 8? Outer marker? What's an outer marker?*

I had no idea. "Sir, this is my first solo...."

"Roger that, 55 X-ray," he answered. "No problem. Just hold your altitude and heading. I'll tell you when to make your turn."

That sounded a lot better to me than the "outer marker" business. I held steady, and after a while the tower controller said, "OK, 55 X-ray, do you see that DC-3 off to your left, there? That's the traffic you're to follow. When he passes under your left wing, turn left."

That was a revelation to me! I hadn't yet learned that waiting to make my turn until the airplane I'm following passes under my left wing ensures I'll never collide with that plane. *Hey, that's cool!* I thought; and with that knowledge I made my three touch-and-go landings as safely and happily as a pig in the sunshine.

Many years have passed since then, and these days I'm not flying a single-engine Cessna anymore. I'm flying a 600-miles-per-hour Citation X that is far more complicated. I've had to learn a lot of additional information, piece by piece, in order to fly that plane, but the revelation I got on my first solo flight still applies. No matter how fast I'm flying, if I'll follow that procedure of letting another aircraft pass under my left wing before I turn, I won't hit it.

I told you all that, so I could say this: What you are about to read in this book is not simply a rehearsal of the first revelations I received in the early years of my ministry. As wonderful as those are, and as life-changing as they were back then, and still prove to be, those first glimpses into THE BLESSING of Abraham were only the beginning. You might say they were the initial lessons I learned in the flight school of The WORD. Those principles still apply but have now become the foundation for new levels of revelation.

As I've moved into those new levels and begun to see the full scope of THE BLESSING, I've felt a little like I did when I started training for the Citation X—as if I were learning to fly all over again. One pilot who went through the classes with me said absorbing the mountains of new information we were being bombarded with was like trying to drink from a fire hose. We had to learn a whole new way of doing things. Sometimes, our brains cramped up trying to retain it all, but the first time I took off in the Citation X, I knew it had been worth the effort. When all the elements I'd been studying in class and practicing in the simulator came together, and I shoved the throttles up and took to the sky in that airplane…what an experience!

There's no way to describe it. All I can say is that every cell in my body felt the power, and I knew that I was about to fly farther and faster than I'd ever flown before.

### Watch Out for the Needle

That's the way we're all going to feel spiritually, once we get the training down and we take off in the revelation of THE BLESS-ING. But, I will warn you, learning to operate in it may, at times, seem new and different. You may be as startled as I was at first, to find out that all the BLESSINGS we've found in The WORD—the BLESSINGS we've studied, believed for and seen manifested in our lives for so many years—are not just random, unrelated expressions of God's goodness. They are not just individual gifts He gives us to take care of our needs as they arise.

Those BLESSINGS are all part of a whole. They are pieces of something bigger and more powerful than anything most of us have ever imagined. Like parts of a watch that work together as one, each of them—from the new birth, to healing, to prosperity, to the power gifts of the Holy Spirit—are all part of a single declaration made by God 6,000 years ago.

They are all the result of one BLESSING—*THE* BLESSING!

The one BLESSING God spoke over Adam and Eve in the Garden of Eden.

The one BLESSING recorded in Genesis 1:28 that set forth God's will for all mankind, for all time: *Be fruitful, and multiply, and replenish the earth, and subdue it: and have dominion....*

With that one BLESSING, God bestowed on the family of man everything they would ever need to become all He had created them to be, and do all He had destined them to do. He released the only BLESSING any of us would ever need. In the following chapters, you'll see how that first BLESSING eventually became THE BLESSING of Abraham. You'll track it down through the generations and see the amazing things that happened to all who received it. You'll get a clearer understanding of how THE BLESSING empowered the true Seed of Abraham, The LORD Jesus Christ, to become the Savior of the world. And, you'll realize, as never before, what the Bible means when it says that through Him, THE BLESSING has been given to us.

What The LORD has taught me about THE BLESSING in the past few years has once again sent shock waves through my spirit. It has changed me as much as the first revelation I received about THE BLESSING of Abraham, back in 1967.

In the following pages, I will take you through the Scriptures, literally from Genesis to Revelation, showing you what God has shown me about what THE BLESSING is and how it operates. You will see, as I did, that the truth of it spans the whole Bible.

Some things you read *will* shake up your thinking. They may even bother you at first. New revelations often do that. They're uncomfortable at first. Sometimes they even make us mad for a while because they upset our religious traditions.

Just the fact that I'm writing an entire book about being BLESSED may ruffle some people's feathers. "Well, I think there's been too much preaching about Christians being BLESSED," they'll say. "We've all gotten too self-centered. Christianity is all about Jesus, it's not all about us."

Those people do have one thing right. From our perspective as believers, life *is* all about Jesus. It's all about loving Him, pleasing Him, advancing His kingdom and giving Him glory.

But, from Jesus' perspective, it's all about us. He didn't die on the Cross to save Himself. He didn't come to earth to fulfill the plan of redemption so *He* could have abundant life. He came so that *we* could have it. He became Abraham's Seed, not so He could inherit God's promise, but that we could. He did it so THE BLESS-ING could come on us and, through us, all the nations of the earth could be BLESSED.

I realize such statements irritate people who think it's pious to be poor and beaten down, but that doesn't bother me. I'm used to it. My preaching has irritated a lot of people through the years. Believe it or not, it's part of my God-given calling. Years ago, when I first went into ministry, The LORD spoke to me about the Holy Spirit-baptized Church and said:

*I have a sleeping giant in the earth and I'm going to wake him up...*

I thought that was great! I was all for it until He finished the sentence.

*...and you're the needle.*

"Lord, why me?" I asked.

*Why not?* He answered.

"OK, let's go!" I said.

Since then, it's happened more times than I can count. I'll be preaching along just enjoying myself, when suddenly, the needle anointing will come on me and I'll say something that wakes people up. Sometimes they get so mad they want to punch me and other times they're glad. On occasion, preachers will come to me later and say, "You made me so angry I decided to go home and study my Bible until I could prove you wrong. But the more I read, the more I realized you were right. What you said was in the Bible all along!" It wasn't me that was right. It was The WORD.

All those preachers were good, God-loving people. Most of them had more formal Bible training than I did, but they'd been so blinded by their religious mindsets, they couldn't see the clear truths of The WORD. Their traditions had made "The WORD of God of none effect"[1] in their lives. The LORD just used me to provoke them into looking at the Bible with a fresh perspective. When they did, they saw the truth, and the truth made them free.

Keep that in mind as you read this book: If some of the things I say needle you, don't just dismiss them, and don't take my word for it. Search The WORD of God for yourself to see if they're true. If The WORD doesn't confirm them, discard them. If it does, let them make you free. Let the reality of THE BLESSING revolutionize your thinking, fuel your faith and send you soaring into new heights of God's will for your life.

Now...let's fire up the engines and fly.

---

[1] Mark 7:13

# Chapter Two

# The One Thing Sin Couldn't Change

"I am The LORD, I change not."
Malachi 3:6
"Jesus Christ the same yesterday, and today, and for ever."
Hebrews 13:8

There's far too much confusion about the will of God these days. Walk into one church and you'll hear that God's will is to BLESS His people—to heal, prosper and pour out His goodness on them in every area of life. Walk into another and you'll hear the exact opposite—that God puts sickness and poverty on His people to teach them lessons, that He leaves them in evil and oppressive situations for reasons only He can understand.

Of course, people have their philosophies and fragments of Scripture to back up what they believe. Every group is convinced they are right. So the arguments continue. The confusion remains...for no good reason.

That's the worst part about it. The entire conflict is unnecessary. The Bible settled the issue for us long ago. It spelled out, with unmistakable clarity, God's will for all mankind, for all time, in the very first chapter of the Book. *In the beginning,* God made His plan known. What's amazing is how we could have missed it for so long.

Isn't it obvious that the Creator of mankind would have made it His first order of business to inform this creation called "man" of His intentions for them? Of course, it is. And that's exactly what He did. Anyone who has read Genesis 1 can verify it. God was quite clear there in His declarations about man's identity and assignment on earth. He left no doubt about His will for man's environment. He created it to be good in every way.

"Yes, but all that changed when sin entered the picture," someone might say.

Without question, sin did change some things. But the one thing it did not change is God. One of the most basic facts of God's nature is that He is the same yesterday, today and forever. James 1:17 calls Him "the Father of lights, with whom is no variableness, neither shadow of turning."

"For I am The LORD," He said in Malachi 3:6, "I change not."

In West Texas we'd say it this way, "He ain't about to change." What He said in Genesis about His will and purpose for mankind, He meant. Period. The devil's plot couldn't change it. The rebellion and failure of Adam could not alter it one iota. Once God has made up His mind and released His WORD—that's it.

When I was a little boy, my father was like that. Once he took a stand on something, as far as he was concerned, the issue was settled. Sometimes I'd question him about it. Sometimes I'd try to change his mind. "But Daddy," I'd say. Then, I'd start explaining all the reasons he should do things my way.

"Did you hear what I said the first time?" he'd answer.

"Yes, Dad, but…"

"What I said the first time still stands. That's the way it is. Do you understand that?"

"Yes, sir," I'd answer, and that would end the discussion. I knew that no matter how hard I pushed him, when my dad knew he was right and he'd made his decision, it never changed. Whatever else he said to me on the subject would simply reaffirm his original position.

If my natural father could be so unchangeable, how much more unchangeable is our heavenly Father? After all, He is perfect in all

His ways. Every decision He makes is the right one. Every plan He comes up with is the best it can be. It's impossible for Him to change. Everything He is and does is right the first time He does it.

That's why the best way for us to understand His will for mankind is to go back to the first thing He said about it. The surest method of finding His plan for us today is to travel back in time and see His *original* plan. Because one thing is sure: God's will for man right now is exactly the same as it ever was. It hasn't changed since the day Adam was created. God still means what He said in the very first verses of the Bible.

### More Than Just a Religious, Three-Letter Word

In the beginning God created the heaven and the earth. And the earth was without form, and void; and darkness was upon the face of the deep. And the spirit of God moved upon the face of the waters. And God said, Let there be light: and there was light (Genesis 1:1-3).

Those familiar verses are more than a biblical history lesson. They set the stage for everything we, as believers, will ever need to know. They give us the first glimpse of God's purpose and plan for our lives. Not only do they provide us with the basic facts about who created the universe and how, but if we study them in the clear light of scriptural truth, they also tell us the "why" behind the Creation.

By telling us God is the Creator of the universe and that He initiated it by releasing light with His WORD, those three simple verses reveal far more than we've realized about the purpose behind it all. For the most part, we've missed that revelation. It has slipped past us because in our day the word *God* doesn't have much meaning. A generic, three-letter word used by all religions, it refers to any deity a person might choose. It is used for Allah or Buddha as well as for The Almighty God of Abraham, Isaac and Jacob.

As Christians we know, of course, that the true God is the God of the Bible. The God in Genesis 1:1 is the One, Eternal, Triune God—The God and Father of our Lord Jesus Christ (Ephesians 1:3).

But even those titles, though correct, fall short of identifying God. They give us little insight into His nature and character. They do not tell us who He is. The Bible does, however. It describes Him in depth and in detail from Genesis to Revelation and, in the end, sums Him up in three breathtaking, yet simple New Testament words:

*"God is love"* (1 John 4:8).

The Old Testament makes the same declaration. It says God is "full of compassion" (Psalm 78:38, 111:4). It says He is "long-suffering, and plenteous in mercy and truth" (Psalm 86:15). "The LORD is gracious," it proclaims, "and full of compassion; slow to anger, and of great mercy. The LORD is good to all: and his tender mercies are over all his works" (Psalm 145:8-9).

One day, while meditating on the phrase "full of compassion," the implications of it exploded in me. It hit me that because God's capacity is infinite, it takes an infinite amount of compassion to fill Him up. It takes all the compassion there is! Compassion is not, then, a feeling or a thing. It is Him.

The magnitude of God's love is staggering. His love is not the on-again-off-again kind of love that human beings can offer us. It's not the kind of love that sometimes "does you wrong." According to Psalm 145:9, "The LORD is [always and forever!] good." The word Lord is capitalized in that verse because it refers to the personal Name of God. It is the Name He revealed to Moses when He told him to lead the Israelites out of Egypt (Exodus 3:13-14). It is the Name He used when He answered Moses' cry to see His glory, and said:

I will make all my goodness pass before thee, and I will proclaim the name of The LORD before thee; and will be gracious to whom I will be gracious, and will show mercy on whom I will show mercy (Exodus 33:19).

The true pronunciation of the Name was lost millennia ago because the Jews held it so sacred they refused to say it aloud. In a vain attempt to translate it, Bible translators rendered it *Jehovah* in English or simply substituted the word Lord. But whether or not we can pronounce it, we can be clear about this: God's Name is good because He is The Good God. He is all the good there is. He is 100 percent good. There is not one trace of bad in Him.

A few years ago, I was studying about weather and came across the term "absolute zero." That's the term used to describe conditions when there is no heat present whatsoever. At absolute zero, cold is all there is. It's as cold as cold can be. Nothing could be colder because absolute zero is 100 percent cold.

If you could measure it on a thermometer, it would be more than 450 degrees below zero. I experienced 50 degrees below zero one time when I was in the Rocky Mountains, and I thought that was seriously cold, but there was still heat in the air. Although I didn't feel it, it was there.

When I read about absolute zero, it occurred to me that God is "absolute good." He is as good as good can be. He is absolute good, absolute love, absolute compassion, absolute mercy, kindness and long-suffering. His goodness is so all-consuming that bad cannot exist in His presence. That's the reason He had to hide Moses in a cave behind a shield of rock when He let His goodness pass before Moses. Though a great prophet of God, Moses was still a fallen man, contaminated (as all have been since Adam) with sin. If God had passed His goodness in front of Moses without protecting him, God's absolute goodness would have burned up the bad in Moses, and he would have made an early exit from the earth.

But God didn't let that happen. He did what was necessary to reveal Himself to Moses while at the same time protecting him. His goodness made a way.

### There's Good News in the First Verse of the Bible

Now, let's look again at Genesis 1:1: "In the beginning God created the heaven and the earth." Keeping in mind what we've just seen about who God is, we could also read the verse this way: *In the beginning, Love created heaven and earth.* Or, *In the beginning, Compassion created heaven and earth.* Or, *In the beginning, Goodness created heaven and earth.* To strike our thinking with maximum impact, we could put them all together and say, *In the beginning the God who is Absolute Love, Compassion and Goodness created heaven and earth.*

We haven't gotten past the first verse of the Bible and we're already seeing good news! We've already learned that Compassion made the universe and it doesn't take a rocket scientist to figure out that if Compassion is behind Creation, then Compassion is the *reason* for Creation. We suddenly know not only that God created all things, we know *why.*

He did it because He needed someone to love.

If you know anything about real compassion, you know that's the truth. Compassion can't be satisfied with selfish endeavors. It needs someone to fellowship with, give to and BLESS. Compassion needs someone on whom it can pour out its goodness. Compassion needs a family.

That fact gives us a whole new perspective on Genesis 1:1. It lets us know that the God of Love is about to create something for the purpose of love. He isn't just making a universe, He is planning a family on whom He can lavish His goodness, and preparing a place for that family to live. God didn't design the universe just for His own enjoyment. He already had a fine dwelling place of His own called heaven. He wanted to build a place for His children that was as wonderful and glorious as His own. He wanted a place where He could visit them, and where He could eventually go and live with them. So He decided to build one.

How did He begin? Verse 3 tells us: "And God said, Let there be light: and there was light." God set things in motion with His

WORD. The New Testament says it this way:

> In the beginning was The WORD, and The WORD was with God, and The WORD was God. The same was in the beginning with God. All things were made by him; and without him was not any thing made that was made (John 1:1-3).

Read those verses again, making the scriptural substitutions we made before and you'll see in them, as we saw in Genesis 1:1, thrilling evidence of what God had in mind at Creation.

> In the beginning was The WORD, and The WORD was with Compassion, and The WORD was Compassion.... All things were made by Compassion; and without Compassion was not any thing made that was made.... And Compassion said... Love said... Goodness said... Light be!

Think of it: Love's WORD created the universe! The earth, the heavens and everything in them were created by Love, with love, for the purpose of love. (That revelation alone wipes out a lot of the lies religion has sold us.) In a most literal way, God built His family a home out of His own love. He brought forth out of His own essence and glory, a place that would reflect His all-consuming desire to BLESS that family and surround them with goodness.

And He did it by saying, *Light be!*

The English translation of the Bible renders that phrase, "Let there be light." But that translation is weaker than the original text. "Let there be light" could leave the impression that God was just making plans out loud. That He was saying, "Hmmm...let's have some light."

The original Hebrew is shorter and more forceful. It reveals the universe exploding into existence at God's direct command. "God said, *'Light be!'* "and light was."

Why is that so important for us to know? Why does God consider revealing to us His method of Creation so vital that He includes it in the third verse of the Bible? Because He's about to bring forth a family of "creators" made in His image; and this divine method of "calling those things which be not as though they were"[2] is a crucial part of His will and plan for them.

It's no coincidence that Genesis 1 tells us again and again that *God said...and it was so.* Like all good teachers, God teaches by repetition. So, for the sake of His students—the sons and daughters who would one day follow His example—He left no room for doubt. He saw to it that the brief summary of Creation in this all-important first book of the Bible would remind us over and over that:

- To bring forth the firmament from the waters, *"God said...*and it was so" (verses 6-7).

- To gather the waters together and let the dry land appear, *"God said...*and it was so" (verse 9).

- To bring forth plant life, *"God said...*and it was so" (verse 11).

- To release the light of the sun, moon and stars, *"God said...*and it was so" (verses 14-15).

- To fill the sea with living creatures, *"God said....* And God saw that it was good" (verse 20-21).

- To bring forth animals from the earth, *"God said...*and it was so" (verse 24).

Speaking is clearly God's creative method. He created and upholds all things by "The WORD of His power."[3] God doesn't just blurt out meaningless babble like people so often do. He doesn't

---

[2] Romans 4:17
[3] Hebrews 1:3

use words lightly. He pours Himself into His words. He fills them with faith and spiritual substance.

When God said, *"Light be!..."* He did more than utter a simple phrase. He set a massive plan in motion. With those words, The Almighty released enough power to cause the universe to explode into being.

He released the power of *Light.*

### What Happened When God Turned On the Light?

How significant was that force called Light?

Far more significant than we've realized.

The Light God spoke forth on the first day of Creation wasn't just visible illumination. It wasn't a kind of night light that lit up the darkness so God could see what He was doing. It wasn't sunshine or moonlight. According to Genesis 1:14-19, the sun and moon were not created until the fourth day.

What was it, then, that God released on day one?

It was the Light of His own glory, the essence of God Himself—of His presence and His substance.

If you're wondering how I got that information, you'll be happy to know I got it from the Bible. It tells us plainly that *God is Light.*[4] It says He is our Light and our salvation.[5] It calls The LORD Jesus Christ, who is the perfect expression of the fullness of God, the "true Light, which lighteth every man that cometh into the world" (John 1:9).

If the Bible means what it says (and it does!) Light is more than just a quality God possesses. It is who He is. It is His very nature. Just as God is Love, God is Light. Both Old and New Testament scriptures confirm it by describing God's appearance in terms of fire, lightning or some other form of light.

---

[4] 1 John 1:5: "This then is the message which we have heard of him, and declare unto you, that God is light, and in him is no darkness at all."

[5] Psalm 27:1: "The LORD is my light and my salvation; whom shall I fear? The LORD is the strength of my life; of whom shall I be afraid?"

- In the wilderness, when God led the Israelites by His presence, He is described as "a pillar of fire, to give them light" (Exodus 13:21).

- When God cut the covenant with Abraham, He appeared as "a burning lamp" that passed between the pieces of the sacrificial animals (Genesis 15:17).

- To the psalmist, God revealed Himself as the One who covers Himself "with light as with a garment" (Psalm 104:2).

- In Ezekiel's vision, God had "the appearance of a man…[with] fire round about…from the appearance of his loins even upward, and from the appearance of his loins even downward…the appearance of fire, and it had brightness round about" (Ezekiel 1:26-27).

- When the prophet Habakkuk saw Him, "His brightness was like the light; He had rays [lightning-like splendor] flashing from His hand, and there His power was hidden" (Habakkuk 3:4, *New King James Version).*

- On the day of Pentecost when God poured His Spirit out on the early disciples, "there appeared unto them cloven tongues like as of fire" (Acts 2:3).

- When the Apostle John received the Revelation and saw God on His throne, he saw lightning and fire around it (Revelation 4:5).

- In John's vision of the New Jerusalem, "the city had no need of the sun, neither of the moon, to shine in it: for the glory of God did lighten it, and the Lamb is the light thereof" (Revelation 21:23).

From Genesis to Revelation, God is Light! So, using Scripture to interpret Scripture, we can assume that in Genesis 1:3 when God said, *"Light be!"* He actually released His own substance (Light) into the void that was space. He released Himself—His own creative, glorious, compassionate, life-filled *glory* (that's one of the Bible words for it) and that glory became the envelope for the universe. It made a kind of container in which all material things began to form—the planets, the stars, the oceans and every other natural element.

In other words, God's Glory-Light became the basis of all matter.

"What do *you* know about it?" someone might ask. "You're a preacher, not a scientist."

Yes, but if you ask scientists who are brave enough to give you an honest answer, they'll tell you much the same thing because science has been catching up with the Bible in recent years. Researchers and physics experts who have the integrity to admit it are now acknowledging that the universe began as a result of a massive explosion of *electromagnetic radiation* (i.e. *light*)[6] [7] and has been expanding ever since. That radiant energy, which includes not only light waves visible to the human eye, but also those that are invisible, became the substance of all material things. Science now acknowledges that what the Bible has told us for thousands of years is true: Light was the original force of the universe and continues to be the ultimate power of all creation.

Do you realize what that means?

It means that God, who is Light—Compassion Himself—used His own glory to make this planet. It means that even "before the foundation of the world"[8] God loved us so much that He decided to build a dwelling place for us out of the very substance of His own Love-filled, Light-filled nature. When God said, *"Light be!"* He did more than ignite the "big bang" that would set the universe in motion. He released the very essence of Himself into this material creation because He wanted the family He was about to create to be eternally surrounded with 100

---

[6] http://imagine.gsfc.nasa.gov/docs/dict_ei.html "electromagnetic waves (radiation)" (9/28/11)

[7] http://imagine.gsfc.nasa.gov/docs/ask_astro/answers/070904a.html (9/28/11)

[8] Ephesians 1:4

percent, absolute Good. He wanted us to be surrounded by His own glory and to be able to say with joy, "in Him we live, and move, and have our being" (Acts 17:28)!

If that doesn't light your spiritual fire, my friend, your wood is wet!

## From Dirt to Divinity

On the sixth day of Creation, everything was ready. The heavens and earth were complete and all the preliminaries finished, so God went to work on the first member of His family. He prepared to create a man.

The first thing He did was form a body "of the dust of the ground."[9] Sometimes, people say God created man from dirt. But that's incorrect. God fashioned the man's *body* from the dust—not the man himself. Once the body was formed, God created the man the same way He'd created everything else:

God *said,* Let us make man in our image, after our likeness: and let them have dominion over the fish of the sea, and over the fowl of the air, and over the cattle, and over all the earth, and over every creeping thing that creepeth upon the earth. So God created man in his own image, in the image of God created he him; male and female created he them (Genesis 1:26-27).

Here again, the English translation is weaker than the Hebrew text. It almost gives us the sense that God was just making plans aloud, that He was saying, "I have an idea. Let's make a man in Our image." But in reality, God didn't create anything that way. He didn't make anything on a whim just to see how it would turn out. He had everything planned to the minutest detail before He started.

When God made the planets and stars, He did it according to the blueprint already formed within Him. When He formed the sea creatures, the birds and the animals, He made each one according to the pattern He'd designed beforehand. When He created man,

---

[9] Genesis 2:7

He did it the same way—with one astounding difference. Instead of making man from an original design, God used *Himself* as the pattern. (See verses 26-27.) When God created man, He actually copied Himself.

He didn't decide to do that at the last minute, either. He had made the decision to create mankind in His image before the foundation of the world. The Bible says that God even had the plan of redemption mapped out and accomplished in His own mind back then. It says that we, as believers:

> …were not redeemed with corruptible things, as silver and gold, from your vain conversation received by tradition from your fathers; but with the precious blood of Christ, as of a lamb without blemish and without spot: *who verily was fore-ordained before the foundation of the world*, but was manifest in these last times for you (1 Peter 1:18-20).

What a Planner! Long before God said, "Let us make man in Our image," He had already created in His heart and mind every human being who would ever be born. He had already foreseen the fact that the devil would tempt Adam and they would sin.[10] Before the universe began, God had settled it in His own heart that He would restore all that would be shattered through their rebellion. He and Jesus had already agreed that Jesus would go to the cross and pay the price for the redemption of their family.

God also knew, way back then, all who would one day receive Jesus as Lord and Savior. He saw us in His heart before we ever existed and chose us "before the foundation of the world, that we should be holy and without blame before him in Love" (Ephesians 1:4). As a result, from before "the beginning" God has seen every born-again believer as made perfectly in His image...and He still sees us that way today. He never accepted that old, sinful image of us that the devil conjured up. He never saw us as old, dirty-dog sinners.

---

[10] The Hebrew word translated *Adam* in the first chapter of Genesis refers to mankind and includes both male and female.

Throughout the ages, God has maintained the inner image of us He had in His heart from the first.

Therefore, it's clear that God wasn't just coming up with a good idea when He said, "Let us make man…." He was giving the command that would bring forth what He had already planned. He was releasing His power through His WORD and bringing His family to life.

He did it the same way He had in Genesis 1:3 when He said, *Light be!…* He said, *"Man be in our image, after our likeness:… and have dominion!"*

As human beings, we can repeat those words in just a few seconds, but it may well have taken God all day to say them because He poured Himself completely into them. He filled them with the totality of His life, His Spirit and His faith. He injected into them what we might call *His divine DNA,* and with those words God "breathed into his nostrils the breath of life; and man became a living soul."[11]

The Bible doesn't give the details surrounding the event, but I firmly believe at that moment a hush fell over all creation. Not a bird sang. Not a bee buzzed. Not a breath of wind fluttered through the trees. The entire universe stood in rapt silence transfixed by what was about to happen.

All creation waited in awe as Almighty God, the Master Creator of the universe, brought forth the family He had planned and chosen before the foundation of the world. No created being in heaven or on earth had ever witnessed such a scene, and it must have seemed inconceivable to all who watched. *Could it really be that God was about to duplicate Himself in this creature called man?*

Multitudes upon multitudes of angels gathered to see the event. Why wouldn't they? They'd been created to serve this family God was about to bring forth.[12] They must have wanted to see who they

---

[11] Genesis 2:7

[12] Hebrews 1:13-14: "But to which of the angels said he at any time, Sit on my right hand, until I make thine enemies thy footstool? Are they not all ministering spirits, sent forth to minister for them who shall be heirs of salvation?"

were supposed to be helping. They must have wanted to see for themselves this divine race whose future existence had already triggered a devastating heavenly war.

That war took place before man was ever created, when Lucifer—the chief musician and most gorgeous angel ever created, the archangel over all music and worship—decided he didn't want to minister as a servant to mankind. He didn't want to use the anointing and talent God had given him to bring loveliness, peace and joy to this family that was about to be created in God's image.

Instead of serving, Lucifer wanted to be served. So, he turned against his Creator, convinced a third of the heavenly host to join him, and tried to imitate God.[13] Using God's own creative method, he attempted to use his words to bring forth a new reality. He said, "I will ascend into heaven, I will exalt my throne above the stars of God: I will sit also upon the mount of the congregation, in the sides of the north: I will ascend above the heights of the clouds: I will be like the most High" (Isaiah 14:13-14).

Unlike the man God was planning to create, however, Lucifer wasn't made in God's image. He didn't have the right to choose his own words and call things that be not as though they were. His declaration was illegal, so rather than raising him up, it brought him down. The very anointing God had put within him turned against him and removed him from his position. When that happened, Lucifer (now known as Satan) gathered up the angels who'd joined in his rebellion and attacked heaven.

It was the biggest mistake he ever made. He and the angels who followed him ended up getting thrown down out of heaven and into nothingness. They were stripped of all rights. From that day to this, they haven't owned anything or belonged anywhere. They eventually stole the authority of man, invaded this planet and became what we know today as the principalities, powers and rulers of the darkness of this world.[14] But the fact is, they're the

---

[13] Revelation 12:4

[14] Ephesians 6:12:"For we wrestle not against flesh and blood, but against principalities, against powers, against the rulers of the darkness of this world, against spiritual wickedness in high places."

lowest form of spirit life on this planet.

I'm jumping ahead a little, but I can't pass up the opportunity to say those foul, fallen spirits don't have any business in a human body. They don't have any business bothering a human mind. They don't belong on the earth, and their time here is rapidly running out. When it's gone, they'll never be back again. In the meantime, don't let them get away with anything in your life. And the next time someone asks if you think there are aliens on the earth, say, "Yeah, they're called devils and demons, and I cast them out every day!"

### Angels Seeing Double

Surely, with a heavenly war just behind them and God at center stage of the universe, breathing (or "spiriting")[15] His WORD of life into this man around whom the whole conflict had centered, every angel in heaven crowded around watching in awe. When God said, "Man, be in Our image, and have dominion...," every angel on hand must have been pondering the questions posed in Psalm 8:

> When I consider thy heavens, the work of thy fingers, the moon and the stars, which thou hast ordained; what is man, that thou art mindful of him? and the son of man, that thou visitest him? For thou hast made him a little lower than the *angels* [or *Elohiym* which literally translated means "God"], and hast crowned him with glory and honour. Thou madest him to have dominion over the works of thy hands; thou hast put all things under his feet (verses 3-6).

The LORD allowed me one day during a season of prayer to see in a vision what happened when man was created. I've not had many visions this dramatic and detailed, so it marked my thinking forever. In my spirit, I saw God standing up, holding Adam's body in front of Him. The first thing I noticed was they were the same size. Adam's form was just like God's except it

---

[15] See *The Chumash*, ed. Rabbi Nosson Scherman, Artscroll Series, Stone Edition, Travel Size (Brooklyn: Mesorah Publications, 1998) p. 11, verse 7, commentary.

was limp and grayish looking. It didn't have much color to it.

When God spoke to Adam, He spoke right into his face. He didn't blow into his mouth to get life into him. He just stood face to face with him. God's nose was right in front of Adam's nose. His mouth was level with Adam's. His eyes—the eyes of Compassion Himself—looking into Adam's eyes, seemed to be pouring into him everything God is. All His love, light, life, goodness and mercy were being infused into this man. God was merging into Adam His very Being!

Adam didn't hear the first words God spoke to him because he wasn't yet alive. But once those words entered him, they did their creative work and, as the Bible says, "Man became a living soul."[16] The Hebrew commentaries put it this way: "He became a living, speaking spirit like God."[17]

As a living, speaking spirit like God, man had the same power to speak that God Himself had. He was full of God's own faith and had the authority to speak creative, compassionate words and exercise dominion with them. Born of God's WORD and created in His exact likeness, man was Love just like God is Love. Man was Light just like God is Light. Man was full of Compassion just like God is full of Compassion. Man was Life just as God is Life. The only difference between man and God was this: Unlike God who is eternally sovereign and independent, man was dependent on God.

In all other ways, God and man were so exactly alike that when the angels saw God and Adam together for the first time, they must have thought they were seeing double. What a shock it must have been to see the Eternal, Almighty God in all His radiant Light and Glory standing face to face with someone who looked just like Him! Someone who had the same radiance and the same fiery presence.[18] Someone who was, as we say in my part of the country, the "spitting image" of God.

---

[16] Genesis 2:7

[17] *The Chumash*, ed. Rabbi Nosson Scherman, Artscroll Series, Stone Edition, Travel Size (Brooklyn: Mesorah Publications, 1998) Vol. 1, Bereishis/Genesis, p. 11, verse 7, commentary.

[18] See *The Chumash*, Vol. 1, Bereishis/Genesis, p. 13, verses 18-25, commentary.

Although that term is a colloquialism, in this case it's the literal truth. One theory is that it originated from the phrase "spirit and image," and that's exactly what Adam was. He was the spirit and image of God Himself. He wasn't just a *little* like God, he was *exactly* like Him. He didn't contain a part of God, he contained everything God is. He was absolutely filled with God.

That fact alone must have stunned the angelic watchers. Before they even had time to gasp in awe at the sight, however, God did something more—something that would once again spark a battle, not in the realms of heaven, but on planet Earth. God crowned this family of man He had created with glory and honor. He made them "to have dominion" over the works of His hands. He put all things under their feet.[19]

> God BLESSED them, and God said unto them, Be fruitful, and multiply, and replenish the earth, and subdue it: and have dominion over the fish of the sea, and over the fowl of the air, and over every living thing that moveth upon the earth (Genesis 1:28).

Those words of BLESSING marked the coronation of mankind. They were the first words Adam ever heard.

They were the most important words God has ever spoken to any man at any time because they carry within them God's unchanging plan and purpose for His family.

They settle, once and for all, the eternal truth that God's will for man is THE BLESSING.

---

[19] Psalm 8:5-6

# Chapter Three

# Project Eden: Filling the Earth With the Glory of God

THE BLESSING of The LORD, it maketh rich,
and he addeth no sorrow with it.
Proverbs 10:22

The word *blessing* has been so stripped of its meaning that most people pay no attention to it anymore. Even though it represents the most important concept in the Bible, and reveals God's will for all mankind, the world has trivialized it into little more than a courtesy comment made when someone sneezes.

*"Ah-choo!"*

"God bless you!" People say it all the time without any idea of what it means.

Even believers, who give the phrase more thought because of its scriptural nature, are often confused by it because it is thrown around in such casual and contradictory ways. On one hand, they hear things like sickness, poverty and calamity referred to as "blessings in disguise," while on the other hand, health, prosperity and protection are called blessings, too. It's no wonder that for all practical purposes, the real definition of the word *blessing* has been lost. Religious double speak has turned it into a term that changes color according to the circumstances surrounding it, with no clear meaning of its own.

In reality, however, the word *blessing* has a definite and distinct identity. Its primary biblical meaning is to say something good about. In Hebrew, a *blessing* is the exact opposite of a *curse,* which means to say something bad about.

The Jews, who were the original readers of the Bible, completely understood that fact. They didn't have the problem many Christians do. They never got blessings and curses mixed up. They knew: If it's good, it's a *BLESSING.* If it's bad, it's a *curse.* You could never convince a Jewish person who knew the Old Testament that things like poverty and sickness were BLESSINGS. If you said to him, "You're going to be sick and broke for the rest of your life and God is going to use that illness and poverty to teach you something," he wouldn't think you had BLESSED him. He'd know you had cursed him.

Most Christians today have been robbed of such clarity. Their minds have been muddled by man-made doctrines so ridiculous they'd never believe them outside of church. Instead of having their minds washed with the water of The WORD, they've been brainwashed by tradition into believing that God actually sends bad things into their lives to bless them.

"I lost my job and went broke," they'll say. "That was when the Holy Spirit was finally able to teach me to put God first in my life. That proves poverty can sometimes be a BLESSING of The LORD."

Such statements may sound spiritual, but they're just plain wrong. Going broke is never a BLESSING. It's a curse.

Certainly, it's great to learn lessons from God. It's exciting to find out that if you seek first the kingdom of God and His righteousness, all these things shall be added unto you (Matthew 6:33). But poverty isn't what teaches us that truth. If it did, every poor person in the world would be a spiritual giant. No, the good things God said in His WORD (specifically, verses like Matthew 6:33) are what teach us to put God first. When we read and obey these verses, we can learn that lesson without having to lose a dime—and *that's* what the Bible calls BLESSING.

The Hebrew definition of the word *good* gives us further proof that a blessing is a purely positive thing. It includes: "beautiful, best, better, bountiful, joyful, kindly, loving, merry, pleasant, prosperity, sweet, wealth and to be well."[20] Since that list does not include even one negative word, we can put behind us forever, the idea that sorrowful, unpleasant, bitter things can be BLESSINGS. It is totally unscriptural.

That truth, by itself, will make us free. But there's another meaning for the word *blessing* that's even more exciting. It's a definition that comes into play when God gets involved. When He is the One speaking, a BLESSING is defined as not only saying something good about someone, but as a *declaration which empowers them to prosper*. Because God's words carry creative power (as seen throughout Genesis 1) His BLESSING does more than express a positive sentiment. It releases the power to bring that BLESSING to pass.

That's the reason THE BLESSING God spoke over mankind in Genesis 1:28 is so significant. God's declaration actually *empowered* man to prosper. It released the divine resources that would make THE BLESSING not just a spiritual reality, but a material reality as well. It endued God's family on earth with all the power they would ever need to:

Be fruitful, and multiply, and replenish the earth, and subdue it: and have dominion over the fish of the sea, and over the fowl of the air, and over every living thing that moveth upon the earth.

### "Go and Finish What I Started!"

Contrary to popular belief, when God spoke those words of BLESSING, He wasn't just commanding Adam and his wife

---

[20] James Strong, *The New Strong's Exhaustive Concordance of the Bible* (Nashville: Thomas Nelson Publishers, 1984) H2896.

to have babies to populate the earth. He was saying much more than that. In Hebrew, the phrase *be fruitful, and multiply* means to increase and have abundance in every way.[21] *Replenish* means to fill up, to perpetually renew, supply and keep full.[22] When God spoke those words, He endowed mankind with the divine power to increase and excel in everything good. He empowered them to fill the earth with that goodness.

Through THE BLESSING, He said: *Prosper and fill this planet with My glory! Finish what I've started here. Fill this place up with Me. Fill it up with compassion. Fill it up with love and life, faith and holiness, and everything good!*

"Wait a minute!" you might say. "I thought the earth was already finished when Adam and Eve were created. I thought God had done everything that needed to be done."

That's what I thought, too, until I studied what the Bible actually says about it. Like most believers, I assumed for years that God had so thoroughly completed the planet that all Adam and Eve had to do was pluck ripe fruit from the trees and enjoy themselves. I figured that because the Garden of Eden was a perfect place, there must not have been much work for them to do.

That would have been true if the Garden had covered the whole earth. But it didn't. Although it was a good-sized piece of property, according to the description given in Genesis, it was only about the size and in the general location of modern-day Iraq. The Bible tells us that God Himself planted it:

> …eastward in Eden; and there he put the man whom he had formed. And out of the ground made The LORD God to grow every tree that is pleasant to the sight, and good for food; the tree of life also in the midst of the garden, and the tree of knowledge of good and evil. And a river went out of Eden to water the garden; and from thence it was parted, and became into four heads. The name of the first is Pison:

---

[21] See Strong's H6509, H7235.
[22] See Strong's H4390.

that is it which compasseth the whole land of Havilah, where there is gold; and the gold of that land is good: there is bdellium and the onyx stone. And the name of the second river is Gihon: the same is it that compasseth the whole land of Ethiopia. And the name of the third river is Hiddekel: that is it which goeth toward the east of Assyria. And the fourth river is Euphrates. And The LORD God took the man, and put him into the garden of Eden to dress it and to keep it (Genesis 2:8-15).

By anyone's standards, the Garden of Eden was massive, and it was, without a doubt, an exquisite place to live. Filled with gorgeous trees that provided food fit for a king, it had a river running through it to keep it lush and green, plenty of gold *(good gold,* the Bible says) and other precious stones. It was, indeed, a BLESSED place—full of everything good and nothing bad.

The rest of the earth, however, was not in the same condition. God had created it with plenty of potential, but it had not yet been cultivated. It still needed to be developed and brought into line with God's perfect will. That's why He included in THE BLESSING, the power to *subdue* the earth and *have dominion* over it. The untamed earth needed supervision and direction. It wasn't yet finished.

God could have done the job Himself. He could have turned the whole planet into a Garden of Eden in an hour, but He had something else in mind. He wanted it to be a "family project"—to watch His sons and daughters become His co-creators and finish out the planet. So He gave them the Garden of Eden as a pilot project to get them started. God's plan was for them to expand it until the earth became the garden spot of the universe. Once earth was finished, they could go to work on the rest of the planets.

I'm convinced that's why there are so many barren, empty planets out there. God made them to be future sites for His family to develop. No wonder human beings dream of exploring the galaxy! No wonder we figured out a way to go to the moon and send spaceships to Mars! We were created to take dominion over the universe and fill every square inch of it with the glory of God.

## Not Just Weed-Pullers

Because God created mankind in His image, by His WORD of dominion, Adam sensed within himself, the desire for dominion the moment he took his first breath. From the beginning, ruling and reigning was a part of his DNA. He wasn't "just a weed-puller in the Garden of Eden." (Someone once said those very words to me, referring to Adam as "God's weed-puller!" I had to exercise great restraint to keep from telling him what an ignorant statement that was.) In the first place, there were no weeds in the Garden of Eden. If there had been, God would have pulled them Himself before He put Adam there. In the second place—and this is much more important—God didn't create Adam to be a servant of the earth. He made him to be a lord over it.

I realize that idea makes religious people nervous, but I don't apologize for it. It upset people in Jesus' day too. The religious people wanted to kill Him for speaking and acting like He had dominion on the earth. When He called God His Father and operated in THE BLESSING by using the same authority the first Adam had before he fell, it aggravated the Pharisees to no end. But, He didn't back down to make them feel better. Instead, He said:

> Is it not written in your law, I said, Ye are gods? If he called them gods, unto whom The WORD of God came, and the scripture cannot be broken; say ye of him, whom the Father hath sanctified, and sent into the world, Thou blasphemest; because I said, I am the Son of God? (John 10:34-36).

Jesus left no doubt about man's authority over the earth. He said that when God spoke His WORD of dominion into mankind, He made us "gods" (little "g") over all that He had created. He gave us authority over everything that flies, walks, crawls, swims and creeps. (I'm especially grateful the creeps are included in that list because flu viruses and cold germs qualify as creeps, so when they try to get on me, I can use my God-given authority to get rid of them!)

"Well, I'm just not convinced I can operate in that kind of dominion, Brother Copeland. Most of the time, I feel more like a weed-puller than a lord."

That may be true—but if you're honest, you'll admit that even while you're pulling weeds, you are longing for dominion. I know that's true because every human being on earth has that longing. Dominion is woven into our very nature. God breathed it into our spirits on day one. That's the reason human beings are always trying to exercise dominion over something. It's the reason why children invent games like "King of the Mountain." Even little children have an innate desire to reign.

I remember when Alex, one of my granddaughters, discovered that desire. She wasn't much more than a toddler at the time. My son, John (her dad), told her to do something, and when it became apparent she wasn't going to follow his instructions, John said, "Alex, you need to obey me."

"Why do I have to obey you?" she asked.

"Because I'm the boss," he answered.

Alex looked at him for a while and gave that some thought. "Then, I want to be the boss!" she announced.

Alex, like all human beings, wanted to be in charge. That's the way mankind is wired. We are all created to be *bosses* on this planet. We are divinely designed to reign. But, as Alex soon found out, it's one thing to have a desire to reign; it's another to be equipped to do it. The desire without the equipping leads to frustration. Try as we may to exercise dominion, if we don't have the power and resources to get the job done, our efforts will fail.

To see how important it is to be equipped for dominion, consider how Jesus transferred His authority to His disciples after His death and resurrection. He did it in two parts. First, He gave them the Great Commission and told them what to do. He said:

All power is given unto me in heaven and in earth. Go ye therefore, and teach all nations, baptizing them in the name of the Father, and of the Son, and of the Holy Ghost: teaching them to observe all things whatsoever I have commanded you: and, lo, I am with you always, even unto the end of the world. Amen (Matthew 28:18-20).

That commission authorized the disciples to preach the gospel worldwide. It instilled in them the desire to do so. But that alone was not enough. They also needed to be empowered or equipped to walk in that authority. So, Jesus commanded them to wait in Jerusalem for part two: *the promise of the Father*. He said to them, "Ye shall receive power, after that the Holy Ghost is come upon you: and ye shall be witnesses unto me both in Jerusalem, and in all Judaea, and in Samaria, and unto the uttermost part of the earth" (Acts 1:8).

The fiery power that came on the disciples at Pentecost, the outpouring of power we call the Baptism in the Holy Spirit, is what equipped the disciples to fulfill the mission Jesus gave them. It empowered them to go into all the world, operate in dominion over all the works of the devil and advance the kingdom of God. It provided them with the same kind of power Adam received when God declared over him the words of Genesis 1:28. It released to them THE BLESSING.

### Our Divine Mandate

I can almost hear you thinking, *What does the Baptism in the Holy Spirit have to do with THE BLESSING Adam received in the Garden of Eden?*

It has everything to do with it; and you'll eventually see the connection. But, for now, let's turn our attention back to the Garden of Eden. Let's see Adam again in our mind's eye as we saw him in chapter 1—in his first split-second of life, standing face to face with God on the center of the world stage, about to receive his mandate from God.

*Mandate* is a term often used in the political realm to refer to that which a government official has been commissioned to accomplish. A president, with a mandate from the people to protect the nation, is authorized and empowered by that mandate. It gives him not only the responsibility for national defense, but it also puts the military resources of the country under his command.

THE BLESSING was Adam's divine mandate. It delivered to him both the responsibility and the resources to fill the earth with God's goodness. It gave him a divine commission and crowned him with all the divine power he needed to fulfill it. When God spoke THE BLESSING over Adam, Psalm 8:5 says, He "crowned him with glory and honour."

Normally, when we think of a crown, we picture a circle of gold set on a person's head. But in Adam's case, the Bible says God crowned Adam by putting His own glory on him. He didn't just dab a little circle of it over him as a kind of halo, but the original Hebrew says God *encircled* or *encompassed* Adam in that glory.

Just imagine it! Adam's eardrums were still vibrating with the first sound he'd ever heard—the sound of Almighty God saying, "Be fruitful, and multiply, and replenish the earth, and subdue it: and have dominion..."—when suddenly he was engulfed by the blazing light of divine glory. He was lit up completely with the fire of God. It shone around him from the inside out, so he was totally encompassed by it.

That's why Adam didn't need material clothing. Although "they were both naked, the man and his wife,"[23] they were not ashamed because they *weren't* naked in the sense that we understand it. They weren't exposed. They were clothed with the radiant glory of God. They couldn't even see their physical bodies. When they looked at themselves and each other, what they saw was the glorious fire of God glistening with every color in existence!

Not only did that glory clothe them with God's light and beauty, it filled them to overflowing with His very essence. It enveloped

---

[23] Genesis 2:25

them in His presence, power, wisdom and love. THE BLESSING crowned Adam and his wife with the same light-energy God used to make the earth. It endued them with the divine power that created the universe. The earth and everything in it is designed to respond to that power. Every tree, and blade of grass, every living thing on the earth and under the sea, recognizes and yields to THE BLESSING because it is the parent force from which they originated.

The moment Adam and his wife received that BLESSING, all creation was under their command. They were totally equipped to fulfill their God-given mission. They had both the authority and the power to exercise dominion over the earth. Crowned with the manifestation of God's glory unique to this universe, they had as much right to use that power as God did. They had just as much divine ability to fill up the earth as God had to create it.

Once they had received THE BLESSING, they had everything they needed to spread the dominion of Compassion (the kingdom of God) into every corner of the earth. They were fully empowered to reign over the whole planet and every living creature in it by the power of love.

I realize that the thought of reigning through love is a novel idea these days. The devil has twisted most people's minds to the point they equate dominion with control. They think the only way to rule is with an iron fist. But God never intended man to dominate His creation that way. He didn't mean for mankind to subdue it with brute force. He planned for them to love this planet into submission, to shine the light of divine compassion on it and speak words of kindness, gentleness and goodness to it until the entire place blossomed into perfection.

### Talking to Trees—With Love

Cynics might claim such a thing would never work. But it does work. I've seen it time and again, not just in my own life, but in the lives of others. My dad, for example, caught hold of this truth many years ago and put it into practice with great success. He didn't have a full revelation of THE BLESSING, but he knew and

believed the words in Deuteronomy 28. He understood that his
land and everything on it was BLESSED, and therefore, it was supposed to prosper.

So, when parasites infested the grove of oak trees in his yard
and started to kill them, my dad took a stand. He refused to give up
on those trees even though the experts told him, "Mr. Copeland, we
have no answer for this problem. You'll just have to accept the fact
that these trees are going to die."

"No, they're not," he answered. Then he went into the house,
got his Bible, and walked around the yard reading Deuteronomy 28
to all his trees. He went to each of them and said, "You are not going to die. You are on my property so you are BLESSED. You will
live and flourish in the Name of Jesus."

Sure enough, every tree in that yard not only survived, but
flourished.

"That was just a coincidence!" someone might say.

No, it wasn't. I got the same results by talking to a tree that was
in even worse shape than his. Gloria and I had planted it because
we were living in a tiny house on a block where there wasn't a tree
in sight. We wanted to beautify the place a little, so we got a tree
that was just a couple of feet tall and stuck it right in the middle of
our front lawn.

The problem was, we were gone a lot of the time so we
couldn't tend to it much. When we were home, we'd water it and
nurse it along but, even so, it started to die. A few months after
we planted it, we came home from a meeting and every leaf had
fallen off the tree. It looked like a broom handle sticking out of
the ground.

I started to pull it up and throw it away, but for some reason, I
thought, *I don't believe I'll do that. I'm not going to let the devil
kill the only tree I have. I believe I'll use what I've been learning
about THE BLESSING, instead.* When I told Gloria about it, she
jumped right on board. "Why don't you start by praying over the
tree in tongues?" I said.

"OK," she answered, and went after it. I'm telling you, that woman can pray in tongues! She has prayed in tongues an hour a day for more than 20 years. She can get the job done.

After she finished and went in the house, I got my Bible and sat down in front of that tree, with it sticking up between my knees. "Hey, tree, you are not going to die," I said. "I'm not going to let you die. I speak life to you. I speak THE BLESSING of God over you. I speak the love of God and the power of God over you…." After I'd talked to it for a while, my head started reasoning: *People in this neighborhood already think you are strange. Now, they have absolute proof. They're all looking out their windows at you and saying, "That idiot is talking to trees!"*

I refused to let it bother me, though. I said to myself, "I'll talk to whomever or whatever I please. It's my tree and I'll preach an entire sermon to it if I want to." So I kept on talking and dragged the hose around to squirt some water on it.

Days passed, and the tree still looked as bad as it ever had. Gloria and I would leave town and come back and there it would be, just a pitiful-looking stick barely clinging to life. I was tempted to give up. *Maybe that tree is so far gone it can't hear me,* I thought. But I just couldn't go for that. Though I didn't know as much about THE BLESSING back then as I do now, I still expected it to work. So I just kept talking…and talking…and talking to that tree.

After a while, God BLESSED Gloria and me with a nicer house and we moved. Years went by without a thought about that little tree. Then one day, The LORD reminded me about it, and I decided to drive by and take a look at it. You should have seen how it had grown! It covered half the yard and a third of the neighbor's. It had blossomed out all over.

I learned something from that experience. I learned that to operate in THE BLESSING, you just speak The WORD. Say about things what God says about them. Then, just go about your business and expect those things to come to pass.

That's what Adam and his wife were originally supposed to do. That's how God meant for them to exercise dominion over the earth: by speaking God's WORD in love. It would have worked, too. Even though they didn't have a Bible, though they didn't even know good from evil, if they had chosen to stick with God's original program, THE BLESSING itself would have taught them what to say. It would have revealed to them everything they needed to know about exercising dominion.

Because THE BLESSING includes not only the glory and power of God, but the Person and wisdom of the Holy Spirit, it would have guided that first man and woman into all truth.[24] They didn't have to struggle along on their own and learn everything by trial and error. They didn't have to sin to find out what evil was. They could have just let the Anointing of God teach them about it.

That's what Jesus did during His life on earth. He grew in the wisdom of God until He understood all there is to know about good and evil, without ever violating God's command. Adam could have done the same thing. If he had just obeyed God and stayed connected to THE BLESSING, he would have had continual access to the wisdom of God, and with that wisdom, reigned on earth as a compassionate king, until the whole planet flourished under his care.

For a very short while, that's exactly what Adam did. His first day on the job, for example, he used the power of THE BLESS-ING to direct the future course of the entire animal kingdom. God brought to him every species "to see what he would call them: and whatsoever Adam called every living creature, that was the name thereof. And Adam gave names to all cattle, and to the fowl of the air, and to every beast of the field" (Genesis 2:19-20).

To understand the significance of those verses, you must remember that to God, a name is everything. As far as He is concerned, whatever a thing is called is what it becomes. Since the animals had no names, they had no direction for life. They did not yet have any unique and definite function. So, God brought them to Adam and let him try his hand at bringing love, life and purpose to them. He let Adam determine the character and chart the behavior of

---

[24] John 14:26 "But the Comforter, which is the Holy Ghost, whom the Father will send in my name, he shall teach you all things, and bring all things to your remembrance, whatsoever I have said unto you."

every bird, and bug, and everything that creeps, crawls and swims.

What a massive task! Just think of Adam standing alongside God, studying a bulky, baffling-looking creature and drawing on God's wisdom to determine what to call it. Imagine Adam saying, "Elephant, *be!*" and the animal answering in response, "Thank you very much, sir," as he walked away, a living, breathing elephant with personality and purpose!

"Brother Copeland, do you actually think the animals talked?"

I don't know. The Bible doesn't specifically say. But they might have before sin entered the picture and messed up everything. (It is interesting to note that when the serpent talked to Eve in the Garden, she didn't express any surprise. She conversed with him as if it were a normal thing to do.) Whether or not the animals talked, however, one thing is certain: They all drew their purpose and character from what Adam spoke over them.

How did he know what to say in that situation? How did he manage to give direction to every creature on earth without any prior training or experience?

He did it by drawing on THE BLESSING. He did it by drawing on the divine energy, wisdom and love that crowned him. Throughout the whole process, Adam was pulling, by faith, on his Father's abilities. God's creativity and compassion were flowing into him, and then out through him into creation. Adam didn't just pull names out of a hat. He drew them out of Love Himself. He was loving the birds as they flew to meet him. He was loving the animals as they came, and BLESSING them all, just as God had BLESSED him.

At that moment, Adam was standing in the center of God's perfect will for mankind. He was in absolute unity and fabulous fellowship with his heavenly Father. He was surrounded by God's goodness and plentiful provision, living a sinless, sickness-free, marvelously abundant life. What's more, he had a worldwide vision and the power to carry it out. He had an international ministry, a divine calling to multiply, be fruitful and fill the earth with the same abundant life God had given him. Commissioned to build

God's family and expand the Garden of Eden until it filled the earth, Adam was on a mission to encompass the world with the glorious BLESSING of God. Divine connection!

Life just doesn't get any better than that.

## The Day God Retired

And God saw every thing that he had made, and, behold, it was very good. And the evening and the morning were the sixth day. Thus the heavens and the earth were finished, and all the host of them. And on the seventh day God ended his work which he had made; and he rested on the seventh day from all his work which he had made. And God BLESSED the seventh day, and sanctified it: because that in it he had rested from all his work which God created and made (Genesis 1:31, 2:1-3).

Once THE BLESSING had been released on Adam, God retired. He rested—not because He was tired but because He was finished. He had completed His work on the universe, poured Himself into mankind, crowned them with His creative power, and given them total authority over the earth. There was nothing more for Him to do. Having turned everything over to His family of subcreators, God intended to relax, fellowship with His sons and daughters, and enjoy the thrill of watching them develop planet Earth into the most marvelous garden anyone has ever seen. When they finished it, He planned to move His heavenly headquarters to Earth and make it His home, so He could dwell there with His family forever.[25]

When you think about it, the fact that God rested on the seventh day—that He actually ended His work and retired—is astounding. As we've already noted, Adam and his wife were still novices in every way at that time. They had no dominion experience. They'd

---

[25] See Revelation 21:2-3.

never subdued a planet before. Yet, God was so confident they could get the job done, He just leaned back, put up His feet and said, "I'm finished, family. Now it's your turn to build Me a home."

How could God put such confidence in them? Because He had confidence in the divine connection. He had given them THE BLESSING, and that BLESSING is divinely designed to create the conditions of the Garden of Eden. Its God-ordained purpose is to provide mankind with everything they need to fill the earth with God's glory. Whenever THE BLESSING is released, it goes to work bringing things into line with the love of God. It goes to work making everything good.

If you want to know how THE BLESSING knows to do that, I'll tell you: God programmed it that way, just like He programmed the ground to make things grow. The ground treats everything like a seed. Put a fence post in the ground and the dirt will go to work decomposing it. It will start gnawing on the fence post like it would gnaw on the husk of an acorn. It will completely rot the bottom off that post trying to open it up so the thing can sprout. Bury an old shoe, and the dirt will do the same thing to it because that's what God programmed dirt to do.

You can see that same pattern throughout creation. Apple seeds bring forth apple trees because they carry inside them the genetic image of apple trees. Watermelon seeds produce watermelon vines because they're designed by God to do so. Animals reproduce according to the DNA they receive from their parents. The golden-retriever puppy, for example, that Gloria and I got for our son when he was a little boy was a retriever from the start. No one had to teach him to run after things. When he was only a few weeks old, we'd pitch something across the yard and he'd run after it. We'd throw a stick into the lake and he'd jump in and start swimming. He couldn't help it. Retrieving was just in him.

THE BLESSING is the same way. It carries within it the blueprint of the Garden of Eden. It's designed by God to reproduce that Garden by empowering God's family to be fruitful, prosper and walk in dominion on the earth. When it's released by faith, that's what it does. Every time. All the time.

So, once THE BLESSING was in place, God rested.

He didn't just rest for 24 hours and go back to work again when Adam sinned. He is still resting today. That doesn't mean He is inactive. It simply means He hasn't changed His mind. He hasn't altered His plan. He has given His WORD that His family is BLESSED and He is resting, assured that the power of that BLESSING will bring His WORD to pass in spite of everything hell tries to do.

Once you understand that fact, you'll begin to understand in a much clearer way, everything else the Bible says. You'll begin to realize everything God has spoken to and for mankind—from Genesis to Revelation—has been in relation to those first words He said to Adam 6,000 years ago. Everything He has done has been for one, central purpose: to get THE BLESSING back where it belongs.

# Chapter Four

# The Day the Light Went Out

(For if by one man's offence death reigned by one; much more they
which receive abundance of grace and of the gift of righteousness
shall reign in life by one, Jesus Christ.).... That as sin hath reigned
unto death, even so might grace reign through righteousness unto
eternal life by Jesus Christ our Lord.
Romans 5:17, 21

Had it not been for the devil, and man's cooperation
with him, the Bible could have been a very short book.
It could have ended with Genesis 2. Any scriptural records written after that would have been filled with stories about God and
His family laughing together, loving each other, and co-creating
throughout eternity—stories about how everyone (except Satan and
his crew) lived happily ever after.

Had it not been for the devil, we would never have seen the
serious side of God.

For years, I thought that was the only side God had. I thought
He was 100 percent serious. I'd seen so much bawling and squall-
ing religion and been around so many people who thought that if
you're not crying and emotionally distraught, you're not getting
anything from God, I just figured He had a solemn temperament.
I knew that He is gracious enough to put up with us when we're

lighthearted and having fun, but I had the idea He wasn't a fun kind of person Himself.

One morning some years ago, however, I discovered I was wrong. During a time of prayer, I broke through into a spirit of praise and started enjoying the presence of God so much that I forgot myself and got giddy. I started giggling, laughing, hollering and jumping around…and right in the middle of it all, the devil broke in on me. "Do you have any idea how dumb you look right now?" he said.

I had to admit, I didn't look very dignified or religious, and for a split second I was tempted to feel sheepish. Then, the story of David flashed across my mind. I remembered how he got so carried away once when he was praising The LORD, that he leapt, danced and threw off his robe right in the middle of the street. He embarrassed his wife so much that she accused him of being vulgar. But David didn't care. He answered by saying, "I am willing to act like a fool in order to show my joy in The LORD. Yes, and I am willing to look even more foolish than this…."[26] That just means, "Woman, you ain't seen nothin' yet!"

Following David's example, I ignored what the devil had said to me. I just shouted louder and kept on rejoicing. When I did, I heard the word of The LORD in my spirit. He spoke to me in a strong, sweet voice that on the inside of me was audible and said, *Kenneth, if it hadn't been for sin, I never would have had a serious thought.*

That statement came as a shock to me. It so contradicted the traditional concept of God, that I wasn't sure if I should believe it. But the more I thought about it, the more sense it made. It dawned on me that according to the Bible, heaven is the place where God's will is done. And there isn't anything in heaven to be serious about. There's no bitterness there, no sorrow there, no danger, no death. In a place like that, you can just have fun all the time.

"But Brother Copeland, this is earth!" you might say. "There's lots here to be serious about."

I know it. But that doesn't change God's nature. It doesn't

---

[26] 2 Samuel 6:21-22, *New Living Translation-96*

make Him any less a joyful, fun-loving Father. It doesn't change His will, either. He wants His will done on earth as it is in heaven (Matthew 6:10). No wonder the Bible tells us again and again to rejoice! No wonder, even under the Old Covenant, God set up feast days and told His people to spend them enjoying themselves, praising Him and having a good time! That's God's nature. That was His original plan—not to set up some sad, sorrowful religion, but to have fun with His family forever.

If Adam and his wife had obeyed God, they could have spent eternity just having a great time. But, they didn't. They deviated from God's instructions, and the results were catastrophic. In the Garden of Eden, as today, everything depended on obedience to God's WORD, so when they turned their backs on that WORD and tried to act independently, they messed up God's plan and things got serious—fast.

Notice, I said they *tried* to act independently. They didn't succeed because, as glorious as they were, the man and woman were not sovereign in their own right. They were not created to be independent. They were designed to operate under the authority of a spiritual Head—to draw their life from God, to be connected to Him and joyfully submit to His loving authority.

God established that relationship with them and gave them the opportunity to maintain it by retaining ownership of one tree in the Garden. He put everything else on earth under their lordship. Every other aspect of creation was theirs to partake in, enjoy and have dominion over. But that one tree—the tree of the knowledge of good and evil—belonged to God, and He told them not to eat the fruit of it. "For in the day that thou eatest thereof thou shalt surely die" (Genesis 2:17).

God's command was so simple, you wouldn't think anyone could misunderstand it, but somehow the woman did. However it happened, she got the idea that they weren't even supposed to touch the tree. But that wasn't true. They *were* supposed to touch the tree. God had commanded them to tend and keep it just like they did the other trees in the Garden.[27] Instead of staying away from that tree, they should have given it extra attention. They should have been especially committed to caring for it because it belonged to God. It represented God's fatherhood and headship over mankind. That's why God placed that tree in the center of the Garden: because their relationship with Him was supposed to be at the center of their lives.

Although Adam fouled things up before God had an opportunity to teach him about it, God intended His tree to be a place where He and His family could fellowship with each other. He meant for Adam and his wife, and ultimately their children and grandchildren, to harvest the fruit of it and bring it to Him as an act of obedience and a confirmation of their love for Him. God wanted them to have the time of their lives returning to Him the fruit of His tree and celebrating the fact that He was then, and is now, the Source of THE BLESSING that was upon them.

If you're wondering how I know that, I found it out by reading the rest of the Book. I found it out by studying what the Bible says about tithing, which is the practice of bringing to God the firstfruits that belong to Him. Throughout scriptural history, God's people have drawn near to Him and connected with His covenant of BLESSING, through the tithe.

Contrary to what some have taught, the concept of tithing didn't originate with the Law of Moses. It originated in the Garden of Eden. That's why in Genesis 4 we find Abel bringing God the firstborn of his flock. Although Abel lived thousands of years before the Law was given, somehow, he learned to tithe. Who taught him? There's only one possible answer. It must have been his father, Adam. Apparently, Adam wanted his children to avoid the heartbreaking, life-wrecking sin he had committed, so he instructed them to give God the first and best portion of their increase.

Abel understood and applied what Adam told him. His brother,

---

[27] Genesis 2:15: "And The LORD God took the man, and put him into the garden of Eden to dress it and to keep it."

Cain, however, didn't. What happened between them as a result, reveals just how vital the principle of tithing truly is. It proves there's more to it than dividing a paycheck by 10 percent and plunking it into a bucket, or legalistically keeping an Old Testament law. Tithing is a covenant interaction between God and man. It represents a spiritual reality that is so powerful, the devil will do everything he can to stop it. That's the reason the first murder in human history was committed over the tithe.

You probably remember the story. When Cain and Abel brought their tithes, God accepted Abel's and refused Cain's. That threw Cain into such a rage that he killed his brother. Why was it so crucial to Cain that God accept his tithe? Because tithing is an act of faith that confirms THE BLESSING—and Cain wanted that BLESSING. He understood that it is the most powerful thing on earth.

There have been a lot of theories offered over the years to explain why Cain's tithe was rejected. Some have suggested that his offering was unacceptable because it wasn't an animal. But that wasn't the problem. Since Cain worked the land, his tithe naturally would have come from the firstfruits of his field. But he didn't bring God the firstfruits. The Hebrew Scriptures indicate he brought the third picking.[28] What Cain gave God was worthless! Anyone who has ever lived on a farm knows what late or third pickings are. They're not good for anything but cow feed. They're shriveled-up leftovers that are tough as leather.

God called that kind of offering a *sin*. But, even so, He didn't condemn Cain right away. He gave him another opportunity and said, "If you do well, will you not be accepted? And if you do not do well, sin lies at the door. And its desire is for you, but you should rule over it."[29] At that point, Cain could have repented and started over, but he wouldn't do it. Instead, he became offended. He let the devil get him so riled up that he finally committed murder.

It's a sad story, but it makes a clear point: The tithe is precious to

---

[28] *The Chumash*, ed. Rabbi Nosson Scherman, Art Scroll Series, Stone Edition Travel Size (Brooklyn: Mesorah Publications, 1998) p. 21.
[29] Genesis 4:7, *New King James Version*

God and powerful for mankind—and the devil hates it. He hates it because it represents THE BLESSING he can never have. He hates it because it establishes God as the spiritual head of His family. It confirms God's people as the rulers who have been given authority over the earth.

Although the devil would like us to think so, God never meant for the tithe to be a kind of religious bondage or a legalistic rule. He meant for it to be an act of BLESSING and rejoicing. If Adam and his wife had walked with God long enough, they could have found that out. They could have had all kinds of fun watching over God's tree. They could have said, "This belongs to our Father! Let's bless it extra. Let's give it more attention than any of the others so when we bring Him the fruit, it'll be the best in the Garden!"

If they'd taken that attitude, God would have taught them everything they needed to know about good and evil. He would have spent much time with them, teaching them how to operate in THE BLESSING. He would have told them all about the universe and all the marvelous angels He had created to help them exercise their dominion over it. God didn't intend for Adam to be ignorant of those things. He planned to instruct them Himself in just the right way at just the right time.

But they didn't give Him the opportunity. They stole! They picked and ate something that did not belong to them (Malachi 3:8). According to the Hebrew sages, they did it the first day.[30] They let the devil convince them that God was holding out on them, and that if they ever wanted to learn the truth about good and evil, they'd have to learn it from him. As we now know, the whole idea was preposterous. The devil can't teach anyone the truth about anything because "there is no truth in him...for he is a liar, and the father of it."[31] Yet he talked Adam's wife into believing otherwise, and here's how he did it...

---

[30] *The Chumash,* ed. Rabbi Nosson Scherman, Art Scroll Series, Stone Edition Travel Size (Brooklyn: Mesorah Publications, 1998) p. 15.
[31] John 8:44

## The Great Deception

Now the serpent was more subtle than any beast of the field which The LORD God had made. And he said unto the woman, Yea, hath God said, Ye shall not eat of every tree of the garden? And the woman said unto the serpent, We may eat of the fruit of the trees of the garden: But of the fruit of the tree which is in the midst of the garden, God hath said, Ye shall not eat of it, neither shall ye touch it, lest ye die. And the serpent said unto the woman, Ye shall not surely die: For God doth know that in the day ye eat thereof, then your eyes shall be opened, and ye shall be as gods, knowing good and evil. And when the woman saw that the tree was good for food, and that it was pleasant to the eyes, and a tree to be desired to make one wise, she took of the fruit thereof, and did eat, and gave also unto her husband with her; and he did eat. And the eyes of them both were opened, and they knew that they were naked... (Genesis 3:1-7).

To understand what the devil had in mind when he devised his plan, you have to remember that when God declared THE BLESSING over Adam on the day he was created, everyone and everything in the universe witnessed the event. Not only did Adam and the ministering angels hear THE BLESSING, but the devil heard it too. When he did, it must have infuriated him. He couldn't stand the fact that the God-like power he so desperately wanted for himself had been freely bestowed on man. He refused to just stand by and watch while the crown of glory, authority and power he had once dreamed of wearing—the crown he had fought and lost everything to gain—blazed in all its divine beauty on this creature called man.

The question was: What could he do about it?

He was smart enough to know he couldn't overthrow this newly created God-like race. He'd learned that lesson the hard way. He'd already tried to break out of the angelic class in which he was created and make himself like God, and it hadn't worked. He'd ended up an angel, still—but a fallen one with no authority over anything. Separated from God, a twisted version of his former self, all the spiritual forces within him had been corrupted. The light of God for which he was named had become darkness. Love had turned to hate, faith had become fear.

Since his outright attack on heaven hadn't worked, this time the devil decided to try a different tactic. He'd use deception to turn things his way. He'd try to convince the man and woman that God didn't really have their best interests at heart, and He couldn't be trusted. He would deceive them into committing high treason and switching their loyalty to him. Then, he would become their spiritual head, and all the power, glory and authority God had given them would be under his command. By hijacking the dominion God had already delivered into man's hands, Satan could, at last, become the god of all the earth.

In part, it was a workable plan, and the devil knew it. He knew that God, who never breaks His WORD, would not, under any circumstances, revoke the authority He had delegated to mankind. He also reasoned that since God had already given Adam the earth and everything in it, if Adam rebelled, God would be caught in a quandary. He couldn't go back to the drawing board and create another man from the dust of the earth without taking back what He had given. Bound by His own integrity, God would find Himself on the outside, looking in.

Proud, no doubt, of the brilliance of his plan, Satan set his scheme in motion by gaining possession of a serpent—one of the animals of the field that Adam had named. Keep in mind that at the time, a serpent wasn't a bad thing. The name wasn't a symbol of evil as it is now. Back then, *serpent* was a wonderful name for a beautiful animal that God had created. The serpent was a delightful creature both God and Adam loved.

That poor serpent didn't know anything about protecting himself. Adam and his wife were his protectors. In characteristic fashion, however, the devil didn't present himself to them and ask permission. He went straight to the serpent and did the same thing he always does. He conned and exploited him, knowing full well he was about to destroy this animal's future forever. The devil used that beautiful creature, ruined him, and then threw him away like a piece of trash. He left him crawling on his belly in the dirt, with a brain less than the size of a walnut, doomed to be despised by mankind all the days of his life.

That's always the devil's mode of operation. He does the same thing today to anyone who will let him. He is still a con artist who feeds people with his lies and exploits them for his own purposes. He is a filthy, heartless, hell-bound, hell-filled creature, and you ought to run him out of your life every time he shows his ugly face.

Actually, that's what Adam should have done. The moment the devil showed up in that snake suit, speaking evil of God and questioning His WORD, Adam should have slammed the devil's face up against the tree of the knowledge of good and evil and said, "You see that tree? That's God's tree. We do with it what He says. Now you shut your lying mouth!" Adam should have laughed in his face when he told them that God didn't want them to be like Him. He should have said, "Hey, we're already like God! Haven't you heard? He made us in His image. What you're doing is trying to make us like you, and you can forget that business because we're not interested!"

Adam could have cursed the devil just like God did later and put him under their feet. God had given him the authority to do it. Had Adam used that authority instead of abdicating it, he could have done at the beginning what the last Adam will do at the end of this age. He could have put an end to the devil's activities right then. He could have jailed him until the time came to throw him in the lake of fire. That's how Jesus is going to deal with him in the millennium.[32] He is going to lock the devil in a hole and slam the lid on it for 1,000 years.

---

[32] Revelation 20:1-3

"Well, I don't think we should put all the blame on Adam," someone might say. "After all, the devil sneaked up on his wife while he was out tending the Garden."

No, that's not how the Book records it. Genesis 3:6 says Adam was there *with* her when it happened. She turned to him and handed him the fruit. He was at Eve's side the whole time and could have straightened out her thinking before she got into trouble because although she was deceived, he wasn't.[33] He walked into that sin with his eyes wide open.

When he did, the unthinkable happened. The light went out. The fiery glory that had illuminated and surrounded Adam and his wife departed. At that moment, they saw their physical bodies for the first time. They realized they were naked, and they felt ashamed. As bad as that was, however, it was only the tip of the iceberg. It was only the part they could immediately see.

What they couldn't see was the distortion that had taken place within them. They could sense it because they felt fear and shame for the first time in their short lives, but they could not possibly have grasped the full implication of what they had done. They couldn't have known the same thing that once happened to the devil was now happening to them. Because they had disconnected from God, the spiritual forces He had put within them were being twisted 180 degrees, becoming the polar opposite of what God intended.

They didn't understand it all, but the horror of it hit them right away. They knew they'd made a catastrophic choice when the light went out. But there was nothing they could do about it. They had unplugged from God and plugged in to Satan, and now there wasn't any way for them to break loose from him. They were like babies who had once been linked by a spiritual umbilical cord to God. Through that cord, God's own love, joy, peace, patience, kindness, goodness, faithfulness, gentleness and temperance had flowed continually into them. But now, that cord linked them to the devil and every foul thing in him was flowing into them. Because

---

[33] 1 Timothy 2:14: "And Adam was not deceived, but the woman being deceived was in the transgression."

they were made to partake of the nature of their spiritual head, the light within them had become darkness. The love had turned to hate. Their faith turned to fear. At that moment, what was said about evil men 4,000 years later, could have been said of Adam and Eve: "Ye are of your father the devil, and the lusts of your father ye will do."[34]

God had warned them it would happen. He told them the day they disobeyed and ate the fruit of God's tree, they would die. He didn't mean that their bodies would immediately stop functioning, and they would cease to exist. People sometimes think that's what He meant because they have such a misunderstanding of death. But the fact is, no spirit being ever ceases to exist. Once spirit beings are created, they are around forever because they are eternal creatures.

Because God is life, to a spirit being, the true meaning of *death* is "separation from God." According to that definition, God's warning came to pass, not when Adam and Eve's bodies finally surrendered to the effects of death some 900 years later, but the very moment they committed sin. The first instant they disobeyed, they disconnected from the life of God and died spiritually.

## The Real Source of the Curse

Although the Bible doesn't say for sure, things might have taken a different course had Adam repented and taken responsibility for what happened. But he didn't. When God came looking for him in the Garden, instead of running to Him and confessing his sin, Adam hid because he was naked and afraid. He cowered behind the bushes and tried to cover up his shame.

Since God is omniscient, Adam couldn't really conceal anything from Him. God knew where Adam was and what he had done, the whole time. He didn't have to wait for Adam to tell Him. He could have come storming in to the Garden, tearing things up and exposing Adam's sin. He could have pulled Adam out of his hiding place and said, "Don't you think I can see you in there, you

---

[34] John 8:44

naked, disobedient man?" But, that's not the way God is. He's
a gentleman. In His kindness, He called out to Adam and said,
"Where are you?" to let them know He was close by. He didn't
want to embarrass them. He knew they felt ashamed, so He dealt
with them with graciousness and sensitivity. He gave them the
opportunity to come to Him on their own, to regain their place by
choosing to acknowledge their sin.

But, they didn't take that opportunity. When Adam came out of
hiding, God asked him the direct question: "Who told thee that thou
wast naked? Hast thou eaten of the tree, whereof I commanded thee
that thou shouldest not eat?" Rather than owning up to his rebellion, Adam blamed his wife. He said, "The woman whom thou
gavest to be with me, she gave me of the tree, and I did eat."[35]

Adam's wife did the same thing when God said to her, "What
is this that thou hast done?" She shifted the blame and answered,
"The serpent beguiled me, and I did eat" (verse 13).

What happened next has been misunderstood for years.
Through misinterpretation of the Scriptures, people have the idea
that God responded in anger to Adam and Eve's sin and denial,
punishing their sin by pronouncing curses on them and then casting them out of the Garden. But nothing could be further from the
truth. The whole message of the Bible is that God still loved Adam
and Eve, even in their fallen state—as He has loved the whole
world ever since. He loved them so much that He was willing to
sacrifice Himself to save them from the spiritual death trap that had
ensnared them. His immediate response was not to punish mankind
for what they had done, but to redeem them from it.

"If that's true, then why did God release the curse?" you
might ask.

God didn't release the curse. Adam did, by putting THE
BLESSING into the hands of the devil. Under demonic control,
THE BLESSING became the exact opposite of what God had cre-
ated it to be. THE BLESSING became the curse.

---

[35] Genesis 3:11-12

Adam had no idea that could happen, and the devil didn't either. He had it figured another way. He thought that by capturing mankind, he could gain access to the power and glory they'd been given to rule the earth. He thought he could elevate himself to their godlike status and get his hands on THE BLESSING. But he was wrong. His conquest of Adam and his wife didn't cause *him* to ascend, it caused *them* to fall. Instead of becoming lord of THE BLESSING he had coveted, the devil's own deadness contaminated its glorious power and he became lord of the curse.

At first, he didn't realize it. He couldn't fully see the deadly consequences of his actions. Neither could the man and woman. All they knew for sure was that the light of God's glory had gone out. They had no way of knowing what would happen to them and to the earth as a result. So, God told them. He spoke to them about the curse they had released through their rebellion. He didn't create the curse by declaration as He did THE BLESSING. (Legally, He could not do that because He had delegated His creative authority on earth to man.) He simply informed the devil first, then Adam and his wife, about the repercussions of what they had done.

And The LORD God said unto the serpent, Because thou hast done this, thou art cursed above all cattle, and above every beast of the field; upon thy belly shalt thou go, and dust shalt thou eat all the days of thy life: And I will put enmity between thee and the woman, and between thy seed and her seed; it shall bruise thy head, and thou shalt bruise his heel.... And unto Adam he said, Because thou hast hearkened unto the voice of thy wife, and hast eaten of the tree, of which I commanded thee, saying, Thou shalt not eat of it: cursed is the ground for thy sake; in [toiling] sorrow shalt thou eat of it all the days of thy life; thorns also and thistles shall it bring forth to thee; and thou shalt eat the herb of the field; in the sweat of thy face shalt thou eat bread, till thou return unto the ground; for out of it wast thou taken: for dust thou art, and unto dust shalt thou return (Genesis 3:14-15, 17-19).

Because Adam had been given dominion over the whole earth, the curse that came through him struck every molecule of matter in existence on this planet. All the dirt, vegetation, every cell of every animal, everything from the minutest detail to the biggest thing on earth was affected by it. According to the Bible, the whole creation groaned under the bondage that came upon it because of mankind's sin.[36]

The fact the curse covered this planet from top to bottom and all the way around, and hit everything that swims, flies, crawls and creeps, reveals in reverse, the true magnitude of THE BLESSING. It confirms the staggering, spiritual capacity God had given to man. It also proves that although the curse carries the devil's nature and influence, he isn't the driving force behind it. He doesn't have that kind of power. He can't do anything at all in the earth without human assistance. On his own, he couldn't have affected 1 square inch of this planet.

Because he is full of pride, he would like for us to think otherwise. He'd like us to believe he's an absolute powerhouse and that we, as human beings, are just unworthy, little worms that God had mercy on. But don't fall for that. It's a lie. Even fallen, unredeemed men and women are more powerful than the devil and can take authority over him to some degree. (They rarely do because he has them deceived and bound by fear, but they have the ability.)

Just one human being has such tremendous spiritual capacity that thousands of demons can live in and around him. If you doubt it, read the New Testament account of the madman of Gadara. He had so many devils inside him that when Jesus cast them out and sent them into a herd of pigs, they drove all 2,000 of those pigs crazy—so crazy, in fact, that they rushed off a cliff and drowned themselves in the sea. That shows just how helpless demons are when they're on their own. Through the man from Gadara, they were able to terrorize the entire region and everyone in it. Once they lost that man's authority, they couldn't even control a herd of pigs.

---

[36] Romans 8:19-22

If one man has that much power in his fallen state, how much power and authority do we, as believers, have? We have *all power and all authority*—because Jesus does, and we are in Him, and He in us. The devil doesn't want you to know it, but this is the truth: *There's nothing bigger in this universe than redeemed man.*

"Oh, Brother Copeland, surely God is bigger than a redeemed man!"

God is the Most High. There's no argument about that. But if you think that lowers our spiritual status, consider this: Through Jesus, the Most High God lifted us up to His level. By seating a born-again, resurrected man at His right hand as an eternal member of the Godhead, the Most High has included all of us who by faith are "in Christ," in the Godhead, too.[37] He has made us part of the Body of Christ and set us "far above all principality, and power, and might, and dominion, and every name that is named, not only in this world, but also in that which is to come."[38] There is a MAN in the Godhead! THE MAN, Jesus!

## A Bitter Pill to Swallow

The principalities and powers mentioned in the verse above are the demonic spirits that moved into the atmospheric heavens around the earth after the Fall of Man. They invaded the spiritual realm of this planet when the curse drove out all the angels who had been created to minister to mankind. As facilitators of THE BLESSING, those angels had to withdraw when THE BLESSING became the curse.

Think of it! All the angels that work for Gabriel, the archangel of God's communication system, were suddenly gone. All the angels under the command of Michael, the archangel of the heavenly hosts, were gone. Their absence opened the way for the devil and his principalities and powers to set up their kingdom. From the

---

[37] Ephesians 2:5-6: "Even when we were dead in sins, hath quickened us together with Christ, (by grace ye are saved;) And hath raised us up together, and made us sit together in heavenly places in Christ Jesus."
[38] Ephesians 1:21

moment Adam sinned until the day of Pentecost described in Acts 2, ministering angels could visit the earth only on specific assignments in specific places. They ascended and descended only in isolated instances as they did on Jacob's "ladder."[39]

It's no wonder the Hebrew root of the word *curse* means "bitterness" because the curse made Adam and Eve's lives bitter in every way. It embittered both the spirit realm and the natural realm. It caused the animals Adam had named to see him as their enemy instead of their benefactor. Even the ground became bitter toward mankind. Instead of joyfully producing abundant fruit for them to eat, it didn't want to grow anything. Adam, who had once lived in a marvelous, beautiful place filled with abundance, was forced to scratch a living out of ground that rebuked him every time he tried to plant it and harvest it. He had to sweat and strain (Hebrew: *toil*) to earn a living, knowing the whole time that God had not designed him to *earn* a living, but to *create* a living.

Every aspect of the curse came as a horrible shock to Adam and Eve. Nothing in them was created to deal with it. Their spirits weren't created to be infested with death and darkness. They were created to be filled with life and light. Their minds weren't made to house things like hatred and fear. They were made for love and faith. Their bodies were designed for health—not sickness and disease.

Death, in all its manifestations, is totally foreign to human beings. The curse is completely contrary to the way God made us. That's why the body fights those things. Our whole system rebels against them because they don't have any business in or on us. When sin, hate, fear and other aspects of the curse invade us, our bodies recognize them as opposing, alien forces and begin to fight them. The body will fight those things until it dies.

Adam must have panicked as the consequences of the curse began to dawn on him. He must have thought, *How am I ever going to get out of this? My seed is bitter, so even my children will be affected*

---

[39] Genesis 28:12: "And he dreamed, and behold a ladder set up on the earth, and the top of it reached to heaven: and behold the angels of God ascending and descending on it."

*by it. The earth is bitter. The animal kingdom is bitter. I've even embittered my relationship with God. Oh, God, how can I ever be Your friend again?*

Before he could even ask those questions, however, they were answered. God answered them before the foundation of the world, when He foresaw that mankind would fall. So, the moment Adam and Eve's sin was revealed and they stood before God, stripped of their former glory, He began revealing His merciful plan. He spoke about the Seed of the woman who would one day crush the serpent's head. He pointed down through the corridor of time to the last Adam, the Redeemer, who would undo what Satan had done through the first Adam. He gave the first clues to the mystery that would be kept secret for thousands of years: that God Himself would become the Son of Man, bear the bitterness of the curse and forever restore THE BLESSING.

Then, God did for His beloved Adam and Eve what had to be done. Sacrificing an animal, He covered their nakedness and shame by making them tunics of skin. Through that sacrifice, He established the first blood covenant. He atoned for their sin and made a way to retain some form of relationship with them. Then, in His great mercy, God ensured that mankind would not live eternally in this fallen state.

> Lest he put forth his hand, and take also of the tree of life, and eat, and live for ever…The LORD God sent him forth from the garden of Eden, to till the ground from whence he was taken. So he drove out the man; and he placed at the east of the garden of Eden Cherubims, and a flaming sword which turned every way, to keep the way of the tree of life (Genesis 3:22-24).

### Living Below the Light Line

Once, when I was fellowshiping with God over those verses, He said to me, *Did you notice I never punished Adam for what he did? I dealt with the circumstances he had created, but I didn't punish him because I'd already put the plan in place to bear his punishment, Myself.*

I'd never thought of it before, but at that moment I realized that even as Adam and Eve left the Garden, and before the foundation of the world, in God's mind, the words of Isaiah had already been written:

> Surely he hath borne our griefs, and carried our sorrows: yet we did esteem him stricken, smitten of God, and afflicted. But he was wounded for our transgressions, he was bruised for our iniquities: the chastisement of our peace was upon him; and with his stripes we are healed. All we like sheep have gone astray; we have turned every one to his own way; and The LORD hath laid on him the iniquity of us all (Isaiah 53:4-6).

That's why I can say with certainty that God did not send Adam and Eve out of Eden to punish them. He sent them out to protect them—and it grieved His heart to do it. Loving them as He did with the unquenchable compassion of a perfect Father, rather than sending them out, He wanted to wrap His arms around them and wipe away their tears. But He could not. Sin had forced a separation between them. The pure and holy fire of His glory would have destroyed Adam and Eve in their fallen state. It would have burned them to ashes because in the presence of pure light, darkness cannot exist. In the presence of pure life, death and everything associated with it is annihilated.

After the Fall, even the molecules of the earth itself—because they had been contaminated by the curse—couldn't bear up under direct contact with the pure presence of God. That's why, generations later, God had to cover Himself with a cloud when He descended on Mount Sinai to give Moses the commandments. He had to hide Himself to protect the earth and the people from being consumed by His glory. Even with the shield of that cloud around

Him, when God sat down on the mountain:

> The smoke thereof ascended as the smoke of a furnace, and
> the whole mount quaked greatly…. And all the people saw
> the thunderings, and the lightnings, and the noise of the
> trumpet, and the mountain smoking: and when the people
> saw it, they removed, and stood afar off. And they said unto
> Moses, Speak thou with us, and we will hear: but let not God
> speak with us, lest we die.[40]

It wasn't that way in the Garden before the Fall, but that's the
effect God had on this fallen creation. It started to come apart in
His presence. Mount Sinai almost exploded because it couldn't
handle the presence of its Creator. Neither could the Israelites.
They were so weakened by sin, just the sound of His voice hurt
them and they ran from Him in fear. It was not God's intention
to frighten or harm them, of course. He came to give them His
WORD. He came to teach them how to live in such a way, they
could reconnect with THE BLESSING. They had no one else to
show them how. So, He visited them Himself, wrapped in a cloud.

Unlike his fellow Israelites, Moses was frustrated with that
cloud. He had such an intense craving to see God face to face
that he prayed, "I beseech thee, show me thy glory!"[41] If God had
answered that prayer outright, Moses would have been physically
destroyed. So, God did the next best thing. He said:

> Thou canst not see my face: for there shall no man see me,
> and live…. Behold, there is a place by me, and thou shalt
> stand upon a rock: And it shall come to pass, while my glory
> passeth by, that I will put thee in a cleft of the rock, and will
> cover thee with my hand while I pass by: And I will take
> away mine hand, and thou shalt see my back parts: but my
> face shall not be seen (verses 33:20-23).

---

[40] Exodus 19:18, 20:18-19
[41] Exodus 33:18

If Moses, who had experienced only cloud-veiled glimpses of God's glory, had such a desperate desire to see The LORD, imagine what Adam and Eve must have felt after the Fall. Imagine how they must have grieved over their spiritual blindness. They had once fellowshiped with God face to face. They had walked with Him and talked with Him in the cool of the day. But through sin and spiritual death, they'd been separated from Him.

Essentially, they were in the same situation Moses was, with one big difference. They knew what they were missing. The splendor of God's glory and the realm of the spirit had once been as tangible and accessible to them as the material realm. Now that whole realm had vanished, and they found themselves trapped by darkness below the *light line*.

What is the light line?

It's the line that separates the spiritual realm from the material realm. It exists because the light God released on the first day of Creation functions on two different levels. The higher level constitutes the world of the spirit, and the lower (or slower) level constitutes the physical world of matter.

The Bible says that at the time of Creation, God made both a seen and an unseen realm. "For by him were all things created, that are in heaven, and that are in earth, visible and invisible...."[42]

The invisible realm above the light line, is where angels and other spirit beings live. Heaven is there. All kinds of glorious things are there. We can't see them with our natural eyes or touch them with our natural hands, but they're there, nonetheless, and just as real (or even more real) as the things in this physical realm.

Above the light line, spirit to spirit is firm and tangible, just as in the natural realm flesh to flesh is firm and tangible. Angels can touch one another. They can see each other. They aren't just floating mists, disappearing and reappearing. Their bodies have form and substance just as ours do, but they are made of spiritual, rather than material substance. Because of that fact, as long as we

---

[42] Colossians 1:16

are in our physical bodies, you and I can't see them. Occasionally, when they are on special assignment at the direction of The LORD, they'll slow down to our speed and make an appearance. But otherwise, our natural senses cannot detect their presence.

When we die, however, and our spirits leave our bodies, all that changes. We will instantly become aware of the spirit realm. It will be as real to us as this earthly realm is now. We'll be able to see, touch and interact with everything and everyone in it. The moment our reborn spirits, which are already functioning at that upper level of light speed, are freed from the encumbrance of our bodies, we will suddenly find ourselves in heaven—absent from the body, and present with The LORD.[43]

"Brother Copeland, will we lose our shape when that happens? Will we just become a ghost or some kind of spiritual cloud?"

No, our spirits aren't a shapeless vapor. They have the same form our natural bodies have. Our spirits fit into our bodies like a hand fits into a glove. So, when we slip out of our bodies, we'll look just like we do now—but a lot better and more glorious. Everything in the heavenly realm is superior to this natural realm. Everything in it shines with the perfection and glory of God.

That's why it was such a blow for Adam and Eve to lose contact with that realm. Before the Fall, the glorious things in the spiritual world were just as real and visible to them as natural things. The fire of God's glory that clothed them was a spiritual substance, but they could see it. The angels who gathered around to serve them were spiritual beings, yet Adam and his wife could see and interact with them. They could look at God and touch Him when He came to walk with them in the Garden. They could hear His voice as clearly as they heard the birds singing. But, when they sinned and spiritual death set in, that changed. They found themselves trapped below the light line and confined to the natural world.

In the 6,000 years that have passed since then, people have become accustomed to that confinement. Many have even come

---

[43] 2 Corinthians 5:8

to believe that the visible realm is all that exists. They deny any reality they can't perceive with their natural senses. But those of us who are born-again children of God know differently because our re-created spirits are in constant contact with the heavenly realm. We may not be able to see that realm with our natural eyes, but with the eye of faith we live, looking "…not at the things which are seen, but at the things which are not seen: for the things which are seen are temporal (temporary, or subject to change); but the things which are not seen are eternal."[44] They never change.

We live, looking forward to the day when we will exchange our temporary, earthly bodies for permanently glorified ones that are like the one Jesus has now. If you've read the New Testament, you know that He has an imperishable, resurrected body—a body with the very glory of God flowing through its veins, a body that is both spiritual and material, and that operates equally well on both sides of the light line.

In His glorified body, Jesus can move at will from the spirit realm to the natural realm. He can appear on earth, as He did to His disciples, seemingly out of thin air, and then vanish as quickly as He came. Yet, He is no ghost. His body is as real and physical as yours and mine. "Behold my hands and my feet," He said to His disciples, "for a spirit hath not flesh and bones, as ye see me have."[45]

That's where all who have made Jesus The LORD of our lives are headed. We are marching toward the day when we, too, will have bodies as alive as our reborn spirits; bodies no longer trapped by the natural effects of the Fall. We are moving toward the time when, clothed inside and out with the glory of God as Adam once was, we can live, forever, in the full spectrum of divine light.

---

[44] 2 Corinthians 4:18
[45] Luke 24:39

# Chapter Five

# Activating Plan B: The Restoration Begins

Howbeit we speak wisdom among them that are perfect: yet not the
wisdom of this world, nor of the princes of this world, that come to
nought: But we speak the wisdom of God in a mystery, even the hidden wisdom, which God ordained before the world unto our glory:
which none of the princes of this world knew: for had they known it,
they would not have crucified The LORD of glory.
1 Corinthians 2:6-8

Nothing the devil did in the Garden of Eden could change
the words God had spoken over man. Despite the Fall
of Adam and Eve, despite the curse that invaded the earth through
their sin, God stood by what He'd said. He didn't back off. He
didn't say, "I guess I'd better scrap THE BLESSING, and do something else."

Instead, He invoked Plan B. He bridged the gap between
Himself and mankind by forging covenant relationships with
those who would believe and honor Him. Through such men and
women of faith, He preserved a bloodline for Himself on the
earth. He established a lineage that would eventually produce
the devil-crushing Seed He had spoken about in the Garden. He
brought forth a covenant people through whom He could one day
fully restore THE BLESSING.

From the beginning, the devil fought hard to destroy those people. Their very existence threatened the demonic kingdom he had set up on earth. He didn't know how, where or when, but according to God's WORD, someday a King would come from their bloodline and overthrow him. A Messiah, born through this covenant race, would strip him of his authority over the kingdoms of the world.

If you think the devil didn't really have that much authority, think again. When he took mankind captive, he became, in a very real way, the god of this world.[46] Through his control of sin-enslaved people, he took possession of the resources of this planet. His rulership over the world's system of commerce and the nations that depended on it was so indisputable that even Jesus acknowledged it. He didn't argue with the devil when he took Him up onto a high mountain during the wilderness temptations and showed Him "… all the kingdoms of the world, and the glory of them." Jesus didn't contradict the devil when he said, "All these things will I give thee, if thou wilt fall down and worship me." Jesus simply answered, "Get thee hence, Satan: for it is written, Thou shalt worship The LORD thy God, and him only shalt thou serve."[47]

It's obvious from that interaction that the devil had the goods to back up his offer. Otherwise, it wouldn't have been a real temptation. Someone couldn't tempt me to do something by offering to give me half of Texas if they didn't own half of Texas. I'd just laugh at them. Jesus would have done the same thing had the devil been lying. He would have said, "You can't give Me something that doesn't belong to you."

Jesus treated the devil's offer like the real thing because it was. Satan actually did have possession of the world's kingdoms and glory. That's why he was so determined to rid the planet of God's covenant bloodline. If he wanted to make his lordship over planet

---

[46] 2 Corinthians 4:3-4: "But if our gospel be hid, it is hid to them that are lost: in whom the god of this world hath blinded the minds of them which believe not, lest the light of the glorious gospel of Christ, who is the image of God, should shine unto them."
[47] Matthew 4:8-10

Earth permanent, he would have to destroy the ones through whom God intended to restore dominion to all mankind.

Every time he tried, however, he ran into one, major problem. He found that God Himself defended His people whenever they were attacked. He protected them at any cost, anywhere, anytime. To preserve that bloodline, God would even destroy the adversaries the devil incited against them. Although it would grieve His heart, He would do it.

"But Brother Copeland, how could God side with one person against another?" you might ask. "Doesn't God love everyone?"

Certainly, He does. God loves the worst criminal just as much as He loves you and me. He loves every man, woman and child on earth, no matter what their race or creed, but He doesn't have a covenant relationship with all of them. He is only in covenant with those who will receive Him and His WORD by faith. He'd be thrilled if everyone would do that[48] but, many won't. God has great compassion for those who reject Him; but if they try to harm His covenant people, He will side against them. He will do whatever it takes to protect His own.

God's commitment to those who are in covenant with Him is much like the commitment of a husband toward his wife. When I married Gloria, for example I made a covenant with her. I committed before God that I would love and care for her. That doesn't mean I don't love other people. But, if someone comes along and tries to hurt Gloria, he'll soon find out I don't have the same kind of relationship with him I have with her. He'll find that even though I love him, I will do whatever is necessary to stop him from harming her.

If you want to know how far God will go to protect His covenant bloodline, look at the great Flood in Genesis 6. It killed almost the entire human race and hit the earth for only one reason. Evil had so increased, it was about to eradicate God's covenant bloodline. For generations, that bloodline had included men who

---

[48] 1 Timothy 2:3-4: "For this is good and acceptable in the sight of God our Saviour; who will have all men to be saved, and to come unto the knowledge of the truth."

called on the Name of The LORD like Enoch, who walked so
closely with God that he was caught up to heaven.[49] But, as mankind
multiplied on the earth, they released so much wickedness that had
the planet not been cleansed of it, it would have swallowed up every
righteous person on earth. By the time Noah came along, he and his
family (a total of eight people) were the only godly ones left.

> And God saw that the wickedness of man was great in the
> earth, and that every imagination of the thoughts of his heart
> was only evil continually. And it repented The LORD that he
> had made man on the earth, and it grieved him at his heart.
> And The LORD said, I will destroy man whom I have cre-
> ated from the face of the earth; both man, and beast, and the
> creeping thing, and the fowls of the air; for it repenteth me
> that I have made them. But Noah found grace in the eyes of
> The LORD (Genesis 6:5-8).

For years, people have interpreted that passage to mean that
God regretted creating mankind. But if that were true, He could
have gotten rid of them by just leaving them alone, allowing them
to continue in their rotten ways and they would have died off
completely in a few years. But God couldn't do that. In His compassion, He had already established His dream. He had decided to
have a family, and He wasn't about to let the devil or anyone else
on earth stop that dream from coming to pass.

God didn't regret man's existence. He regretted that man was
living on the earth under the curse instead of THE BLESSING. He
grieved (felt anguish and deep, heart-felt pain) because mankind—
this awesome reproduction of Compassion Himself—had totally
blotted Him out of their minds. They had become so consumed
with sin, they thought of nothing else. They had not one thought
about their Creator. No wonder He was grieved! Wouldn't you be?

Even so, God took no pleasure in destroying those people.[50] He

---

[49] Genesis 5:24
[50] Ezekiel 33:11: "Say unto them, As I live, saith The LORD God, I have no pleasure in the death of the wicked; but that the wicked turn from his way and live."

wanted them to turn from their wicked ways and be saved. That's
why He made Noah a "preacher of righteousness,"[51] as well as a
boat builder. Through Noah, God kept calling out to mankind even
though they wouldn't listen to Him. That shows just how patient
and merciful He is. As wicked as those people were, it grieved His
heart to put an end to them. But they left Him no other choice.

Had he not washed the earth of them, those devil-consumed
people would have completely overrun the place. They would have
demolished any hope of THE BLESSING ever being restored. God
couldn't and wouldn't let that happen. He put up with them until
the last possible moment. He waited until there was only one family, eight people on earth who gave Him any thought.

> And God looked upon the earth, and, behold, it was corrupt;
> for all flesh had corrupted his way upon the earth. And God
> said unto Noah, The end of all flesh is come before me; for
> the earth is filled with violence through them…. And, behold,
> I, even I, do bring a flood of waters upon the earth, to destroy
> all flesh, wherein is the breath of life, from under heaven; and
> every thing that is in the earth shall die. But with thee will I
> establish my covenant… (Genesis 6:12-13, 17-18).

Once the flood was over and the tide of wickedness had been
stemmed, mankind got a fresh start. Noah and his family stepped
out of the Ark onto an earth that had been given a reprieve from the
works of the devil. Remembering, no doubt, the stories he'd been
told about Adam's sin in the Garden of Eden, the first thing Noah
did was honor God and fellowship with Him over the tithe. He
built an altar to The LORD and brought of every clean beast, and
of every clean fowl and offered burnt offerings.

> And God BLESSED Noah and his sons, and said unto them,
> Be fruitful, and multiply, and replenish the earth. And the

---

[51] 2 Peter 2:5: "And spared not the old world, but saved Noah the eighth person, a preacher of
righteousness, bringing in the flood upon the world of the ungodly."

fear of you and the dread of you shall be upon every beast
of the earth, and upon every fowl of the air, upon all that
moveth upon the earth, and upon all the fishes of the sea; into
your hand are they delivered (Genesis 9:1-2).

If that BLESSING sounds familiar, it's because God said to
Noah and His family the same thing He said to Adam in Genesis
1:28: *Be BLESSED! I empower you by declaration, to excel in
everything good! Prosper and fill up the earth, have dominion over
everything in it!*

Noah needed that BLESSING. Everything on earth had been
wiped out except his family and one boatload of animals. We think
the devastation of category 4 and 5 hurricanes is massive—and it
is!—but it doesn't even begin to compare to what Noah saw. When
he stepped off the Ark, there wasn't one trace of civilization left
anywhere. He must have looked around and thought, *How are we
ever going to get this place restored? How are we going to make it
habitable again?*

God answered those questions when He gave him THE
BLESSING. With that BLESSING, He equipped this one, little
family to turn the whole planet back into a Garden of Eden. For a
moment, things were like they'd been before the Fall of Adam. All
mankind was once again BLESSED. Since Noah and his sons—
Shem, Ham and Japheth—represented all the races and nations that
would ever inhabit this planet, THE BLESSING could have been
passed on through them to all the families of the earth.

Like Adam and Eve, however, Noah and his sons messed things
up. Noah made the mistake of getting drunk. That opened the door
for Ham to sin. Then Japheth started living, not by faith in THE
BLESSING, but by his own wits and human strength. Before long,
he and Ham had invented their own system of commerce. They
came up with the Babylonian-style, fend-for-yourself, dog-eat-
dog, lie-cheat-and-steal economy we see in the world today. (More
about that later.)

Only Noah's first son, Shem, stuck with God. So, it was

through the bloodline of Shem that a man named Abram was born. And it was through Abram—who would later be known as Abraham—that God made His next, mysterious move toward forever restoring THE BLESSING.

## I Will BLESS Them That BLESS You

Now The LORD had said unto Abram, Get thee out of thy country, and from thy kindred, and from thy father's house, unto a land that I will show thee: And I will make of thee a great nation, and I will BLESS thee, and make thy name great; and thou shalt be a BLESSING: And I will BLESS them that bless thee, and curse him that curseth thee: and in thee shall all families of the earth be BLESSED. So Abram departed, as The LORD had spoken unto him; and Lot went with him: and Abram was seventy and five years old when he departed out of Haran (Genesis 12:1-4).

When God first spoke to Abram, he was a resident of the heathen city of Ur, a city of moon worshipers, located not far from modern-day Baghdad. Why would God choose to reveal Himself to such a man? Because He was searching for a man who would teach his children. He was looking for someone who, by passing along his faith to his family, would perpetuate the lineage of THE BLESSING. Apparently, Abram was the only man He found. In him, God saw the spark of faith that, fueled by the fire of The WORD, could turn into a light for the nations.

He ignited that fire by saying the same thing to Abraham He'd said to Adam. It was the same thing He'd said to Noah and his family. God declared to Abraham THE BLESSING. He empowered him to prosper and excel in everything good and set him in the place of dominion by saying, "Whoever does good to you, I'll do good to them. Whoever comes against you, I'll come against them. I'll back you 100 percent." Then, He commissioned Abraham, just as He'd commissioned Adam, to take THE BLESSING worldwide.

He said, "In thee shall all families of the earth be BLESSED."

I know I'm repeating myself here, but this is a vital point. For years, most Christians have seen no connection between Adam's BLESSING and Abraham's BLESSING. Looking at the Bible as a collection of disjointed incidents, we've viewed scriptural history as if God were making it up as He went along—coming up with one BLESSING for Adam, another for Noah, another for Abraham and so on. We've had the idea that God has dozens of different blessings. But it's time we straightened out our thinking. If we, as New Testament believers, are going to understand God's will for us, we must settle the fact that the first BLESSING He gave mankind is THE BLESSING for all time. It will never change because He never changes.

Once Abraham received THE BLESSING, things in his life started changing. In obedience to God's instructions, he left the place where he was raised and moved away from his moon-worshiping relatives. God wanted to get him away from their ungodly way of thinking so Abraham could start thinking in line with THE BLESSING. We, as believers, should do the same thing. If we want to learn how to walk in THE BLESSING of God, we have to separate ourselves from our unbelieving friends and relatives. We love them and pray for them from a distance until we've renewed our own minds with God's WORD to the point where we can influence *them,* instead of letting them influence us.

That's what Abraham did. He packed up and followed God into an absolute wilderness. He moved to a foreign land where he had no family, no established business connections, nothing to depend on but THE BLESSING. From a natural perspective, Abraham was a prime candidate to go broke. He was headed to a country that was in famine. No salary was waiting for him there. No one was looking to give him a helping hand. Where he was going, no one cared whether he lived or died. But, none of that mattered because Abraham had THE BLESSING, and the Bible lets us know in no uncertain terms, it worked! Everywhere Abraham went, THE BLESSING did its job. It created the conditions of the Garden of Eden. It brought forth such abundance that within a very short time, "Abram was very rich in cattle, in silver, and in gold."[52]

The effects of THE BLESSING even spilled over onto Abraham's nephew, Lot, who traveled with him. Between them, their households and livestock multiplied until the land where they were living couldn't support both of them. They had to separate.

> And Abram said unto Lot, Let there be no strife, I pray thee, between me and thee, and between my herdmen and thy herdmen; for we be brethren. Is not the whole land before thee? separate thyself, I pray thee, from me: if thou wilt take the left hand, then I will go to the right; or if thou depart to the right hand, then I will go to the left. And Lot lifted up his eyes, and beheld all the plain of Jordan, that it was well watered every where...*even as the garden of The LORD,* like the land of Egypt, as thou comest unto Zoar. Then Lot chose him all the plain of Jordan; and Lot journeyed east: and they separated themselves the one from the other. Abram dwelled in the land of Canaan, and Lot dwelled in the cities of the plain, and pitched his tent toward Sodom (Genesis 13:8-12).

Those verses confirm that THE BLESSING on Abraham turned land where he was living into "the garden of The LORD." If Lot had been smart, he would have given Abraham that garden spot and taken the less fruitful land for himself. He should have figured out by then that by blessing Abraham, he would be blessed. After all, it was THE BLESSING on his uncle that had made them all rich. Everyone got along well, they stayed healthy and things worked great as long as Uncle Abraham was around. But somehow, Lot didn't catch on to that, so he took the best land for himself, left Abraham, and moved to the city of Sodom.

Things didn't go well for Lot after that. In fact, the next thing the Bible tells us about Lot is that he and his household were in very big trouble.

---

[52] Genesis 13:2

## Who Taught These Guys How to Fight?

A group of four kings banded their forces together and attacked the region where Lot and his family lived. The leader of the group—a man named Chedorlaomer—was an extremely bad character. An international bully, he forced other nations to either serve him or pay the consequences. When some cities he'd strong-armed rebelled against him, he got mad. Together with three other kings, he put forth an army and went storming through the countryside killing people. His forces were so fierce, they defeated everyone in their path: "the Rephaims in Ashteroth Karnaim, and the Zuzims in Ham, and the Emims in Shaveh Kiriathaim...the Horites in their mount Seir...all the country of the Amalekites, and also the Amorites, that dwelt in Hazezon-tamar" (Genesis 14:5-7). In other words, Chedorlaomer's army was a serious military force.

When he attacked the region of Sodom, the five kings who governed that area rose up to defend themselves.

> ...and they joined battle with them in the vale of Siddim; with Chedorlaomer the king of Elam, and with Tidal king of nations, and Amraphel king of Shinar, and Arioch king of Ellasar; four kings with five. And the vale of Siddim was full of slimepits; and the kings of Sodom and Gomorrah fled, and fell there; and they that remained fled to the mountain. And they took all the goods of Sodom and Gomorrah, and all their victuals, and went their way. And they took Lot, Abram's brother's son, who dwelt in Sodom, and his goods, and departed (verses 8-12).

Taking Lot captive turned out to be the worst decision King Ched and his band of bad kings could have made because when Abraham heard about it, he went after them. He armed the 318 trained servants who had been born in his house, attacked Ched's forces by night and defeated them so completely that the Bible called it a "slaughter."[53] (Abraham's 318 fighting men represented just a portion of his servants. Can you imagine how many he had altogether? There were a lot of servants in his household—and THE BLESSING was providing for them all!)

When the battle was over, Abraham's household army had not only whipped the four-king, military machine that had conquered everyone in that part of the world; they had stripped them of all their spoils. "And he brought back all the goods, and also brought again his brother Lot, and his goods, and the women also, and the people" (verse 16).

Talk about an upset! How on earth were Abraham and his servants able to pull off such an overwhelming victory? Where did they get the war technology to do that?

From THE BLESSING.

"Brother Copeland, surely you aren't saying that THE BLESSING taught them how to fight!"

That's exactly what I'm saying. What's more important, the Scriptures indicate the servants born in Abraham's house were trained warriors. Who trained them? Abraham couldn't have done it. He wasn't a military man. If a soldier or commander from another army had come in to train them, Abraham's servants wouldn't have had an edge on Ched's army at all. They would have been using the same battle strategies that he, and everyone else, was using. Clearly, someone taught Abraham's men military tactics no one else knew. Who was it?

It was the Spirit of God.

The anointing of THE BLESSING revealed to them strategies and tactics of war no one had ever heard of before. It empowered them to subdue and have dominion over whatever and whomever came against them. The Bible doesn't tell us how God trained Abraham's servants, but they wound up knowing how to fight so effectively that a few hundred of them could rout an army of thousands. When they showed up at Ched's camp in the night, he

---

[53] Genesis 14:17

and his troops didn't know what to do but die or run. Abraham's commandos ruled the night. Of course, that wasn't the only time such a thing has happened. The Bible tells about many men who were trained to fight by God Himself. David, for example, said it was The LORD who gave him military strength. He declared it was THE BLESSING of God on him "which teacheth my hands to war, and my fingers to fight."[54]

If anyone ever knew how to fight, it was David. He was only 17 years old when he killed the biggest man in the world. He didn't do it just by chance, either. He was able to take Goliath down because he fought by faith in his covenant with God. He had been trained by THE BLESSING. David had such faith in that BLESSING that when all the other Israelite soldiers were cowering in their tents, David was asking, "What are they going to give to the man who kills this guy?"

His question offended his brothers, who were military men. They accused him of being arrogant. But their rebukes didn't dampen David's enthusiasm. On the contrary, when he found out that the man who conquered Goliath would get the king's daughter as his wife and live tax-free for the rest of his life, he got even more excited. A pretty girl and money—that's a 17-year-old boy's dream! So he went to King Saul and said, "I'm going to kill the giant for you."

At first, Saul thought David was out of his mind. "Why, you're nothing but a little boy," he said. "Goliath has been a man of war for years."

David's answer told the story. "Your servant has killed both lion and bear; and this uncircumcised Philistine will be like one of them, seeing he has defied the armies of the living God."[55] When Saul heard that, he realized this young man had some experience fighting covenant battles. He'd seen how THE BLESSING worked in real combat. By the Anointing of God, David had bested opponents with much greater natural strength than his own. During his

---

[54] Psalm 144:1
[55] 1 Samuel 17:36, *New King James Version*

sheep-tending days, he'd jerked lions and bears around by their chin hair. He'd killed them single-handedly when they attacked his sheep.

In the clearsighted simplicity of youth, David couldn't see any difference between Goliath and the animals he'd slain. Those animals had no covenant with God, and the fact that the Philistine was uncircumcised indicated he had no covenant, either. The way David saw it, he had THE BLESSING, and his opponent didn't. So Goliath—fierce warrior that he was—didn't stand a chance.

When David went out to fight, Goliath shot his mouth off just like the devil always does. He cursed and mocked the wild, young kid with the slingshot and staff.

> Am I a dog, that thou comest to me with staves?... Come to me, and I will give thy flesh unto the fowls of the air, and to the beasts of the field. Then said David to the Philistine, Thou comest to me with a sword, and with a spear, and with a shield: but I come to thee in the name of The LORD of hosts, the God of the armies of Israel, whom thou hast de-fied. This day will The LORD deliver thee into mine hand; and I will smite thee, and take thine head from thee; and I will give the carcases of the host of the Philistines this day unto the fowls of the air, and to the wild beasts of the earth; that all the earth may know that there is a God in Israel. And all this assembly shall know that The LORD saveth not with sword and spear: for the battle is The LORD's, and he will give you into our hands (verses 43-47).

Do you see what David was doing? Can you catch the spirit of what he was saying? He was talking about THE BLESSING that was on him. He was declaring his God-given dominion. He even said, "News of this BLESSING is going worldwide!" He was right, too. His victory over Goliath turned out to be one of the most-often told stories of all time.

What I like most about this story is the way it ended. After David felled the giant with his slingshot, he climbed up on the giant's chest and cut his head off. Then, he grabbed the giant's head by the hair and started running, swinging it as he went. Want to know where he ran? To Goliath's hometown! Can you imagine it? David and the Israelite army chased the entire Philistine army back to the birthplace of their defeated champion.

When it was all over, David took Goliath's armor and hung it up in his room. That's what the Bible says (verse 54), and it proves he was just like every other 17-year-old boy who puts his trophies on his bedroom wall. He was a typical teenager in every way but one: His faith was not in himself but in THE BLESSING that was on him. He believed in the power of THE BLESSING of Abraham, which was THE BLESSING of Adam, which is THE BLESSING of God.

### The Tithing Connection

Amazing as it may seem, when Abraham and his servants whipped Ched's army, he didn't yet have a full revelation of everything THE BLESSING included. He understood that it caused him to prosper financially because wherever he went, the area flourished and he became richer. He also knew that THE BLESSING empowered him to triumph over his foes (and over the foes of his relatives, which was a good thing for Lot). Every time anyone came against him, His covenant word from God was enforced—"I will BLESS them that bless thee, and curse him that curseth thee" (Genesis 12:3)!

Abraham didn't know the full magnitude of THE BLESSING, however, until he brought Lot and his family home after the slaughter of Chedorlaomer. On that day, the king of Salem went out to meet him:

> And Melchizedek king of Salem brought forth bread and wine: and he was the priest of the most high God. And he BLESSED him, and said, BLESSED be Abram of the most high God, possessor of heaven and earth: And BLESSED be the most high God, which hath delivered thine enemies into thy hand. And he gave him tithes of all (Genesis 14:18-20).

Underline these verses in your Bible. Draw stars around them. Do whatever you have to do to signify this is vital information! Why is it so important? Because through Melchizedek, God revealed to Abraham the stunning, good news that THE BLESSING had made him possessor of heaven and earth. Through this one-of-a-kind, Old Testament priest, God made it clear to Abraham that he'd become heir of Adam's BLESSING. He'd been given dominion over everything! The Bible calls that revelation *The Gospel.*

"How could that be the gospel? Jesus hadn't even been born when Melchizedek said those things."

That's true, but even so, the New Testament says that "the scripture, foreseeing that God would justify the heathen through faith, *preached before the gospel unto Abraham,* saying, In thee shall all nations be BLESSED."[56] According to those verses, Abraham heard The Gospel the first time when God declared to him THE BLESSING in Genesis 12. But he didn't get the full impact of it until Melchizedek ministered it to him. That's when he realized that through THE BLESSING, God was giving him possession, not just of the land of Canaan, but of the whole world.

As non-Hebrew-speaking Christians, most of us have never realized that's what Melchizedek said. We thought he was referring to God as possessor of heaven and earth. But, he wasn't. He was talking about God's covenant man. He was referring to "Abram of the Most High God" as possessor.

If you have a hard time believing that, don't take my word for it. Read Romans 4. It calls Abraham "the heir of the world."[57] Doesn't the word *heir* mean "a person who possesses something?" That's what it means in Texas. That's what it means wherever you live. And that's what it meant to Abraham. Can you imagine how that news must have hit his ear? *Who, me? Possessor of heaven and earth? How is that possible?* He couldn't wrap his mind around it all at once. He had to walk it out with God one step at a time. But

---

[56] Galatians 3:8

[57] Romans 4:13: "For the promise, that he should be the heir of the world, was not to Abraham, or to his seed, through the law, but through the righteousness of faith."

he believed God. He believed it because the priest who declared those words over him was ministering the bread and the wine, which represented the body and blood of a covenant sacrifice. Those things symbolized the most serious, unbreakable commitment in existence.

What's more, Melchizedek wasn't just any priest. He was *the* representative of God on the earth at the time. As readers of the New Testament, we recognize him as an Old Testament type of Christ who operated under the priestly anointing that belongs to Jesus. According to the book of Hebrews:

> This Melchisedec, king of Salem, priest of the most high God, who met Abraham returning from the slaughter of the kings, and BLESSED him; to whom also Abraham gave a tenth part of all; first being by interpretation King of righteousness, and after that also King of Salem, which is, King of peace; without father, without mother, without descent, having neither beginning of days, nor end of life; but made like unto the Son of God; abideth a priest continually. Now consider how great this man was, unto whom even the patriarch Abraham gave the tenth of the spoils (Hebrews 7:1-4).

I've heard it preached that Melchizedek actually was Jesus, that he didn't have a mother or father, that he wasn't born and didn't die. But that's not true. The author of Hebrews was simply saying that Melchizedek didn't come from the tribe of Levi like the other priests in Israel. He had no natural pedigree. There's no official record of the beginning or end of his priesthood because he was handpicked by God Himself.

It sounds mysterious, but Jewish history solves the mystery for us. He was Noah's son Shem.[58]

Even more important than who he was historically, however, is

---

[58] *The Chumash*, ed. Rabbi Nosson Scherman, Art Scroll Series, Stone Edition Travel Size (Brooklyn: Mesorah Publications, 1998) p. 65.

what he did. What makes Melchizedek an Old Testament type of
Jesus is the fact that he was anointed, both to declare THE BLESS-
ING and to receive the tithe:

> And verily they that are of the sons of Levi, who receive the
> office of the priesthood, have a commandment to take tithes
> of the people according to the law, that is, of their brethren,
> though they come out of the loins of Abraham: But he whose
> descent is not counted from them received tithes of Abra-
> ham, and BLESSED him that had the promises. And without
> all contradiction the less is blessed of the better. And here
> men that die receive tithes; but there he receiveth them, of
> whom it is witnessed that he liveth (Hebrews 7:5-8).

Any way you look at it—from the Garden of Eden on, THE
BLESSING and the tithe are connected. Adam learned it the hard
way. Abel learned it from Adam. Noah knew it, and so did Abraham. So, when Melchizedek ministered THE BLESSING to him,
he did what his great-grandfather many times over should have
done in the Garden. Before he took any of the spoils of his victory
over Chedorlaomer, he brought a tenth of it to God. He wasn't crying about it, either. He wasn't thinking about how much he needed
that extra 10 percent.

He was thinking, *I'm richer than I've ever been! The whole
earth, some way or another, is mine!* As Abraham took his tithe to
the priest who was anointed to receive it, he was receiving revelation of the tremendous wealth that belonged to him because of his
covenant with God. Notice, Abraham didn't get that revelation
in Sunday school. He didn't get it while he was out herding his
flocks. He received it tithing!

If you don't learn anything more about it, you need to know
this. If you're not tithing, you're living under the curse because it's
when you bring your tithe to God that you connect, by faith, with
the anointings provided by THE BLESSING. When you tithe (if
you do it scripturally), you go to Jesus, your Melchizedek, and He

comes to you. You take to Him what is His, and He brings to you what is yours. Tithing time is Communion time. I am so confident in the power of it, that if the only thing standing between me and absolute starvation was my tithe, I would smile and give it to God. I'd give it with confidence and joy because the covenant interaction of tithing is what opens the door for me to receive everything I could ever need to take care of myself and my family.

### The Fire and the Blood

Right after Abraham received his expanded revelation of THE BLESSING, the king of Sodom approached him with what he thought was a "real deal." "Give back my people who were captured," he said. "But you may keep for yourself all the goods you have recovered."[59]

Chedorlaomer's invasion had hit that king hard. He'd lost everything—all the wealth of his city, the people, the livestock—and he was trying to come up with a way to regain his throne and power over the people. He probably figured if he could get the people back, he could work them, tax them or whatever else he had to do to get wealth again. But Abraham didn't want any part of that kind of thing. He didn't need to have any part in it! Standing there with the sound of THE BLESSING pounding in his ears and the realization that he, through his covenant with the Most High God, had become heir of the world, Abraham made one of the boldest confessions of faith in the Bible. He answered the Sodomite king:

> I have lift up mine hand [my covenant tithe] unto The LORD, the most high God, the possessor of heaven and earth, that I will not take from a thread even to a shoelatchet, and that I will not take any thing that is thine, lest thou shouldest say, I have made Abram rich (verses 22-23).

One translation says, "Never let it be said that any man made

---

[59] Genesis 14:21, *New Living Translation*

Abraham rich, but God!" Abraham was BLESSED, and he knew it. He wasn't about to let anyone or anything rob him of that BLESSING. He wasn't about to mess around with some low-integrity, two-bit scheme that might bring dishonor to God's Name.

That kind of attitude thrills me, and what's more important, it thrills God. He gets excited when His people talk and act that way. He got so stirred up listening to Abraham declare his confidence in THE BLESSING that in the very next chapter, He spoke to Abraham in a vision about his heart's greatest desire. He assured His covenant man that he and Sarah would have a child of their own, an heir to whom they could pass on THE BLESSING.

Abraham had struggled for decades with that issue. Because his wife had been barren all their married lives, he hadn't been able to figure out how God could make him a "great nation."[60] Though God had promised it, the thought boggled his mind. So, on the heels of Abraham's bold confession of tithe and faith, God did what was necessary to help him take his next step of faith. He appeared to Abraham and said:

> He that shall come forth out of thine own bowels shall be thine heir. And he brought [Abraham] forth abroad, and said, Look now toward heaven, and tell the stars, if thou be able to number them: and he said unto him, So shall thy seed be. And he believed in The LORD; and he counted it to him for righteousness. And he said unto him, I am The LORD that brought thee out of Ur of the Chaldees, to give thee this land to inherit it. And he said, Lord GOD, whereby shall I know that I shall inherit it? And he said unto him, Take me an heifer of three years old, and a she goat of three years old, and a ram of three years old, and a turtledove, and a young pigeon (Genesis 15:4-9).

What happened next changed Abraham forever. He took the animals as God instructed, prepared them as covenant sacrifices,

---

[60] Genesis 12:2

and with his physical senses suspended in a kind of vision sleep, he watched while God came down and made covenant with him. He saw the flaming fire of God's glory pass through the pieces of the sacrificed animals. I'm convinced he saw God's footprints as He walked the traditional figure eight in the pathway of blood.

When Abraham saw the fire of God in the midst of that blood and heard Him swearing the covenant oath to him, suddenly THE BLESSING took on an even greater meaning—a blood-sworn oath. He realized that God was saying, "I swear by Myself. I will die before I will ever break My WORD to you. I will shed My own blood like these animals have shed theirs, if necessary, to see to it that through your Seed all the families of the earth are BLESSED."

That dark night, the fire and the blood anchored Abraham's soul forever in God's promise. From that point on, he never doubted God again. With all human reason for hope being gone, Abraham:

> ...believed in hope, that he might become the father of many nations, according to that which was spoken, So shall thy seed be. And being not weak in faith, he considered not his own body now dead, when he was about an hundred years old, neither yet the deadness of Sarah's womb: He staggered not at the promise of God through unbelief; but was strong in faith, giving glory to God; and being fully persuaded that, what he had promised, he was able also to perform (Romans 4:18-21).

# Chapter Six

# Tracking the Bloodline of THE BLESSING

BLESSED is the man that feareth The LORD, that delighteth
greatly in his commandments. His seed shall be mighty upon earth:
the generation of the upright shall be BLESSED.
Psalm 112:1-2

Once Abraham locked his faith on to God's blood-sworn
oath and believed, without wavering, that THE BLESS-
ING would bring forth a son for him and Sarah—despite that they
were about 100 years old—Isaac was born. Abraham raised his son
just like God said he would. He taught him God's ways and trained
him in the life and power of THE BLESSING.

Through the years, as Isaac grew, he watched THE BLESS-
ING work in his father's life. He saw it prosper him financially, so
that by the time "Abraham was old, and well stricken in age…The
LORD had BLESSED Abraham in all things."[61] Isaac witnessed
that THE BLESSING made Abraham great and brought him an
abundance of everything good.[62]

No doubt, as a youngster, Isaac heard the stories from Abraham and Sarah about the dangers they'd come through in safety
because of THE BLESSING. He heard about the kidnapping of Lot

---

[61] Genesis 24:1
[62] See Genesis 24:35.

and Abraham's slaughter of Chedorlaomer's forces, the arrival of Melchizedek and THE BLESSING he spoke over Abraham as he tithed. He'd heard about King Abimelech who took Sarah to make her his concubine and how God appeared to Abimelech in a dream, saying, "If you touch that woman you're a dead man because she is another man's wife" (Genesis 20:3-7).

Abraham must have told Isaac time and again about the night God took him outside, directed his eyes to the sky and promised him an heir who would bring forth descendants as numerous as the stars. That was the night God guaranteed His promise by appearing in His fiery glory and walking the covenant path of blood. Abraham had, no doubt, described the scene so many times, Isaac felt as if he had been there.

Of course, Isaac did more than just hear the stories. He lived some of them. He was there the morning Abraham rose early to climb Mount Moriah and make an offering to The LORD. He heard his father tell his servants, "You stay here. The boy and I are going up to worship, and afterward we'll be back" (Genesis 22:5). Isaac had trudged up the mountainside carrying the wood for the burnt offering, unaware that God had spoken to his father the night before and instructed him to offer his son on the altar. Isaac had no idea he was to be the sacrifice. How could he?

There were no tears running down Abraham's face that day. He showed no trace of grief or loss. Things seemed so normal that Isaac's only question was, "Where is the lamb for the offering?"

Abraham had answered, "My son, God will provide Himself a lamb."

Sure enough, He did. At the last moment before Isaac was to be sacrificed, the angel of The LORD called out from heaven and said:

"Do not lay your hand on the lad, or do anything to him; for now I know that you fear God, since you have not withheld your son, your only son, from Me." Then Abraham lifted his eyes and looked, and there behind him was a ram caught in a thicket by its horns. So Abraham went and took the ram, and offered it up for a burnt offering instead of his son. And Abraham called the name of the place, The-LORD-Will-Provide (Genesis 22:12-14, *New King James Version*).

Once the sacrifice was made, God reaffirmed THE BLESSING as He had so often before in Abraham's life.

By Myself I have sworn, says The LORD, because you have done this thing, and have not withheld your son, your only son—BLESSING I will BLESS you, and multiplying I will multiply your descendants as the stars of the heaven and as the sand which is on the seashore; and your descendants shall possess the gate of their enemies. In your seed all the nations of the earth shall be BLESSED, because you have obeyed My voice (verses 16-18, *New King James Version*).

It was THE BLESSING that had kept Abraham's steps sure and steady as he'd climbed the mountain to sacrifice Isaac that day. It empowered him to obey with confidence what would have been to a man of lesser faith, a heartbreaking command. This is a vital point: Abraham didn't obey God so he could get THE BLESSING. He obeyed God because he had faith in the covenant of BLESS-ING God had already given him.

When he prepared to offer up his precious son, his thoughts were fixed on the promise of God: *In Isaac shall thy seed be called.* Abraham was so convinced God would keep His promise that he fully expected God to resurrect his son from the dead. He believed the power of THE BLESSING would raise Isaac right up out of the sacrificial ashes. THE BLESSING would make a way for God's promise to be fulfilled.

Let's look at it from Hebrews 11:17-19:

By faith Abraham, when he was tried, offered up Isaac: and he that had received the promises offered up his only begotten son, of whom it was said, That in Isaac shall thy seed be called: accounting that God *was* able to raise him up, even from the dead; from whence also he received him in a figure.

That's what it means to be fully persuaded—that his God could and would do all that He had promised.

That was Isaac's heritage of faith. He grew up seeing, hearing and believing that THE BLESSING always had and always would turn every situation in Abraham's favor.

### Walk Around Like You Own It

It's one thing to see THE BLESSING work for someone else. It's another thing altogether, to believe it will operate the same way for you. Isaac found that out when his father died. After enjoying a life of abundance in the household of Abraham, he ran head-on into a situation that was totally foreign to him. He found himself in a condition of lack because the land where he lived (the land God promised to Abraham's descendents) had fallen into famine. Unaccustomed to walking in THE BLESSING on his own, Isaac packed up his household and did the only thing he knew to do. He headed for Egypt to get food.

God, however, stopped him in his tracks and changed his mindset forever. He appeared to him and said:

Go not down into Egypt; dwell in the land which I shall tell thee of: Sojourn in this land, and I will be with thee, and will BLESS thee; for unto thee, and unto thy seed, I will give all these countries, and I will perform the oath which I sware unto Abraham thy father; and I will make thy seed to multiply as the stars of heaven, and will give unto thy seed all these countries; and in thy seed shall all the nations of the earth be BLESSED; because that Abraham obeyed my voice, and kept my charge, my commandments, my statutes, and my laws (Genesis 26:2-5).

When Isaac heard those words, the Almighty God appearing and speaking directly to him, his hair must have stood straight up. His knees went weak. His heart jumped right up into his throat. This was The LORD speaking to *him*. This was the Most High—the fiery God who had appeared to his father and said, "Surely BLESSING I will BLESS thee, and multiplying I will multiply thee."[63]

I believe, at that moment, the revelation hit Isaac like an 18-wheeler. *THE BLESSING of Abraham now belonged to him.* By virtue of the bloodline through which he'd been born, he had become the full heir of that BLESSING. God was saying to him, as He had said to his father, "I WILL perform for *you* the oath I swore…. So, go and sojourn in the land I've given you."

Sojourn doesn't refer just to traveling around. To *sojourn in the land* means to walk around in it like you own it. A sojourner doesn't act as if he's a stranger or tiptoe around as if he might not belong there. He takes the attitude of ownership. It doesn't matter whether people there accept him or not—it's his!

God was telling Isaac, "If you'll walk around with that attitude of faith, I WILL do for you exactly what I did for your father. I WILL give you everything I gave him."

Oh, how believers today need to catch that revelation the way Isaac did! We need to realize that every promise in the Bible is God's blood-sworn oath to us. Because in Jesus, all His promises are yes and amen,[64] God has said to us, just as surely as He said to Isaac, "I *WILL PERFORM* in your life THE BLESSING of Abraham. I heal you! I prosper you! I create the conditions of Eden around you, and you will carry THE BLESSING to people everywhere you go!"

It's time we believed that and started sojourning in the land. We ought to walk around in faith acting like healing belongs to us (regardless of symptoms to the contrary). We should walk around like prosperity is ours (regardless of the figures in our checkbooks). If we'll do that, God WILL get those things to us. It is His WILL for us.

---

[63] Hebrews 6:14
[64] 2 Corinthians 1:20

"But, Brother Copeland, what if those things are not God's will for me?"

They *are* His will for you! The Bible says so, and He put an end to any argument about it when He stood in the blood of the covenant sacrifice and said, "It is My will to BLESS you with THE BLESSING of Abraham!"[65] When God said that to Isaac, he believed it. He took God at His WORD and stayed in the Promised Land, in spite of the famine. Putting his faith in THE BLESSING, he sowed in that land and reaped a hundredfold harvest in the same year, and "the man began to prosper, and continued prospering until he became very prosperous; for he had possessions of flocks and possessions of herds and a great number of servants. So the Philistines envied him" (Genesis 26:13-14, *New King James Version).*

The last thing Isaac wanted was a fight with those Philistines. He was a peace-loving man. But, because they were jealous of THE BLESSING that was on him, they persecuted him unmercifully. They fought with his servants. They stole his water wells. When he found a place to settle down, they pushed him out of it.

That kind of thing always happened to the heirs of THE BLESSING. Everywhere they went, people dealt them unmitigated misery. But Isaac just kept believing and obeying God. He did everything possible to live at peace with the people around him. He refused to get into strife with them, and in the end he came out on top. Eventually, the Philistines made a covenant with him and said, "We have seen that you are now THE BLESSED of The LORD."[66] THE BLESSING in and on Isaac overpowered the famine in the land and at the same time, made Isaac very great.

### The Deceiver Who Became a Prince of God

Through Isaac, THE BLESSING was passed down through the bloodline to his sons, Jacob and Esau. Had they both lived by faith in it, it would have produced the same results in their lives that it had for their father and grandfather. As it turned out, however,

---

[65] Galatians 3:14
[66] See Genesis 26:28-29.

the two brothers treated THE BLESSING in startling and different ways. The elder one, Esau, thought so little of it that one day
when he was hungry, he traded it away for a bowl of stew. Just like
Adam, he gave up THE BLESSING for something to eat.

His brother, Jacob, on the other hand valued THE BLESSING
and wanted it so badly that he lied and cheated to get it. Of course,
he shouldn't have done that. He didn't need to. As the seed of Abraham, THE BLESSING already belonged to him. He could have
just walked in it by faith. Instead, he tricked his father and enraged
his brother with a BLESSING-stealing scheme he and his mother
thought up. As a result, he had to run for his life, leaving home with
nothing but the clothes on his back and a stick in his hand.

You'd think God wouldn't want anything to do with him after
that. You'd think He'd go looking for someone else to BLESS. But
He didn't. He honored the blood covenant He'd made with Abraham and his seed. God saw in Jacob a man who had faith in THE
BLESSING (but no idea how to live in it). So, while Jacob was on
the run, God appeared to him in a dream. He gave him a vision of
a ladder connecting heaven and earth, with angels ascending and
descending on it.

> And behold, The LORD stood above it and said: "I am The
> LORD God of Abraham your father and the God of Isaac;
> the land on which you lie I will give to you and your de-
> scendants. Also your descendants shall be as the dust of the
> earth; you shall spread abroad to the west and the east, to
> the north and the south; and in you and in your seed all the
> families of the earth shall be BLESSED. Behold, I am with
> you and will keep you wherever you go, and will bring you
> back to this land; for I will not leave you until I have done
> what I have spoken to you."...Then Jacob made a vow, say-
> ing, "If God will be with me, and keep me in this way that I
> am going, and give me bread to eat and clothing to put on,
> so that I come back to my father's house in peace, then The
> LORD shall be my God. And this stone which I have set as

a pillar shall be God's house, and of all that You give me I will surely give a tenth to You" (Genesis 28:13-15, 20-22, *New King James Version*).

That night, God freely gave to Jacob THE BLESSING he'd tried and failed to get by deception. He declared over him his blood-sworn inheritance; and Jacob responded—just as Abraham and Isaac had—by promising God the tithe.

With THE BLESSING activated in his life, Jacob expected things to start looking up—and in some ways, they did. He soon found his way safely to his Uncle Laban's house where his mother had sent him. She had decided Jacob could find a wife and lay low there until Esau cooled off and gave up the idea of killing him. In part, that's what happened. Laban and his family received Jacob with joy. He married both of Laban's daughters, and ended up working on Laban's ranch for 20 years.

There was just one problem, however. Laban was not an honest man. From the moment Jacob went to work for him, Laban began cheating him. He made promises to Jacob and broke them. He defrauded him of his wages. But even so, THE BLESSING kept working on Jacob's behalf. It gave him wisdom and understanding. At times, it opened his eyes to the realm of the spirit as it had the night he saw the angelic ladder. It enabled him to see what God was doing and hear His voice, so he'd know what to do. Through it all, Jacob learned to depend on that BLESSING more and more. He learned to press in to it by faith so that everything he did prospered.

As his employer, Laban enjoyed the benefit of that prosperity, and as long as Jacob worked for him, he grew richer…and richer… and richer. So, when Jacob decided it was time for him to go back home, Laban tried to talk him out of it. "I have learned by experience that The LORD has BLESSED me for your sake,"[67] he said.

In his attempt to keep Jacob (and THE BLESSING that was on him) around a little longer, Laban eventually agreed to let Jacob

---

[67] Genesis 30:27, *New King James Version*

start keeping some of the livestock for himself. After that, even Laban's trickery couldn't stop Jacob from increasing. His portion of the estate multiplied so much that Laban's sons became envious. "Jacob hath taken away all that was our father's;" they said, "and of that which was our father's hath he gotten all this glory."[68]

Actually, Laban's sons had just as much right to THE BLESSING as Jacob. They too, were the family of Abraham. They could have said, "Jacob, if you'll teach us how to operate in THE BLESSING, we'll stop cheating you. We'll treat you well and pay you whatever you want." Instead, they got mad and accused Jacob of stealing their family's money.

They were wrong, though. Jacob didn't steal anything. He just lived by faith in THE BLESSING and it kept increasing him until it absorbed everything they had. When Jacob left Laban and returned to his homeland, he went back a very wealthy man. He returned in THE BLESSING of God, no longer known as Jacob, *The Deceiver,* but as Israel, *A Prince of God.*

### Behold, the Dreamer Cometh

Every one of Israel's children could have followed in his footsteps. They all could have walked in THE BLESSING. But, only one chose to do it—the little guy named Joseph.

From the time he was a child, Joseph believed he was BLESSED. The son of his father's old age, he had a special place in his daddy's heart. It's easy to imagine him walking around in the special coat Jacob had made him, happy, enjoying life and saying, "I am BLESSED!"

Such faith always delights the heart of God, but often aggravates others, and that was especially true in Joseph's case. His carefree confidence and his father's love for him so irritated his brothers that "they hated him, and could not speak peaceably unto him" (Genesis 37:4).

No matter how much their father's favoritism hurt their feelings,

---

[68] Genesis 31:1

Joseph's brothers had no excuse for that kind of behavior. Though Joseph was the apple of their daddy's eye and had a special, rainbow-colored coat and they didn't, Joseph was their little brother! They should have loved him. Instead, they refused to say a civil word to him.

That, in itself, was bad enough. But when Joseph told his brothers about a dream he'd had that indicated God was planning to promote him, things got worse. He might have been wiser to keep the dream to himself—but he was a teenager. Teenagers don't know much about keeping their mouths shut, so he said to them:

> Hear, I pray you, this dream which I have dreamed: For, behold, we were binding sheaves in the field, and, lo, my sheaf arose, and also stood upright; and, behold, your sheaves stood round about, and made obeisance to my sheaf. And his brethren said to him, Shalt thou indeed reign over us? or shalt thou indeed have dominion over us? And they hated him yet the more for his dreams, and for his words (Genesis 37:6-8).

That dream absolutely infuriated Joseph's brothers. From their perspective, he was just their little brother trying to lord it over them by claiming to hear from God. They weren't about to believe he had some kind of special spiritual insight.

Relatives often feel that way when God starts to use someone in their family. I found that out for myself when I first went into the ministry. My aunt Macky, who is a believer, told some of my relatives that I prophesied in my meetings. They were appalled.

"Do you mean to tell me Kenneth is a prophet?" they asked.

"Yes, I believe he is," she answered.

"Are you saying he speaks for God?"

"Yes, I believe he does."

"That can't be!" they argued. "He's our kinfolks!"

They weren't trying to be mean. They just couldn't wrap their minds around the idea that God could work through one of their relatives. When my aunt told me about their reaction, I thought,

*Every prophet is somebody's relative! There's never been a prophet
who just fell out of heaven and started ministering. Even Jesus
Himself had relatives.*

Joseph's brothers struggled with that fact. They couldn't accept
the idea that God had called one of the youngest members of their
family and was beginning to speak to him. The very thought of it
made them more jealous than ever. They didn't realize God wasn't
speaking to Joseph for his own benefit. He wanted to use that
young man to minister to his family. He wanted to say something
to them through him. They didn't have the written WORD then
and couldn't just pick up the Bible and find out about God as we
can. God was establishing Joseph as a prophet in their midst so He
could manifest Himself to them on a regular basis.

But, that never occurred to them. They just thought Joseph was
an arrogant teenager who knew he was his father's favorite, so they
were offended. It was one of the biggest mistakes they ever made.
Had they been walking in any kind of humility toward God, or had
used any spiritual sense, they would have said, "Hey, we're *all* the
seed of Abraham. We've all inherited THE BLESSING. Maybe
God is trying to speak to us here and help us. Maybe there's a famine coming that we need to know about or something."

That would have saved them a lot of trouble.

How much better if they'd knelt down together and prayed,
"Lord, what are You saying here through our little brother? Thank
You for BLESSING him. We love him. We're willing to receive
what You want to say through him, so just speak on, Lord!"

Think about the heartache that would have saved them. It
would have opened the door for God to direct the family so that
they wouldn't have had to go down to Egypt when the famine
came. They would have been prepared. But they didn't do it. They
didn't put any faith in God, in THE BLESSING, or in Joseph. Instead, they let their hatred intensify to a murderous pitch.

Joseph didn't react to their hostility the way you'd expect.
When his father asked him to go out to check on his brothers who
were tending the sheep in the fields, to make sure they were all

right, he said, "Here I am. I'm ready to go." Most people would
have said, "Forget about that! After the way those heathens treated
me, I'm not going to do anything for them. They can starve to
death out there in the pasture as far as I'm concerned."

Had Joseph taken that attitude, he would have been in the same
boat his brothers were in. He would have cut himself off from THE
BLESSING by stepping out of love and into strife. That's what
Satan wanted Joseph—and all of us—to do. He knows as long as
we're walking in love, THE BLESSING of Abraham that's ours
through Christ Jesus will keep working in our lives.

It doesn't matter how people treat us, if we'll just keep walking in love toward them, they can't steal our BLESSING. Joseph is
proof of that. In spite of their mistreatment, he went out to see about
his brothers in the field. He kept on trying to bless them. When he
found them, instead of thanking him, "they conspired against him to
slay him. And they said one to another, Behold, this dreamer cometh.
Come now therefore, and let us slay him, and cast him into some pit,
and we will say, some evil beast hath devoured him: and we shall see
what will become of his dreams" (verses 18-20).

Joseph's brothers didn't realize it, but when they mocked "the
dreamer," they mocked God. They ridiculed the covenant message
He'd sent them and attacked the messenger! It was a sad scene
when you think about it. There was Joseph, walking up with a big
grin on his face, glad to see his brothers. But they weren't smiling
back. They jumped on him, ripped off his coat of many colors and
began beating him.

Jacob must have taught Joseph and his brothers some things
about walking in THE BLESSING because Joseph didn't even
fight back. In the face of all the pain his brothers caused him, he
never attempted to hurt them.

Joseph's brothers would have killed him but one of them, Reu-
ben, intervened and said, "Let's not kill him. Let's just throw him
in a hole and leave him there."

Then they took him and cast him into a pit. And the pit was

empty; there was no water in it. And they sat down to eat a meal. Then they lifted their eyes and looked, and there was a company of Ishmaelites, coming from Gilead with their camels, bearing spices, balm, and myrrh, on their way to carry them down to Egypt. So Judah said to his brothers, "What profit is there if we kill our brother and conceal his blood? Come and let us sell him to the Ishmaelites, and let not our hand be upon him, for he is our brother and our flesh." And his brothers listened (verses 24-27, *New King James Version*).

THE BLESSING was working on Joseph's behalf. Why do you think that caravan showed up at just the right time to give the brothers the idea to sell Joseph instead of leaving him in that hole to die? It was working for Joseph, just as it works for us, 24 hours a day, seven days a week. THE BLESSING, under God's direction and power, caused that caravan to leave at the proper day and hour to be right there when Joseph needed it.

Some people would claim that was just coincidence. But I've discovered in my own life, the more I walk by faith in THE BLESSING, the more "coincidences" pile up in my favor.

### Running Away From Sin

That's the way it was with Joseph. Even before he got into trouble, THE BLESSING was preparing his deliverance. It started maneuvering him back into a place of prosperity the moment the slave traders pulled him up out of that hole. It was THE BLESS-ING that brought him into the house of a wealthy, influential Egyptian officer named Potiphar. Though Joseph went into that household as a slave, it wasn't long before he was promoted because Potiphar saw that Joseph had THE BLESSING on him.

By Joseph's generation, people all over that part of the world had heard about THE BLESSING of Abraham. So, when Potiphar saw that everything Joseph did was a wild success, he knew exactly what was going on, and he put that BLESSED young man in charge of his entire estate.

Under Joseph's supervision, the cattle increased. The horses, camels, sheep and goats multiplied. The crops multiplied. Everything Joseph put his hand to began doing better than it had before.

Keep in mind, he was still just a teenager. He'd never been trained to buy and sell livestock. He'd never earned a degree in ranch management. But THE BLESSING on him taught him what he needed to know. THE BLESSING taught him how to make the best deals, how to increase crop production and how to manage the money. Potiphar was so thrilled with what was going on that he didn't even bother to keep track of what Joseph was doing. He made him his CEO and said, "Have at it, young man. Do whatever you want to do."

As always, however, the devil was on hand to throw a wrench into the works. He used Potiphar's wife, who "cast longing eyes on Joseph, and...said, 'Lie with me.' But he refused and said to his master's wife, "'Look, my master does not know what is with me in the house, and he has committed all that he has to my hand. There is no one greater in this house than I, nor has he kept back anything from me but you, because you are his wife. How then can I do this great wickedness, and sin against God?'" (Genesis 39:7-9, *New King James Version*).

How Joseph responded in this situation is a major key. He realized (more than most New Testament believers today) the consequences of sin. He knew that sin of any kind hinders THE BLESSING. That's the reason God is so against it. It's not because He doesn't want us having fun. God hates sin because it kills THE BLESSING. It chokes off The WORD in our spirits and dims the light of God within us. It turns down the power and anointing until it becomes feeble and inoperative in our lives. Sin is the enemy of THE BLESSING, and if we persist in it, it will eventually kill us.

As New Testament believers, Jesus is our High Priest, so if we sin, we can go to Him and repent. He will not only forgive us, but cleanse us from all unrighteousness and reinstate THE BLESSING in our lives. He will restore us to the condition where it can operate at the level it's supposed to. Thank God for that!

But what's better is to refuse to sin in the first place. We ought to run from every form of it.

That's what Joseph did. When Potiphar's wife tried to grab him, he left his garment in her hand and ran outside.

> And so it was, when she saw that he had left his garment in her hand and fled outside, that she called to the men of her house and spoke to them, saying, "See, he has brought in to us a Hebrew to mock us. He came in to me to lie with me, and I cried out with a loud voice. And it happened, when he heard that I lifted my voice and cried out, that he left his garment with me, and fled and went outside." So she kept his garment with her until his master came home. Then she spoke to him with words like these, saying, "The Hebrew servant whom you brought to us came in to me to mock me; so it happened, as I lifted my voice and cried out, that he left his garment with me and fled outside." So it was, when his master heard the words which his wife spoke to him, saying, "Your servant did to me after this manner," that his anger was aroused. Then Joseph's master took him and put him into the prison, a place where the king's prisoners were confined. And he was there in the prison (verses 13-20, *New King James Version*).

## Prospering in Prison

When Joseph found himself behind bars as a result of that woman's lies, he could have become bitter. When he realized he'd once again been unjustly stripped of his dignity and position, he could have said, as many do, "I just don't know why God let this happen to me. I've done the best I can. I've done what my daddy and granddaddy taught me. I tried to bless my brothers. I worked for Potiphar and made him rich. What do I get in return? I get bought and sold and thrown around like a piece of meat. It's just not fair."

Had Joseph taken that kind of unbelieving attitude, he'd have cut himself off from THE BLESSING and spent the rest of his life rotting in a prison cell. But, thank God, he didn't. He picked himself up and kept walking in his calling. He didn't waste time thinking about the things people had done to him. He didn't let the prison walls around him dominate his mind. He was too busy meditating on THE BLESSING. He went to bed thinking about it and got up in the morning thinking about it.

THE BLESSING was his profession. He worked it all the time and expected it to do the same thing in prison that it did anywhere else. He expected it to remove the curse and begin creating the conditions of Eden wherever he went—and that's exactly what happened. Even when he was locked up in an Egyptian prison:

> The LORD was with Joseph and showed him mercy, and He gave him favor in the sight of the keeper of the prison. And the keeper of the prison committed to Joseph's hand all the prisoners who were in the prison; whatever they did there, it was his doing. The keeper of the prison did not look into anything that was under Joseph's authority, because The LORD was with him; and whatever he did, The LORD made it prosper (verses 21-23, *New King James Version*).

Joseph had never been a prison warden. He'd never been in charge of criminals. But, just as it had in Potiphar's house, THE BLESSING gave him the wisdom he needed. It taught him to make even a prison prosper.

THE BLESSING is doing the same thing today. I've seen it. I preached in a prison in Louisiana that at one time, was the meanest penitentiary in the nation. People called it "America's Devil Island." The only warden who has lasted more than five years in the prison's 100-year history, is a born-again Christian. At this writing, he's been the warden there for 15 years. The reason for his longevity is he pastors that prison instead of just being warden over it. The last I heard, 2500 of the 5200 inmates are born again.

The 18,000 acres of prison grounds produce the finest crops

and livestock around. The cows are prospering. The fields are prospering. The inmates produce all their own food and build all their own buildings. They don't need outside assistance. They don't even have to call in contractors or electricians. They have their own!

While I was ministering there, they were having a craft show and rodeo. The warden told me they made $250,000 from the craft show. In the past few years, the prison has built new buildings with their own money. They even have four churches there. From any cell window in any cellblock in the prison, you can see a church steeple. They have a closed-circuit radio station throughout the prison that makes gospel preaching and gospel music available all the time.

They even have a Bible seminary there. When the first group of 82 students graduated, the warden thought, *What am I going to do with 82 preachers in this prison?* Then The LORD showed him. He said, *Send those preachers out two by two as missionaries in the other units.* Today, those prison preachers are out evangelizing the penitentiaries of Louisiana.

While preparing to minister at that prison, I was marveling at what God had done there and The LORD spoke to me about it. He said, *If everyone in this penitentiary realized that by receiving Jesus as Lord and Savior they could have THE BLESSING of Abraham, it could turn this prison into a Garden of Eden because that's what THE BLESSING does. It will turn hell on earth into heaven on earth. It will do it in a household, in a business, a university or a church. If everyone in this prison would live by faith in THE BLESSING, there would be people trying to get in instead of trying to get out.*

After walking around the place, I found it easy to believe. Already, with just half the inmates born again, the peace of God is on that prison. Everywhere I went, people were getting along. Even on death row (or "life row," as some of the inmates call it) I heard, "Hey, Brother Copeland. How are you doing! Praise The LORD! Glory to God!"

## From Prisoner to Prime Minister...Overnight

That's the kind of thing that was going on in the prison where Joseph was warden. The anointing on him just kept working, making things better. In the course of time, two of Pharaoh's servants ended up there—a butler and a baker. Both had a dream, "each man's dream in one night and each man's dream with its own interpretation."

> And Joseph came in to them in the morning and looked at them, and saw that they were sad. So he asked Pharaoh's officers who were with him in the custody of his lord's house, saying, "Why do you look so sad today?" And they said to him, "We each have had a dream, and there is no interpreter of it." So Joseph said to them, "Do not interpretations belong to God? Tell them to me, please" (Genesis 40:6-8, *New King James Version*).

Like the born-again warden in Louisiana, Joseph cared about the inmates in his prison. He walked in compassion toward them. He noticed when they were sad and wanted to help them. Since he had some experience with dreams, he went to The LORD and got the interpretation for them. Instead of helping him in return and mentioning him to Pharaoh when they got out, however, they forgot about him. Joseph didn't let it get to him, though. He just stayed in that prison and kept working THE BLESSING.

One morning, two years later, Pharaoh had a dream.

Why do you think he had that dream? Did God just look at him and say, "I'm tired of that Pharaoh sleeping so well. I'm going to give him a dream"? No, that dream was a manifestation of THE BLESSING at work on Joseph's behalf. It opened up Pharaoh's mind and made him realize he needed help. When he went looking for that help in the form of a dream interpreter, his once-imprisoned butler told him about Joseph.

Then Pharaoh sent and called Joseph, and they brought him quickly out of the dungeon; and he shaved, changed his clothing, and came to Pharaoh. And Pharaoh said to Joseph, "I have had a dream, and there is no one who can interpret it. But I have heard it said of you that you can understand a dream, to interpret it." So Joseph answered Pharaoh, saying, "It is not in me; God will give Pharaoh an answer of peace" (Genesis 41:14-16).

Notice, Joseph didn't start backtracking at that point, saying, "Well, I'm just a little Hebrew. What do I know about kings and their dreams? I'm not sure I'll be of any help to you." He said, in essence, "Pharoah, whatever you need to know, God will show me. He'll give me the interpretation."

To many people an attitude like that seems haughty. It irritates them to see someone with that kind of boldness and faith. Like Joseph's brothers, they get mad at believers who have it. But Joseph wasn't haughty. He was just confident in God. He knew the One he believed in. He knew how to pull aside and get God's wisdom. He'd learned how to function in THE BLESSING.

Joseph didn't wake up that morning saying, "Oh yeah, I am going to be prime minister of Egypt by nightfall!" He was just walking with God. He had no plan to fight his way up the corporate ladder to leadership. He was just living by faith, loving people, helping them and expecting to be BLESSED. He had no idea when he walked in to Pharaoh's palace on a one-day furlough from prison, that within 24 hours he'd be in charge of the nation's finances. But that's what happened. Pharaoh made Joseph his second-in-command on the spot. It was the smartest thing he ever did because through the plan Joseph introduced into the Egyptian government, Pharaoh became owner of all the land in the nation—and kept the people from starving to death in the process.

I've heard some preachers say that's the reason Joseph was sent to Egypt. God knew there was going to be a famine, so He sent him to a prosperous, heathen nation to provide food for his family. But,

God didn't send Joseph to Egypt to get blessed. Joseph brought THE BLESSING to Egypt. It was BLESSED because of him. Instead of destroying the nation, the worldwide famine made it rich—all because Joseph was there.

As long as the Egyptian people and the Pharaohs remembered Joseph and THE BLESSING he'd been to them, things went well for them and for the Israelites who moved there during Joseph's time. But, there came a day when the Egyptians forgot where their prosperity came from. Instead of honoring the descendants of the man who had once interpreted the crucial dream that saved the nation, the Egyptians turned God's BLESSED bloodline into slaves. They burdened and troubled them so much that they cried out to God for deliverance.

That's when THE BLESSING moved them out.

# Chapter Seven

# Ten Commandments of Love: Teaching the Israelites to Live in THE BLESSING

See, I have set before thee this day life and good, and death and evil;
in that I command thee this day to love The LORD thy God, to walk
in his ways, and to keep his commandments and his statutes and his
judgments, that thou mayest live and multiply: and The LORD thy
God shall BLESS thee in the land whither thou goest to possess it.
Deuteronomy 30:15-16

The Egyptians weren't the only ones who forgot about
Joseph and how THE BLESSING on him exalted their
nation. During the 400 years the Israelites lived in Egypt, they forgot THE BLESSING, too. Unlike Abraham, they weren't diligent
to teach their children about it. They didn't have a written Bible
to remind them about what it was and how to live in it. They had
handed-down traditions, and through the years, those were almost
wiped out. It's no wonder that eventually the Israelites stopped
putting their trust in the God of Abraham, Isaac and Jacob, and
started thinking like the people around them. They had begun to
blend into the society in which they lived and began looking to
Egypt for their blessing.

When they did that, they threw open the door to all kinds of
misery because the Egyptians were so far into sorcery and witchcraft

that they had a god for everything.

Living in the middle of that kind of culture influenced the Israelites until they began thinking and behaving in ways that stopped THE BLESSING from protecting them.

The Bible says that when sin comes in death comes with it; [69] and the Israelites found that out during their last 35 to 50 years in Egypt. During that time, they lived under deadly oppression, suffering unthinkable horrors. They were enslaved. Their babies were murdered. In every conceivable way, their lives were made bitter and hard.[70]

But though the Israelites had forgotten God, He had not forgotten them. So when they sighed and cried in their bondage, "God heard their groaning, and God remembered his covenant with Abraham, with Isaac, and with Jacob. And God looked upon the children of Israel, and God had respect unto them" (Exodus 2:24-25). He appeared in a burning bush to an Egyptian-raised Hebrew named Moses, and called him to deliver the Israelites out of the bondage of the curse and back into THE BLESSING.

### Learning Covenant Conduct

When The LORD first called Moses, he was totally ignorant of God. He'd been raised, not as a son of Abraham, but as a prince of Egypt. Although he was aware of his Israelite heritage and wanted to help his fellow Hebrews, he had no idea that there was a right and a wrong way to do it. So, as a young man, when he saw an Egyptian beating an Israelite, he murdered the Egyptian and buried him in the sand.

It wasn't exactly what God had in mind. But, of course, Moses didn't know that. What he did know was that once news of the murder got out, Pharaoh was sure to come looking for him (Exodus 2:15), so he went into hiding and spent 40 years herding sheep on the backside of the desert in a place called Midian. It was there God appeared to him and said:

---

[69] Romans 5:12
[70] Exodus 1:14, *New King James Version*

> I am the God of thy father, the God of Abraham, the God of
> Isaac, and the God of Jacob.... I have surely seen the afflic-
> tion of my people which are in Egypt, and have heard their
> cry by reason of their taskmasters; for I know their sorrows;
> and I am come down to deliver them out of the hand of the
> Egyptians, and to bring them up out of that land unto a good
> land and a large, unto a land flowing with milk and honey
> (Exodus 3:6-8).

When God told Moses He wanted to bring His people into *a
good land*...a land flowing with milk and honey, He wasn't just
saying He had a particular piece of real estate He wanted to give
them. He was saying much more than that. He was declaring
His intention to restore to Israel the conditions of the Garden of
Eden—conditions which can come only by THE BLESSING.

To do that, God would not only have to take the Israelites out
of Egypt, He would have to get Egypt out of them.

That's why God didn't just pull the Israelites out of Egypt and
take them straight into the Promised Land. He took them by way of
the wilderness to teach them that He was their Source of BLESS-
ING. When they were hungry, He gave them manna from heaven to
eat. When they were thirsty, He poured millions of gallons of water
out of a rock. He shaded them with a cloud by day and lit their
camp with His fire by night. He gave them supernatural victory
over the army of the Amalekites (Exodus 17:8-13).

Then, He did the most important thing of all. He called Moses
to the mountaintop to give him the commandments.

The tone of those commandments and the reason God gave
them has been totally misunderstood through the years. People
have assumed God gave them with a threatening voice and
clenched fist. They've seen the commandments as legalistic whips
God used to keep His people in line.

But nothing could be further from the truth. God gave
those commands to Israel to teach them what Abraham, Isaac,
Jacob and Joseph had once known. He wanted to teach them to

live by faith in THE BLESSING.

God's tone was not, "You had better do these things or else!" He was saying, "Here's how people who have a covenant with God conduct themselves. Here's how BLESSED people act in a land of milk and honey." God's heart wasn't to burden them with restrictive rules that would make their lives difficult. He wanted to help them learn how to live in covenant with Him and keep THE BLESSING intact.

I remember when I first saw that. I'd been reading the instructions God gave the Israelites in Exodus and noticed He used the words *commandment* and *covenant* interchangeably. In Exodus 15:26, for example, Moses said, "If thou wilt diligently hearken to the voice of The LORD thy God, and wilt do that which is right in his sight, and wilt give ear to his *commandments,* and keep all his statutes...." A few chapters later, in Exodus 19:5, God expressed the same idea by saying, "Now therefore, if ye will obey my voice indeed, and keep my *covenant....*" That puzzled me. "Lord, I don't understand," I said. "How is a commandment a covenant?"

After praying about it a little while, I heard The LORD—not audibly but in my spirit—say, *Kenneth, when those words were written, I'd already made covenant with those people. I'd been in covenant with them for 400 years—ever since the time I declared THE BLESSING over Abraham and his seed.*

When He said that, I saw it. The commandments were given inside the framework of the covenant of BLESSING. God had that covenant in mind when He gave them. When He gave the first commandment and said, "Thou shalt have no other gods before me,"[71] He wasn't just being demanding. He was telling them He was the only God they would ever need. He was saying, "You don't have to look to anyone else to meet your needs. You don't need to go begging some idol to help you. You don't need to look to governments or anything else in the world to take care of you. You don't even have to try to meet your own needs. You can put all your

---

[71] Exodus 20:3

trust in Me. I am your Covenant Partner and will look after you better than anyone else ever would or could." That's not just some kind of rule or legalistic bondage. That's good news!

If we read them the way God intended, every commandment carries that kind of gospel and is a reflection of what God has pledged to do for His covenant people. When He said, "Thou shalt not kill" or a more accurate translation, "Thou shalt do no murder," He was saying, "If someone does you wrong, I'll protect you. I'll defend you. You don't have to take matters into your own hands; just bring the situation to Me. I'll uphold you in it while dealing with your adversary in the most merciful way possible."

"Thou shalt not commit adultery," carried the same message of love. God was saying, "Don't take your neighbor's wife. That will stop THE BLESSING on your life. What's more, it's not necessary. If you want a wife, ask Me for one. I'll provide you with the best woman around. Put your faith in Me and I'll give you a mate who's divinely made for you."

"And don't steal. Why should you steal when you can come to Me and I'll give you the desires of your heart? I will give you an abundance of every good thing."

Every commandment was given in love because God is love.

You'd think the Israelites would have known that and been full of faith in God's ability to take care of them, waiting with eager anticipation to learn the ways of this loving God who had already done so much for them.

But they weren't. Instead, while Moses was on the mountain with God:

> The people gathered themselves together unto Aaron, and said unto him, Up, make us gods, which shall go before us; for as for this Moses, the man that brought us up out of the land of Egypt, we wot not what is become of him. And Aaron said unto them, Break off the golden earrings, which are in the ears of your wives, of your sons, and of your daughters, and bring them unto me. And all the people brake off the golden

earrings which were in their ears, and brought them unto Aaron. And he received them at their hand, and fashioned it with a graving tool, after he had made it a molten calf: and they said, These be thy gods, O Israel, which brought thee up out of the land of Egypt (Exodus 32:1-4).

Amazing as it seems, just a few weeks after God turned the most powerful nation on its ear to give these people their freedom, they went back to worshiping idols as they had back in Egypt. What's worse, when Moses caught them at it and demanded an explanation, Aaron lied, actually claiming that the idol had shown up of its own accord. "The people gave me their gold. I put it into the fire, and out came this calf!" he said.[72]

I know that situation was serious, but I have to admit, sometimes I have to chuckle about what Aaron said. It proves that human nature never changes. I used to make up the same kinds of lies as a child. You probably did too.

That's what Aaron did. Of course, God and Moses and everyone who's ever read that claim in the thousands of years since, know it's not true. We know the calf didn't come from that fire.

Where did it come from?

It came from Egypt—not the land of Egypt the Israelites had left behind, but from the Egypt they carried inside them. That calf was a product of their old, unrenewed, slavery-influenced, fear-filled minds and hearts. Because the inner image of that golden calf (and all it represented) went with them when they left the land of bondage, when they were under pressure, it came out.

### Clearing Up the Confusion

This is why it was so important for God to get the commandments to the children of Israel. It explains why He went to such great lengths to describe to them in detail their covenant of BLESSING and how it operates.

---

[72] Verse 24

He wanted to renew their minds because whatever they carried on the inside would eventually come out. If they carried a mindset of bondage, they'd turn even the Promised Land into a place of bondage. But if they carried within them the mindset of BLESS-ING, that BLESSING would create a Garden of Eden wherever they went.

The same thing is true for us as New Testament believers, but we have a major advantage. We have a regenerated spirit that's been made righteous. We have available to us the mind of Christ.[73] We have the very image of Jesus inside us. God has "BLESSED us with all spiritual BLESSINGS in heavenly places in Christ."[74] (We'll talk more about that in the next few chapters.)

If we'll just believe what the Bible says about us and walk in the covenant of love, THE BLESSING will produce the conditions of the Garden of Eden around us as surely as it did for the Israelites in the Promised Land. In fact, it will do even more for us than it did for them. Because we carry THE BLESSING inside us wherever we go, God can send us to the hardest, thistle-growing, demon-infested place, and we can go with joy. We don't have to argue with Him about it. We don't have to complain and drag our feet. We can go in faith knowing that God is sending us there not to live in squalor but to release THE BLESSING that's within us and turn that dark corner of the world into a milk-and-honey kind of place.

"Oh, Brother Copeland, you're not being practical. There are some places even THE BLESSING won't work."

If there are, I've never seen them, and I've been to a lot of places. I've seen THE BLESSING work everywhere from the wilds of Africa to the urban jungles of America. One time Gloria and I were in Los Angeles with a minister friend of ours, touring a really tough neighborhood where that church had some outreaches. Right in the middle of part of the city filled with drug dealers and crack houses, he pointed out a little lady who was out sweeping the sidewalk with her broom.

---

[73] 1 Corinthians 2:16
[74] Ephesians 1:3

"That woman isn't afraid of anyone," he said. "She keeps this whole block clean. There's not a drug dealer in Los Angeles who will touch her. If anyone tries to peddle drugs near her house, she'll point her finger in his face and say, 'I'm telling you right now, you aren't touching this place in the Name of Jesus! I plead the blood!'"

You can't tell that little woman THE BLESSING won't work in her neighborhood. She's already proved it does. It's turned her block into the nicest, neatest, safest spot in that part of the city.

Jesse Winley, one of the great faith men of the 20th century, did much the same thing when he began a ministry years ago in the middle of the worst part of Harlem. The area was so dangerous that one time some chain-carrying, knife-wielding gang members came after him while he was preaching. They scared the congregation so much that everyone ran off except Jesse Winley. He jumped off the platform, charged right up to those gang members and stuck his Bible out at them like a sword. When he did, the power of God fell on them and they all threw down their weapons and said, "We didn't know it was real, Brother Winley! We didn't know it was real!"

Jesse Winley ended up starting a church in that area called Soul Saving Station. Before he went home to be with The LORD, the members of that congregation held the best jobs in the government of New York City because they'd learned to walk by faith. They used THE BLESSING of God to take dominion over that area and ended up turning that part of Harlem around.

The Israelites faced much the same challenge as they headed toward the Promised Land. Though it was already a good and prosperous place, it was inhabited by violent and corrupt people. If they were going to successfully occupy that land, THE BLESSING would have to be in full operation in their lives. They'd have to know what THE BLESSING would do for them and understand how to cooperate with it. So, God spelled those things out in the form of His written WORD. He not only gave them commandments to live by, He also provided them with a detailed description of THE BLESSING so that they could imprint it on their minds and hearts.

Because they'd become so confused while living in Egypt about the difference between good and evil, God didn't just say, "I BLESS you. Be fruitful, multiply and have dominion." He cleared up any misconceptions the Israelites might have had by telling them just what the multiplication and dominion released through THE BLESSING looks like. He said:

> And it shall come to pass, if thou shalt hearken diligently unto the voice of The LORD thy God, to observe and to do all his commandments which I command thee this day, that The LORD thy God will set thee on high above all nations of the earth: And all these BLESSINGS shall come on thee, and overtake thee, if thou shalt hearken unto the voice of The LORD thy God. BLESSED shalt thou be in the city, and BLESSED shalt thou be in the field. BLESSED shall be the fruit of thy body, and the fruit of thy ground, and the fruit of thy cattle, the increase of thy kine, and the flocks of thy sheep. BLESSED shall be thy basket and thy store. BLESSED shalt thou be when thou comest in, and BLESSED shalt thou be when thou goest out. The LORD shall cause thine enemies that rise up against thee to be smitten before thy face: they shall come out against thee one way, and flee before thee seven ways. The LORD shall command the BLESSING upon thee in thy storehouses, and in all that thou settest thine hand unto; and he shall BLESS thee in the land which The LORD thy God giveth thee. The LORD shall establish thee an holy people unto himself, as he hath sworn unto thee, if thou shalt keep the commandments of The LORD thy God, and walk in his ways. And all people of the earth shall see that thou art called by the name of The LORD; and they shall be afraid of thee. And The LORD shall make thee plenteous in goods, in the fruit of thy body, and in the fruit of thy cattle, and in the fruit of thy ground, in the land which The LORD sware unto thy fathers to give thee. The LORD shall

open unto thee his good treasure, the heaven to give the rain unto thy land in his season, and to BLESS all the work of thine hand: and thou shalt lend unto many nations, and thou shalt not borrow. And The LORD shall make thee the head, and not the tail; and thou shalt be above only, and thou shalt not be beneath; if that thou hearken unto the commandments of The LORD thy God, which I command thee this day, to observe and to do them (Deuteronomy 28:1-13).

When God declared that BLESSING to Israel, He wasn't coming up with something new. He was simply telling them what was included in THE BLESSING they had inherited as the seed of Abraham. He was confirming to them the original BLESSING— the one He had first released on mankind in the Garden of Eden. That BLESSING had actually belonged to the Israelites all along. It was their birthright, but because they didn't have faith in it and hadn't lived according to its principles, it hadn't been operating in their lives.

The same is true of the curse God talked to them about in the last part of Deuteronomy 28:

But it shall come to pass, if thou wilt not hearken unto the voice of The LORD thy God, to observe to do all his commandments and his statutes which I command thee this day; that all these curses shall come upon thee, and overtake thee: Cursed shalt thou be in the city, and cursed shalt thou be in the field. Cursed shall be thy basket and thy store. Cursed shall be the fruit of thy body, and the fruit of thy land, the increase of thy kine, and the flocks of thy sheep. Cursed shalt thou be when thou comest in, and cursed shalt thou be when thou goest out (verses 15-19).

That curse wasn't anything new, either. It had been operating on the earth for thousands of years. Ever since Adam's sin, it had overtaken anyone not protected by THE BLESSING. So when

God described that curse to the Israelites, He wasn't saying, "If you don't keep My rules, I'm going to destroy you, and here's how I'm going to do it." He was saying, "The curse is out there. It's already on the world; and if you go the way of the world instead of walking in THE BLESSING, it's going to overtake you."

That seems very simple to me. We don't have any trouble understanding that if it's raining outside and we want to keep dry, we have to stay inside. Why should we have trouble understanding that if the curse is in the world and THE BLESSING is in God, we'll be BLESSED and curse-free as long as we stick with God?

Some people have thought the verses say God will send the curse.

If you study that out, you'll find that what God actually said is that He would *permit*[75] that curse to come into their lives if they opened the door to it through unbelief and disobedience. Why would He permit it? Because He didn't have a choice. God had given mankind a free will. When He created us in His image, He left it up to us to choose THE BLESSING or the curse. (See Deuteronomy 30:19.)

God has never chosen the curse for anyone. Never in the history of the world has He ever put someone in Satan's hands.

### Don't Buy the Lie About Job

I know you're thinking, *What about Job? Didn't God give the devil permission to go after him?*

No, He didn't. That lie has been taught for years and has absolutely wreaked havoc with people's understanding of God. Good Christian people have quaked in their boots, wondering if God is going to open the door to the devil and let him come into their lives to test their faithfulness. So let's clear up that misunderstanding right now. Let's take a look at what really happened to Job.

The first thing the Bible teaches about him is that THE BLESSING of God was operating in his life. If you want to talk about someone

---

[75] Robert Young, *Young's Analytical Concordance to the Bible* (Peabody, Mass.: Hendrickson Publishers) Excerpt From Prefatory Note to the First Edition.

who was fruitful, multiplied and had dominion—it was Job. He not only reverenced God and steered clear of evil, he prospered in every conceivable way. He had a wife and a beautiful family—seven sons and three daughters. His finances had multiplied to the point where he was the wealthiest man in the East. He had the respect of the community, and even had a healing ministry.

No question about it, Job had lived by faith in THE BLESSING of God for years. His life bore the fruit of it.

After his children grew up, however, he stepped out of faith and into fear. He began worrying that when they got together at one another's houses to celebrate, they were sinning against God. He developed such a terror of it that every time one of them had a party, "Job sent and sanctified them, and rose up early in the morning, and offered burnt offerings according to the number of them all: for Job said, It may be that my sons have sinned, and cursed God in their hearts. Thus did Job continually."[76]

Job had the same, mistaken religious idea many people have today. He thought if he worried about his children, he was being a responsible parent. But, in reality, he was just opening the door to the devil by failing to trust God. He wasn't making his sacrifices in faith. He was making them in fear and unbelief.

I've done it myself. There have been times when I've found myself confessing The WORD of God as hard and fast as I could, but instead of confessing in faith, I was doing it in fear.

One time, I'd come up on a financial deadline for the ministry and was several thousand dollars short. *Whew! I've got to have this money in the next couple of days or I'm in trouble!* I thought. I got under so much pressure that I decided to get in my boat, go out to the middle of the lake near our home, anchor it there and declare The WORD over the situation. After I'd been standing in my boat out there awhile declaring, "My God meets my needs according to His riches in glory," again…and again…and again, The LORD finally managed to get a word in edgewise.

---

[76] Job 1:5

*Kenneth, will you shut up?* He said.

I obeyed and sat down.

*Now, just hush and let Me bring this thing to pass.*

When He said that, it dawned on me that even though I was confessing scriptures, my words had been stout against Him because I was releasing fear as I said them. When I got quiet and just determined to trust God, my faith opened the door for Him to move on my behalf and He was able to provide the money right on time.

Job was in that same kind of situation. He was doing something that looked right, but he was doing it in fear. Instead of having God's faithfulness on his mind while he was making his sacrifices, he had the curse on his mind, and it eventually generated such terror in his life that he said, "The thing which I greatly feared is come upon me, and that which I was afraid of is come unto me. I was not in safety, neither had I rest, neither was I quiet; yet trouble came."[77]

If Job had been walking in faith where his children were concerned, he would have made one sacrifice for them and then said, "Father, I'm rolling all the care of my children over on You. From this moment on, I'll never worry about them again. You said You'd take care of them and I believe You. You said they'd be BLESSED and I trust You to keep Your WORD."

Then, instead of staying home and making a religious fuss over them, he could have shown up at their parties and said, "Hey! I came down here to spend some time with you. Let's have some fun together—and while we're at it, I'll teach you some things The LORD has taught me about living in THE BLESSING."

When the devil brought Job's situation up before The LORD, he wasn't sharp enough to pick up on all that. All he knew was this man had THE BLESSING on him (the devil described it as a "hedge around him") that was producing healing power, children, wealth and success. He wanted to get his hands on it so he said:

---

[77] Job 3:25-26

Doth Job fear God for nought? Hast not thou made an hedge about him, and about his house, and about all that he hath on every side? thou hast BLESSED the work of his hands, and his substance is increased in the land. But put forth thine hand now, and touch all that he hath, and he will curse thee to thy face. And The LORD said unto Satan, Behold, all that he hath is in thy power; only upon himself put not forth thine hand. So Satan went forth from the presence of The LORD (Job 1:9-12).

Those verses tell us two important things. First, they reveal that the sin the devil wanted Job to commit was the sin of cursing God. He'd already been working on Job to get him thinking that his children were cursing God. Job's wife eventually sided with Satan and said, "Why don't you just curse God, and die!"[78] The devil figured out that if Job cursed God, that hedge around him would fall, he'd lose THE BLESSING and the devil could steal everything he had.

But Job never did that. He made a lot of other mistakes. He said more wrong things than he did right, during that season of his life. But he never cursed God. That's why the Bible says, "In all this did not Job sin with his lips."[79]

The second thing we learn from these verses is that God didn't say to the devil: "Here, I put Job in your hands. Do whatever you want to him."

The fact that the devil even suggested it just shows how foolish he is. God wasn't about to stretch out His hand against Job. He never agreed to do what the devil suggested.

What He said to the devil was, "Behold, he is already in your hand."

Today, we don't use the word *behold* very much. We don't walk down the street and say, "Did you behold that car? Oh, behold! Isn't it beautiful?" So we don't really know what the word means. But if you look it up in any of the translations—Hebrew, Greek,

---

[78] See Job 2:9.
[79] Job 2:10

English, Spanish or any other translation—you'll find out it always means, "Look and see. Wake up and pay attention."

God was saying to the devil, "Job has already opened the door to you." God was just telling the devil the truth. Job had already broken down his protective hedge with his own fear. He had already put himself into the devil's hand. God wasn't going to lie about that. As much as He loved Job, God wasn't going to be dishonest because of him. That's just not the way God works. He's the truth-teller, not the liar.

Once the devil realized Job had crippled the power of THE BLESSING in his life, he went after Job and caused all kinds of trouble. He killed Job's children. He killed his cattle. He stripped the man of his wealth and hit his physical body with sickness. Then, he brought Job's good friends around to tell him that God did it all to him. All of that was designed to pressure Job into cursing God. But even though he said some foolish, unbelieving things while all that was going on, he stood up and shouted, "I don't care if God were to kill me! I'd serve Him anyway."

If you've read the story, you know how it ended. God sent a young preacher to help straighten things out. I've always enjoyed reading about that young man. He'd been sitting there listening to Job and his friends and when he'd heard all the unbelief he could take, he rose up and ripped into the situation with The WORD of God. He preached some faith into Job and in the process, God Himself got stirred up.

He appeared in a whirlwind, finished correcting Job's thinking, then turned to Job's friends and said, "You've spoken wrongly about Me! You'd better hope My servant Job will pray for you or you'll be in deep trouble."

When Job heard that, he stepped right back in to the place of faith and compassion. He believed God, loved his friends and prayed for their healing. The next thing you know, the hedge went back up and THE BLESSING roared back into operation. It destroyed the disease and destruction and reversed the effects of the curse Satan had brought on Job. It went back to work creating the conditions of the Garden of Eden around him, restoring everything he'd lost, and then doubling it. Job ended up twice as strong in every way as he had been before.

## Not Just Protection—Dominion!

Job learned his lesson about THE BLESSING and the curse the hard way. The Israelites didn't have to do that. God spelled out the way things worked in meticulous detail, so they could do what He said and keep their BLESSING hedge high and intact.

Actually, had they listened with the ear of faith, they would have been as thrilled with God's description of the curse as they were with His declaration of THE BLESSING, realizing that the curse was a list of things they were protected from. When they heard that "every sickness, and every plague"[80] is part of the curse, they could have shouted, "Glory! If we'll just live by faith and obey The WORD, we won't have to put up with the flu anymore!" When they heard that under the curse they would experience fear of heart,[81] they could have said, "Hey, we'll never be afraid of anything or anyone again!" That's the kind of response God wanted them to have.

He also wanted the difference between THE BLESSING and the curse to be so indelibly engraved on their hearts, He made a major production out of it. He instructed half of the Israelite leadership to stand on Mount Gerizim and declare THE BLESSING and the other half to stand on Mount Ebal and declare the curse. He never wanted them to get the two confused, so He presented them in a dramatic way. With millions of Israelites watching and listening, He said:

> I call heaven and earth to record this day against you, that I have set before you life and death, BLESSING and cursing: therefore choose life, that both thou and thy seed may live (Deuteronomy 30:19).

---

[80] Deuteronomy 28:61
[81] Verse 66

If you think just because those verses are in the Old Testament, they don't apply to us today, think again. The promises included in THE BLESSING work now just like they did back in Moses' day. If we'll take hold of them by faith, they'll have the same effect on us they had on the Israelites who believed them. They'll cause us to excel and prosper wherever we live (in the city, in the country, or both). They'll even give us dominion over our livestock, so we can see to it that they're BLESSED.

"But, Brother Copeland, most of us don't have livestock."

Don't you have pets? Sometime, your dog or cat or fish or parakeet may need you to minister THE BLESSING to them. The first time I found that out was when Angelo, the little dog we gave our daughter Kellie, got his tail broken. That little dog couldn't have weighed more than 2 or 3 pounds, but he thought he was the boss of everything in sight—including the big Labrador named Major that belonged to our son, John.

When Major was a puppy, Angelo got away with pushing him around. Angelo would yap and nip at his heels and Major would do whatever Angelo wanted him to do. But one day, that changed. It dawned on Major that he outweighed Angelo by at least 50 pounds or more, so when Angelo started aggravating him, he just picked up all four feet and fell on Angelo, flattening the smaller dog beneath him.

I was right there watching and I could hear Angelo's muffled yips coming from under Major's barrel chest, but I was laughing too hard to do anything about it. Finally, I realized something had to be done so I pushed Major aside and rescued Angelo. When I did, I saw that his little tail that normally curled over his back was straightened out and pushed to the side.

About that time, Kellie came running in and saw him. "Oh, Daddy, pray for Angelo's tail! It's broken! Pray, Daddy, pray!"

At that moment, I couldn't pray for anything. I was still laughing too hard. So Kellie grabbed Angelo in disgust and said, "I'll get Mama to pray."

I felt kind of ashamed of myself and asked The LORD to

forgive me for not praying for Angelo, but things turned out all right for him anyway. Just a few minutes later, after Gloria prayed for him, he came running through the house, barking, with his tail curled back again and Kellie running behind him shouting, "Angelo's healed!"

You can believe what you want, but I was there. I saw that dog's broken tail and I saw it made right again. God healed that noisy, little dog. That sounds like a wild story until you realize it's what we're supposed to do. We're supposed to have dominion and BLESS the animal kingdom, and every other area of creation under our influence.

As for the curse, it's still out there...but it's under our feet. If we choose to lie down and submit to it, we can. God will let us do it. But we don't have to because Jesus has delivered us from it once and for all. That's the marvelous difference between us and God's Old Covenant saints. As the servants of God, they were protected from the curse by the blood of animals. In their day, Satan still had authority over this planet and was ruling over it as the god of this world.

But when Jesus came, He defeated the devil and pulled him down out of his place of authority. "Having spoiled principalities and powers, he made a show of them openly, triumphing over them in it."[82] By taking on Himself the sin of all mankind...

> Christ...redeemed us from the curse of the law, being made a
> curse for us: for it is written, Cursed is every one that hangeth
> on a tree: That the BLESSING of Abraham might come on
> the Gentiles through Jesus Christ; that we might receive the
> promise of the Spirit through faith (Galatians 3:13-14).

As New Covenant believers, we are not only protected from the curse, we have dominion over it. It has no authority over us unless we yield to it.

The devil will push you hard at times to get you to yield to the

---

[82] Colossians 2:15

curse. He'll put symptoms of sickness and other parts of the curse on you to try to get you to receive it. That's when you have to dig your heels in to THE BLESSING, refuse to let him lie you out of it, and fight the good fight of faith.

During my early years in ministry, I was preaching in Shreveport, Louisiana, and a pain hit me in the groin that absolutely doubled me over. I didn't know nearly as much about THE BLESSING back then, but one thing I did know was that sickness was a part of the curse, and Jesus had delivered me from it. So, I resisted the devil over that pain for three weeks. The whole time I preached in Shreveport, when I'd step onto the platform, the anointing would hit me and I'd feel fine. But as soon as I finished the service, it would come back and I'd hurt so badly, I could hardly stand it.

When I flew home and stepped out the door of the airplane, still feeling that pain, I heard the devil say, "It's a mile from this gate to your car. If you're fool enough to walk that distance, you'll cut a blood clot loose in your groin and I'll kill you before you can get home."

I knew my covenant. I wasn't going to listen to his lies so I just said, "That'll be the day." I told him to shut up, and started quoting healing scriptures.

About that time, a man pushing a wheelchair walked up to me. To this day, I don't know where he came from. I hadn't said anything to anyone about needing a wheelchair. "You need this, don't you?" he said.

"No, thank you, sir!" I answered, and then said to myself, "Healed men don't ride in wheelchairs."

I took three or four steps and the pain hit me again. "See there?" the devil said, "I'm going to kill you between here and the gate."

"Devil, you don't have the power to kill anyone!" I snapped back. "I am born again. I am filled with the Holy Spirit. Greater is He who is in me than he who is in the world. You're not going to kill me today. You're not going to kill me tomorrow. You're not going to kill me the day after that. My life is hidden in Christ Jesus and I am redeemed from the curse. So you shut your lying mouth, and get out of my presence."

I walked all the way to the car with Gloria and my mother and father, who'd come to meet me at the plane. On the way home, I did something I'd never done before and have never done since. I said to my parents, "Don't take me all the way home. Just take me to your house and I'll sleep there."

I went upstairs as soon as I got there and went to sleep—pain and all. I didn't know it, but after I fell asleep, my mother came and sat at the foot of the bed. She stayed there praying until about 2 a.m., when I sat straight up in the bed and said, "Glory be to God!"

"That did it!" said my mother, and she walked out of the room. I jumped up, danced a little dance around the bed, went back to sleep and never had another pain. Sometimes, it takes that kind of faith fight to walk in THE BLESSING. But it's a good fight because it's a fight we win!

### Some People Throw Rocks

If the children of Israel had done that kind of thing, believing God and trusting THE BLESSING to work for them, even in the midst of contrary circumstances, they could have marched right through the wilderness and into the Promised Land. They could have overcome every enemy that rose up against them. They could have whipped every giant in sight and made themselves at home in the land of milk and honey, without having to spend 40 years in the wilderness.

"I don't know about that," someone might say. "They didn't know much about living by faith, and they faced some pretty tough circumstances."

That's true, but God had fully equipped them to meet the challenge. Joshua and Caleb proved it. They stood up against all their unbelieving, complaining, fearful friends, neighbors and relatives who refused to go into the Promised Land. They believed THE BLESSING when everyone around them said it wouldn't work.

And they spake unto all the company of the children of Israel, saying, The land, which we passed through to search it, is an exceeding good land. If The LORD delight in us, then he will bring us into this land, and give it us; a land which floweth with milk and honey. Only rebel not ye against The LORD, neither fear ye the people of the land; for they are bread for us: their defence is departed from them, and The LORD is with us: fear them not (Numbers 14:7-9).

Do you know how those unbelieving people responded to Joshua and Caleb's words of faith? They grabbed rocks and wanted to stone them. That doesn't surprise me at all. I've found out through the years that people who choose not to believe and walk in THE BLESSING of God often throw rocks at those who do. People get mad about it; and that's what those wilderness-wandering Israelites did. They groaned and dug in their heels for 40 years. God had to let that whole generation—with the exception of the two men of faith—die in the desert.

God didn't want that to happen. He tried His best to get them to go into the Promised Land. He'd spoken to them again and again, saying, "Will you please come on?" But when it came time to cross over, they refused to believe God would do for them what He said He'd do.

At that point, God closed the door. He finally said to them, "Your children will go in to Canaan along with Joshua and Caleb, but you'll never see it." That might sound harsh but God had no alternative. He couldn't afford to let that group in to the Promised Land. They would have destroyed it with their unbelief.

The New Testament tells us how God felt about the choice the Israelites made and urges us not to follow in their footsteps. It says:

(Harden not your hearts, as in the provocation, in the day of temptation in the wilderness: when your fathers tempted me, proved me, and saw my works forty years. Wherefore I was grieved with that generation, and said, They do always err in their heart; and they have not known my ways. So I sware in my wrath, They shall not enter into my rest.) Take heed, brethren, lest there be in any of you an evil heart of unbelief, in departing from the living God (Hebrews 3:8-12).

Those of us who love The LORD should remember those words. We should never forget that when we choose the path of unbelief, and fail to receive by faith THE BLESSING that belongs to us as His children, it doesn't only hurt us, it grieves the heart of our heavenly Father. In His great love and compassion, He has been working for thousands of years to get THE BLESSING back on His family. He has given His WORD, shed His blood and poured out His Spirit—all for one reason:

So the world He so loved from the very beginning could at last be BLESSED.

# Chapter Eight

# The Day All Heaven Broke Loose

For unto us a child is born, unto us a son is given: and the government shall be upon his shoulder: and his name shall be called Wonderful, Counsellor, The mighty God, The everlasting Father, The Prince of Peace. Of the increase of his government and peace there shall be no end.... And it shall come to pass in that day, that [the enemy's] burden shall be taken away from off thy shoulder, and his yoke from off thy neck, and the yoke shall be destroyed because of the anointing.
Isaiah 9:6-7, 10:27

One day is with The LORD as a thousand years, and a thousand years as one day (2 Peter 3:8). So, for God, it was less than a week between the Garden of Eden and the birth of Jesus.

For the devil, however, the time crawled. He spent 4,000 years watching for and dreading the arrival of the long-promised Messiah. Four fear-filled millennia wondering about the One, God had told him was coming after the Fall of man in the Garden.

With every passing day, the questions must have hounded him: Who would it be—this Seed of the woman who would come through the bloodline of THE BLESSING to crush his head? Which Seed of Abraham would prove Himself able to fulfill the divine promise: "...in thee shall all families of the earth be BLESSED" (Genesis 12:3)?

Whomever He turned out to be, the prophets had made it clear He would be anointed with the power to destroy the sin-forged yoke the devil had used to enslave the human race. According to the prophets, this Anointed One would rip all authority and power out of his hands and put it back into the hands of mankind where, according to God's first words, it rightfully belonged.

The devil had murdered one godly man after another in his attempts to abort the fulfillment of such prophecies. Time and again, he'd tried his best to obliterate the entire Hebrew race, or turn them into covenant-forsaking, sin-bound idol worshipers so THE BLESSING on them would be blocked.

Despite the devil's feverish opposition, THE BLESSING always remained active through at least a remnant of them. Throughout the ages, there was always a man or woman or group of stubborn believers who refused to let go of it. Through them, THE BLESSING kept working, generation after generation.

As a result, the devil could find no way to undo what Abraham had done the day he hiked up the mountain to offer Isaac as a sacrifice to God. Nothing could stop the divine response that had been authorized when, by faith in THE BLESSING, Abraham took his only begotten son and laid him on the altar as an offering for sin, fully expecting God to raise him from the dead.[83] By offering Isaac, Abraham had activated the principle of covenant that obligated God to do the same in return. He opened the door for God to offer up *His* only Son as a sacrifice for mankind.

That, of course, was the reason God asked Abraham to offer Isaac in the first place. He did it to set the plan of redemption irrevocably in place.

Although it took a few thousand years for that plan to unfold, eventually it did. On one historic night in Bethlehem, the Son of God Himself stepped through the door that had been opened by Abraham's faith in THE BLESSING. After marching down

---

[83] Hebrews 11:17-19

through the generations, THE BLESSING gave birth to a tiny, sin-less baby wrapped in swaddling clothes, lying in a manger.[84]

## The Way to the Garden Is Open Again

And there were in the same country shepherds abiding in the field, keeping watch over their flock by night. And, lo, the angel of The LORD came upon them, and the glory of The LORD shone round about them: and they were sore afraid. And the angel said unto them, Fear not: for, behold, I bring you good tidings of great joy, which shall be to all people. For unto you is born this day in the city of David a Saviour, which is Christ The LORD (Luke 2:8-11).

Ignore the images you've seen on so many Christmas cards. Forget the glitter and the drawings of sissified, singing angels. These verses recount one of the most earth-shaking events of all time. They contain an announcement more shocking than any that had been heard since God BLESSED Adam in the Garden of Eden—an announcement that thrilled heaven, stunned earth and threw hell into a panic.

The announcement wasn't delivered by some little twinkle-toed angel holding a choir book, either. It came from the angel of The LORD himself—Jesus' own, personal angel.

That angel's eternal assignment is to help Jesus in everything He does. He had been with Mary throughout her pregnancy, protecting and watching over her on that long trip from Nazareth to Bethlehem.

The angel of The LORD was the one who orchestrated every-thing surrounding Jesus' birth. He oversaw the sanctification of the manger. He released the glory of The LORD there and purified it. Every dirty, death-inspired germ had to wait outside.

When the angel showed up to announce Jesus' birth, contrary to what some Christmas carols claim, he wasn't crooning. He

---

[84] Luke 2:12

didn't just hover in the night sky holding a birthday candle and sing to a few sleepy shepherds. He came blazing on the scene so surrounded by the radiance of God that it lit up the whole region. People all around must have awakened in their homes thinking it was daylight. Some of them may have gone outside to find out why it was as bright as noon in the middle of the night.

When that glorious angel spoke, I'm convinced his voice shook the earth. The fields vibrated with his words as he delivered the message of Almighty God: "I bring you good tidings of great joy, which shall be to all people" (verse 10).

*Good tidings* means "good news."[85] It refers to *the gospel*. That angel was saying, "I'm bringing you the gospel [good news] of great joy."

You and I take those terms for granted because we've lived our lives in the gospel dispensation. But those shepherds had never experienced any kind of supernatural joy. True joy is a result of the inner working of the Holy Spirit. It comes from having God inside you. In those days, it was difficult to even imagine such a thing.

It was all those shepherds could do just to wrap their minds around the news that the Savior—the Deliverer the Jews had hoped and prayed for so long—had finally been born. That alone was almost more than they could grasp.

But that wasn't all the angel of The LORD was telling them. He was announcing the restoration of THE BLESSING to the whole human race. That huge, glory-radiating messenger was proclaiming the news that the serpent-crushing Seed of Abraham, the Anointed One, had come to bring the joy of The LORD, not only to the Jews, but to *all people*.

He was announcing to the sin-cursed human race that had fallen in the Garden of Eden and lived in a cursed world for 4,000 years, that the way to the Garden was open once again.

---

[85] James Strong, *The New Strong's Exhaustive Concordance of the Bible,* (Nashville: Thomas Nelson Publishers, 1984) G2097.

## Reeling From the Revelation

As soon as the angel of The LORD got that message out, all heaven broke loose:

> And suddenly there was with the angel a multitude of the heavenly host praising God, and saying, Glory to God in the highest, and on earth peace, good will toward men (verses 13-14).

There's no record in The WORD of God that this happened at any other time. But on the night Jesus was born, the angels were so excited, they couldn't keep quiet any longer. They shouted down the archangel himself and went wild praising God and shouting about peace on earth and good will toward men.

Notice, they didn't say anything about good will *among* men. They weren't shouting about the kind of natural peace that comes from the absence of earthly violence. No, their excitement was generated by something greater.

They were reeling from the revelation that the war between heaven and earth was over. The Garden of Eden incident was finished. The battle that started when Satan stole Adam's BLESSING and fought heaven with it, had been won. Those angels were saying, "There's peace now between God and mankind. The sacrifice for sin has come to earth and through Him, God's good will has been extended to all mankind!"

The night Jesus was born, earth's atmosphere reverberated with the answer to the question Satan had asked Eve thousands of years earlier in the Garden:

*"Hath God said?"*

Heaven's hosts rocked this planet with the news, *"Yes, God has said!"*

THE BLESSING was the first thing God ever said to mankind; and He'll never change it. THE BLESSING is God's perfect will for humanity. Jesus is the perfect will of God for humanity. He is THE BLESSING manifest in the flesh. He is the incarnation of the divine words: "Be fruitful, and multiply, and replenish the earth, and subdue it: and have dominion...."

Even before Jesus had finished His mission on earth—before He went to the cross and completed the plan of redemption—God sent His angels to say, "Good news, everyone! THE BLESSING is back!"

That's how God always operates. He calls things that be not as though they were (Romans 4:17). He declares the end from the beginning. And, as always, the end He declared came to pass just as He said it would. Thirty-three short years later, the devil was whipped and the curse conquered—all by the power of THE BLESSING.[86]

## No Divine Privileges

"Wait a minute," you might say, "I thought Jesus did those things by the divine power that belongs to Him as the Son of God."

No, the Bible says that when Jesus came to earth, He stripped Himself of all divine privileges. He laid aside the power that belonged to Him as a member of the Godhead, "became like men and was born a human being."[87]

That means every miracle Jesus performed and every work of ministry He accomplished on earth was a manifestation of THE BLESSING in operation. He healed the sick, cast out demons and raised the dead—all by faith in THE BLESSING of Abraham and the promises it included.

It's amazing, but true: Jesus did everything the Father had called Him to do, not as the Son of God, but as the *Son of man*. The New Testament leaves no doubt about it, telling us again and again that Jesus referred to Himself in that way:

- When He healed the paralytic, He said, "That ye may know that *the Son of man* hath power on earth to forgive sins, then saith he...Arise, take up thy bed, and go unto

---

[86] Galatians 3:13-14; Colossians 2:15
[87] Philippians 2:7, *The Amplified Bible*

thine house" (Matthew 9:6).

- When speaking to His disciples, He asked, "Whom do men say that I *the Son of man* am?" (Matthew 16:13).

- When He talked about His crucifixion, He said, "*The Son of man* must suffer many things..." (Mark 8:31).

- When He explained His earthly mission He said, "*The Son of man* is not come to destroy men's lives, but to save them" (Luke 9:56).

- When He spoke to the Jews who questioned His identity, He said, "When ye have lifted up *the Son of man*, then shall ye know that I am he, and that I do nothing of myself; but as my Father hath taught me, I speak these things" (John 8:28).

By referring to Himself as the Son of man, Jesus was in no way denying His divinity. He wholly affirmed Peter's revelation that, "Thou art the Christ, the Son of the living God" (Matthew 16:16). Yet, it was not His divinity that Jesus emphasized. It was His humanity.

By calling Himself "the Son of man," Jesus was actually saying to His Jewish listeners who knew that *man* and *Adam* were the same Hebrew word: "I am the One who walks in Adam's BLESSING. I am the last Adam."[88]

"But, I thought Jesus walked in THE BLESSING of Abraham," you might say.

He did! As we've already seen, Adam's BLESSING and Abraham's BLESSING are the same. The reason that BLESSING is referred to in the New Testament as "THE BLESSING of Abraham" is because it was Abraham's faith and his covenant with God that made the way for Jesus to come to earth. Jesus' birth, life,

---

[88] See 1 Corinthians 15:45.

ministry, sacrifice for our sin and His resurrection, were all possible because Abraham believed and received THE BLESSING—not just for himself, but for his Seed.

Notice the word *Seed* is singular, not plural. It not only refers to the Jewish people who are Abraham's natural heirs, but according to Galatians 3:16, THE BLESSING of Abraham and every promise included in it were specifically directed toward one particular Heir—Jesus.

> Now to Abraham and his seed were the promises made. He saith not, And to seeds, as of many; but as of one, And to thy seed, which is Christ.

In light of this, you can see why Galatians 3:8 says that God was preaching *the gospel* unto Abraham when He said, "In thee shall all nations be BLESSED." With that one statement, God proclaimed the good news that Jesus was coming to get THE BLESSING back for all nations, to demonstrate its true power and make it available again to every man, woman and child on earth who would put their faith in Him!

### Yoke-Destroying, Burden-Removing Power

It's no wonder Jesus laid aside the power of His divinity when He came to earth. He didn't come to demonstrate His power as God's Son. He came to release and restore the power of THE BLESSING.

If His purpose had been to prove His divinity, He would have worked miracles as a child. He was just as much the Son of God at 4 years old as He was at 30. But the Bible makes it clear that He didn't work a single miracle until after the Holy Spirit came on Him during His baptism in the Jordan River. At that moment, Jesus stepped into the full power of THE BLESSING:

> And, lo, the heavens were opened unto him, and he saw the Spirit of God descending like a dove, and lighting upon him:

and lo a voice from heaven, saying, This is my beloved Son, in whom I am well pleased (Matthew 3:16-17).

When Satan heard those words, the fight was on. He knew exactly who he was facing. He knew the baby born three decades earlier in Bethlehem had grown into the One with the power to bring him down. He responded right away by following Jesus into the wilderness and bombarding Him with temptations. But Jesus overcame every one of them with the powerful words, "It is written...."

Returning in the power of the Spirit to Galilee, He showed up at the synagogue in Nazareth and made the announcement that turned the religious world upside down:

The Spirit of The LORD is upon me, because he hath anointed me to preach the gospel to the poor; he hath sent me to heal the brokenhearted, to preach deliverance to the captives, and recovering of sight to the blind, to set at liberty them that are bruised, to preach the acceptable year of The LORD (Luke 4:18-19).

Notice, Jesus didn't proclaim He was the divine Son of God. He announced that He was *anointed*.

Because The WORD *anointed* isn't used in ordinary speech today, most people don't know what it means. But the definition is simple: "to smear on, rub into or pour all over." In a spiritual sense, a person who is anointed is one who has the power of God on him.

In Jesus' day, people understood that, so they knew He was telling them that the Holy Spirit had come on Him to undo what the devil had done in the Garden of Eden. God had poured out on Him the same power the first Adam had been given—the power to create the conditions of the Garden wherever he went.

"Well, I don't see how you come up with that," someone might say. "There's nothing about the Garden of Eden in those verses."

The exact words may not be there, but let me ask you this: Were any of the evil things Jesus said He was anointed to overcome present in the Garden of Eden? Was any poverty, sickness, brokenheartedness, blindness or bondage there?

Certainly not! So, when Jesus declared that the Spirit of The LORD was upon Him to empower Him to get rid of such things, He was saying, in essence, "I've come to bring back the Garden."

That's what the anointing does! It removes the burdens and destroys the yokes of the enemy.[89] It gets rid of every work of the devil and brings God's will to pass on earth as it is in heaven. Since God's will is and always has been THE BLESSING, you might say that the anointing is THE BLESSING on the move.

And when Jesus came on the scene, THE BLESSING moved as never before! Because He perfectly kept the commandments of God, it flowed through Him without hindrance. In time past, that had been impossible. Although THE BLESSING could come on Old Testament saints like Abraham, Isaac and Jacob, it couldn't flow from within them because their spirits were contaminated by sin. They hadn't been born again.

Jesus, however, was different. His spirit was pure, so THE BLESSING moved through Him from the inside out. That's why He could say, "...the Father that dwelleth in me, he doeth the works."[90]

THE BLESSING had such free course in Jesus that it could pour through Him in full force without any kind of reserve or measure. So, everywhere He went, He brought the Garden of Eden with Him. If anyone would listen to Him and put their faith in His Anointing, THE BLESSING on Him would drive the curse out of their minds and bodies and fill them with life.

The only thing that could stop THE BLESSING from flowing to them through Him was unbelief. The people of Nazareth found that out. Jesus was just as anointed there as He was everywhere

---

[89] Isaiah 10:27
[90] John 14:10

else He preached. But instead of receiving the anointing by faith, the people in Nazareth said:

> Is not this the carpenter, the son of Mary, the brother of James, and Joses, and of Juda, and Simon? and are not his sisters here with us? And they were offended at him…. And he could *there do no mighty work,* save that he laid his hands upon a few sick folk, and healed them. And he marvelled because of their unbelief (Mark 6:3-6).

Most Christians are under the impression those people balked at Jesus' divinity or that they refused to believe He was the Son of God. But, according to the Bible, Jesus didn't tell them He was the Son of God. He told them, "The Spirit of The LORD is upon me, because he hath anointed me…" (Luke 4:18). That's the message Jesus preached everywhere He went.

In places where the people believed it—like the area of Capernaum—THE BLESSING flowed like a river. People would follow Him around for days listening to Him teach, and multitudes would get healed. They would go without food for days just to be in His meetings. If they were too hungry to make it home, Jesus would take a few loaves and fish, multiply them by releasing THE BLESSING and feed the whole crowd.

In places like Nazareth, where people wouldn't believe, however, Jesus *could do no mighty work* (verse 5). He wanted to—but couldn't because unbelief slams the door on THE BLESSING.

## Dominion in Action

The people in Nazareth not only refused to believe Jesus was anointed, they got so mad at Him, they tried to push Him off a cliff. But, they couldn't do it because even surrounded by doubters, He continued walking by faith in THE BLESSING as He always did. He kept believing it was on Him and expected it to function with every step He took and every word He spoke.

As a result, those people couldn't lay a hand on Him. THE

BLESSING operating on Him blocked Him from their sight and so, "passing through the midst of them [He] went his way."[91]

THE BLESSING worked like that for Jesus everywhere He went. His entire ministry was a manifestation of those first words God spoke over Adam: "Be fruitful, fill up the earth, have dominion and subdue it."

- When a storm threatened His boat, Jesus "rebuked the wind, and said unto the sea, Peace, be still. And the wind ceased, and there was a great calm" (Mark 4:39).

- When people with sickness and disease reached out to Him in faith, Jesus took dominion over it and "healed them all" (Matthew 12:15).

- When He went fishing with Peter, Jesus took dominion over the fish and gathered up such a net-breaking, boat-sinking load that Peter "was astonished, and all that were with him, at the draught of the fishes which they had taken" (Luke 5:9).

- Even death itself bowed its knee to Jesus' dominion. When it clamped its hands around Lazarus and dragged him to the grave, Jesus broke its grip with the power of THE BLESSING and said, "Lazarus, come forth" (John 11:43).

In addition to living in the power of THE BLESSING, Jesus taught the people who came to hear Him how to do it. He said, "BLESSED are the merciful...." "BLESSED are the pure in heart...." "BLESSED are the peacemakers...."[92] (The message

---

[91] Luke 4:30
[92] Matthew 5:7-9

we call "The Sermon on the Mount" is all about how to connect with and release the power of THE BLESSING!)

Parents who attended Jesus' meetings brought their children and asked Him to lay His hands on them because they wanted that BLESSING on their children. They knew when Jesus took them in His arms, put His hands on them and BLESSED them,[93] it wouldn't be just a religious ritual, but a powerful thing.

When I get to heaven, I'm going to ask The LORD how the little ones Jesus BLESSED turned out. I'm going to read the heavenly history books and find out what amazing things those children accomplished.

That may sound silly to you, but I've seen firsthand the kind of boldness and power that comes on little children who understand the power of THE BLESSING. I've seen born-again, Spirit-filled first-graders who can absolutely put the devil in his place.

My own children have done it more times than I can count. One of the first times I saw it happen, Gloria and I were driving across Fort Worth one stormy evening to preach at a church across town. John, who was about 4 years old, and Kellie, who was 6, were riding in the back seat.

Overhead, a sky full of dark, greenish-looking clouds churned and threatened to turn ugly, so we were keeping an eye on them. Sure enough, as we pulled out onto the road, two tornadoes dropped down out of one of the clouds. We saw them both and I started shouting, "No, you don't! In the Name of Jesus whose I am and whom I serve, you get back up there where you belong!"

When I quieted down, I could hear John and Kellie behind me screaming at the top of their lungs with the same kind of confidence, "Yeah, you get out of here in the Name of Jesus!"

At that instant, both those tornadoes bounced back up into the clouds. They looked as if they had springs on them.

"Brother Copeland, surely you don't believe those kids did that?" Why not?

---

[93] Mark 10:16

THE BLESSING on them is the same BLESSING that's on me. It's the same BLESSING that stilled the storm on the Sea of Galilee, and it works for every born-again, Holy-Ghost baptized member of God's family—whether they're 6 years old or 60—the same way it worked for Jesus.

By simple faith, THE BLESSING is ours—through Him.

# Chapter Nine

# From the Cross to the Throne

Forasmuch then as the children are partakers of flesh and blood, he also
himself likewise took part of the same; that through death he might destroy him that had the power of death, that is, the devil; and deliver them
who through fear of death were all their lifetime subject to bondage.
Hebrews 2:14-15

That Jesus lived and ministered on earth in the power of
THE BLESSING is an indisputable, scriptural fact. But it
needs to be made clear that He did not do it just to give mankind
an example to follow. He didn't take on human flesh so He could
show people how to live a BLESSED and godly life. Anyone who
understands human nature knows such an idea is ridiculous.

To expect fallen humanity to live like Jesus did by following
His good example would be like expecting a stubby-legged, sway-
backed donkey to win the Kentucky Derby by following the good
example of a racehorse. It will never happen. It can't happen. No
matter how much a donkey might want to be like a racehorse, it
will never win the Derby because it's born of the wrong bloodline.
And no matter how much people want to live like Jesus, if they are
born of the lineage of Adam, they will never be able to do it because they are born of sinful seed.

That's why God didn't send Jesus to be our example. He sent

Him to be the firstborn of a whole new breed.

Conceived in the womb of a virgin, Jesus was not just a spectacular and spiritually successful member of the fallen Adamic race. He was God's own Son—the second member of the Godhead—clothed in a body of flesh that pulsed, not with the sin-contaminated blood of Adam, but with sinless blood generated by The WORD of His heavenly Father. He was the Pure Seed who would give rise to a whole new species of humanity—a God-born race of men, women and children with spirits as holy and full of divine glory as His own. A reborn race as pure as God Himself, completely untainted by the bitterness of the curse.

What Jesus came to earth to accomplish was sheer, supernatural genius. It was a plan so perfect and so perfectly hidden in God that, try as he might, the devil in all his craftiness could not figure it out. It was "a mystery...which God ordained before the world unto our glory: which none of the princes of this world knew: for had they known it, they would not have crucified The LORD of glory."[94]

Had the devil and his crew been able to detect even the faintest inkling of what was going to happen when Jesus went to the cross, they would have left Him alone. They would have realized that one sinless life alone could never turn back the flood of evil that had been released through the Fall of Man. They would have known that Jesus' earthly ministry, powerful as it was, could not liberate a sin-enslaved world.

Had they not been blinded by their own pride and spiritual darkness, they would have paid closer attention when Jesus declared: "Verily, verily, I say unto you, Except a corn of wheat fall into the ground and die, it abideth alone: but if it die, it bringeth forth much fruit...for this cause came I unto this hour" (John 12:24, 27).

Somehow, the whole demonic kingdom missed the point of those words. They failed to grasp it was not Jesus' life but His

---

[94] 1 Corinthians 2:7-8

*death* that would fill the earth with sons of God like Himself. It was through His crucifixion and resurrection that He would strip Satan of his authority and set earth's captives free.

The hosts of hell were totally ignorant of that fact when they stirred up the mob in Jerusalem and urged them to cry, "Crucify Him!" It never occurred to them that they were about to be ambushed by Almighty God. They just figured that by killing Jesus, they could get Him out of the way.

When their attempts began to succeed, they must have been mystified. They'd tried to kill Him many times and been unable to do it. Why was He suddenly submitting to torture and pain? Why, instead of asking God to send legions of angels to protect Him, was He letting sinners jerk His beard out by the roots? Why was He simply bowing His head beneath the skull-piercing crown of thorns, yielding His back to the flesh-ripping scourge, and offering His hands to the iron nails?

They didn't know what you and I know—that Jesus did it all to pay the price for the sin of all mankind. He gave Himself willingly, to become the sacrificial Lamb for the whole world. He poured out His pure, sinless blood on purpose, to establish a new covenant between God and man—a covenant that would reconcile them and restore THE BLESSING forever.

## A Miraculous Transfer

What the new covenant cost Jesus goes beyond what the natural mind can comprehend. Even the most gruesome depictions of His physical sufferings don't begin to touch the fullness of the price He paid because His greatest agonies were not physical but spiritual. He didn't just die a fleshly death, He took into Himself every sin mankind ever committed—past, present and future. He absorbed into His own spotless spirit, every foul, demonically inspired thought, action and deed of humanity and suffered the full consequences of them.

- "For he [God] hath *made him to be sin for us,* who knew no sin; that we might be made the righteousness of God in him" (2 Corinthians 5:21).

- "Christ hath redeemed us from the curse of the law, *being made a curse for us:* for it is written, Cursed is every one that hangeth on a tree" (Galatians 3:13).

- "All we like sheep have gone astray; we have turned every one to his own way; and The LORD *hath laid on him the iniquity of us all"* (Isaiah 53:6).

"But, Brother Copeland," you might say, "how could sin get into Jesus' spirit if He never committed any sin?"

Our sin got into His spirit the same way His righteousness gets into ours when we're born again. It was transferred by a miracle of God that was released through faith in His WORD.

Jesus received spiritual death the same way we receive spiritual life: by believing in His heart and confessing with His mouth that what God said would come to pass. He stood in faith on The WORD that The LORD would lay on Him the iniquity of us all, stepped out in obedience to it by going to the Cross, and The WORD did its work.

When it did, Jesus' body became so twisted and disfigured by the effects of sin, He didn't even look human. His spirit underwent such torture and pressure that "his visage was…marred more than any man, and his form more than the sons of men."[95] No human spirit has ever gone through the horror He did. That's why the centurion who witnessed Jesus' death said, "Truly this was the Son of God"![96]

The centurion had probably seen hundreds of people crucified, but never seen anything like what happened to Jesus. The only thing he could figure was what the Pharisees had said was

---

[95] Isaiah 52:14
[96] Matthew 27:54

true. This man must have committed some kind of blasphemy. He claimed to be equal to God, and now God, in His wrath, was punishing Him. That's what most of the people who watched Jesus die believed. While He was hanging on the Cross paying the price for their sins, bearing their guilt on Himself, they claimed He was being "smitten of God."[97]

Even the devil must have eventually come to that conclusion. He had no other explanation for what was going on. He must have been thinking, *I don't know what terrible thing this man did, but somehow he has sinned in a way that has turned God totally against him.* If he had any doubts about that, they were erased when, after Jesus died physically, His sin-deadened spirit descended into hell.

"Oh, come on now," someone might say. "Jesus didn't go to hell. He finished the work of redemption when He was on the Cross. He said so, Himself."

No, when He said *It is finished,* He wasn't talking about redemption. Everyone who's heard the gospel knows that the plan of redemption wasn't finished until after the Resurrection. So, Jesus couldn't possibly have been referring to that. What He declared on the Cross was the end of the age of justification by animal sacrifice. He announced that with the shedding of His blood, the Old Testament type and shadow of the Passover Lamb had been fulfilled. Mankind no longer had to slaughter animals to atone for their sin. The One, true, sacrificial Lamb of God had come. The Old Covenant was finished.

Small wars have been fought between theologians over what happened next. Debates have raged over the question of what happened after Jesus *yielded up His spirit*[98] on the cross. Did He die spiritually or not? Did He go immediately to Paradise or plunge into the bowels of hell?

The Bible clearly answers those questions. The first few chapters of Genesis settle the fact that Jesus died spiritually. Those chapters prove that spiritual death—not just physical death—is the

---

[97] Isaiah 53:4
[98] Matthew 27:50, *New King James Version*

true penalty for sin. It's obvious that in Genesis 2:17, when God said to Adam in the Garden of Eden, "In the day that thou eatest thereof [of the tree of the knowledge of good and evil] thou shalt surely die," He wasn't talking about the death of Adam's body. Adam didn't die physically the day he ate from the tree. He lived for another 930 years.

The death God warned Adam about was spiritual death. It's the inward death that takes place when a spiritual being is separated from God. That's what spiritual death is—separation from God. Adam experienced it the moment he sinned. He was immediately cut off from his fellowship with the Father, and the light of God's life and glory within him was snuffed out.

For Jesus to become our *substitute,* He had to go through the same kind of separation. He had to die, not just physically, but spiritually, and descend into hell to suffer the whole penalty of sin.

It shocks some people's religious sensibilities to think of Jesus in hell, but that doesn't change the fact that He went there. The Scriptures verify it again and again. They tell us that He descended "…into the deep [or the bottomless pit]" before He was brought up from the dead (Romans 10:7); and that "his soul was not *left in hell,* neither his flesh did see corruption" (Acts 2:31). Psalm 18, which paints a detailed, prophetic picture of what Jesus went through between the cross and the throne, declares, "The sorrows of hell compassed me about: the snares of death prevented me" (verse 5).

Not only did Jesus go to hell, He sank to the deepest, darkest part of it to suffer everything that was necessary on our behalf. We'll be forever glad He did, too—because had He not gone to hell, we would have to. Had He stopped short of paying that price, we would have to pay it ourselves.

The only reason we can walk debt-free through heaven's gate is because He paid it all.

## A Massive, God-Ordained Trap

Actually, it was the spiritual suffering Jesus was facing that He agonized over in the Garden of Gethsemane. When He said, "O my Father, if it be possible, let this cup pass from me,"[99] He wasn't asking to be spared the physical torment of the Cross. He wouldn't have sweat drops of blood over the thought of His body dying. That wasn't the major part of what He was facing. The thing He dreaded and felt such sorrow about was being separated from His Father and going to hell on behalf of mankind.

Never in all of human history had anyone gone to hell and gotten out. No man had ever done what He was about to do. No man had ever given himself up to spiritual death and then been made spiritually alive. Yet, Jesus took that step of faith. He went to the Cross believing that by the power of God's WORD He would be the first man ever born again from death to life, the first man to ever emerge triumphant from the depths of hell.

When He took that step, every demonic spirit in existence, every principality and power, every ruler of the darkness of this world, every wicked spirit in heavenly places came after Him. They swarmed around Him expecting to annihilate His spirit and lock Him up in that pit so He could never get out. They sneered and exalted themselves over His tortured, emaciated, death-wracked spirit, thinking that somehow they had outsmarted the Anointed One and done away with THE BLESSING once and for all.

But the whole thing was a trap. A massive, God-ordained trap. Jesus, the Holy Spirit and the Father Himself had suckered all those demons in there at the same time for one reason: to strike them down with a single stroke.

Just as God knew they would, they took the bait…then the trap snapped shut. The voice of God Almighty roared across the universe, shaking the very guts of hell and striking like lightning into Jesus' shriveled, sin-plagued spirit:

Thou art my Son, this day have I begotten thee…. And again, I will be to him a Father, and he shall be to me a Son…. Let all the angels of God worship him.[100]

---

[99] Matthew 26:39
[100] Hebrews 1:5-6

According to the book of Hebrews, those are the words God spoke when He raised Jesus from the dead. Those are the words that brought the First-begotten again into the world.

"But, Brother Copeland, don't those verses refer to Jesus being begotten of God when He was born in Bethlehem?"

No, God didn't become Jesus' Father when Mary gave birth to His physical body. Jesus had been the Son of God throughout eternity. In Bethlehem, He simply took on a human form. That's where "The WORD was made flesh, and dwelt among us."[101]

It was after He'd been separated from God by spiritual death and the sin of mankind that God said, *"Again,* I will be to him a Father, and he shall be to me a Son." It was when the power of God resurrected Jesus' spirit in the pit of hell and He was born again that He became "the *first begotten* of the dead."[102]

At that moment, Jesus was brought to life by God's words of dominion, just as Adam was in the beginning. God called Him *Son* and rocked the universe with the command, "Let all the angels worship Him!" When He did, every angel including Satan himself, fell at Jesus' feet. They didn't like it, but they had to do it anyway. That whole, filthy, demonic horde sank weak-kneed in Jesus' presence as His spirit was regenerated by the power of God's WORD.

In a flash, the demonic party was over. The spirits of darkness that had been reveling over the mistaken idea that Jesus was forever whipped, scattered and quaked like the cowards they are. He towered over them, looking like God Almighty Himself, speaking with God's own voice, eyes blazing with His glory, highly exalted and having been given the Name that is above every name:

That at the name of Jesus every knee should bow, of things in heaven, and things in earth, and things under the earth; and that every tongue should confess that Jesus Christ is Lord, to the glory of God the Father (Philippians 2:10-11).

---

[101] John 1:14
[102] Revelation 1:5

That's when Jesus started to kick some demonic backside. He went into combat mode behind the gates of hell and won every fight. He defeated *every* demon, *every* principality, *every* power.

Then, "having spoiled principalities and powers, he made a show of them openly, triumphing over them in it."[103] He put the devil and his defeated forces on public display. The New Testament terminology likens it to how the Roman army paraded their conquered foes through the streets of Rome. While jubilant crowds cheered in victory, vanquished kings and military leaders became spectacles as they were marched through the city as prisoners, bound with chains and with yokes around their necks. They were put on display as trophies of conquest for all to see.

Jesus did essentially the same thing to the devil. After He conquered him and took the keys of death and hell away from him, Jesus paraded the devil down the avenues of hell in full view of the heroes of faith who watched in awe from the upper regions of the dead, in the place the Bible calls *Paradise.*

All the prophets of the Old Testament—those faith hall-of-famers listed in Hebrews 11—were there in the grandstands that day, cheering wildly as Jesus defeated Satan, abolished death and brought forth life and immortality.[104] They must have been having an absolute fit of joy while all that was going on. I can almost hear them shouting, *"Put it on him, Jesus! Whip him again!"*

Those Old Covenant saints were thrilled, not only because the battle was being won, but because it was being won by a born-again man—a man as human as they, or you or me—a man who had been dragged deeper into hell than any other and who had borne *all* sin.

This born-again man overpowered the entire demonic kingdom, destroying him that had the power of death, that is, the devil; and delivered them who through fear of death were all their lifetime subject to bondage.[105]

---

[103] Colossians 2:15
[104] 2 Timothy 1:10
[105] Hebrews 2:14-15

What's more, this same born-again, resurrected man is the second Person of the Godhead today. He didn't become something else when He ascended back into heaven. He is still a man. He will forever be a man. He has the same body He had while ministering on earth. It's glorified now, of course. The blood that once flowed through His veins was poured out in sacrifice for us and replaced with the glory of God, but it's the same flesh-and-bone body He had when He went to the Cross.[106]

He proved that to Thomas after the Resurrection when He held up His hands and showed him the nail holes in them. Those holes are big enough to stick your fingers through. The Roman nails that made them weighed over 2 pounds apiece, and the head of each was big enough to cover the entire palm of Jesus' hand.

This is the startling truth of Christianity—that God's Son became a man forever and there is a resurrected, glorified man in the Trinity! He is the Champion of champions. He is the Victor of all, and He is our representative. We have been brought into the Godhead through Him.

## A Fresh Interest in Uncle Fred

When Jesus had defeated the devil and his forces in the pit of hell, He turned to all the Old Covenant believers who'd been held captive by death and preached the gospel to them. He declared to them, as He did later to the disciples, "All authority has been given to Me in heaven and on earth."[107] They believed it and were born again.

When they did, Jesus said, "Come on, family. We're getting out of here."[108]

I like to think He linked arms with Abraham on one side and David on the other and marched the whole shouting, singing, rejoicing crowd out of captivity and into glory. When He escorted them through heaven's gate, the heavenly Father—

---

[106] See Luke 24:39.
[107] Matthew 28:18, *New King James Version*
[108] See Ephesians 4:8.

Compassion Himself—must have run to meet them, shouting, "They're home! They're home! They're home at last!" Then, they had the most marvelous reunion celebration you can imagine—a celebration they'd been looking forward to for 4,000 years.

From there, Jesus went back to the earth and spent 40 days ministering to people.[109] He wasn't the only one who did, either. The Bible says that "many bodies of the saints which slept arose, and came out of the graves after his resurrection, and went into the holy city, and appeared unto many."[110]

Wouldn't that be something? Just think what a shock it would be to see Uncle Fred who has been dead for 25 years, walk in while the family is sitting at the breakfast table and say, "Good morning, everyone!" I'd guess Aunt Minnie and Cousin Jeffrey and everyone else who had once made fun of Uncle Fred's faith would suddenly have a fresh interest in what he had to say!

You can believe what you want about it, but I'm persuaded that the same kind of thing will happen at the Rapture of the Church. Jesus set the pattern, and we're going to follow it. In the 40 days after our bodies are resurrected and glorified, I am convinced we'll make some appearances on earth, preach the gospel to some people and have the most amazing move of God we've ever seen.

"But, doesn't the Bible say we'll be caught up in the twinkling of an eye?" you might ask.

No, it says we'll be changed from mortality to immortality in the twinkling of an eye.[111] It doesn't say we'll go to heaven that quickly. But you can read The WORD, study it out for yourself, and come to your own conclusion about it.

### One Final Request

Even after Jesus poured out the blood of the New Covenant, defeated the devil, released the captive saints and cleansed the

---

[109] Acts 1:2-3
[110] Matthew 27:52-53
[111] See 1 Corinthians 15:51-53.

heavenly utensils of worship from the contamination of Satan,[112] wiping every trace of him out of heaven, Jesus wasn't quite finished with the work of redemption. He had one more thing to do. He had to fulfill the promise He made to His disciples just before He went to the Cross: "I will pray the Father, and he shall give you another Comforter, that he may abide with you for ever" (John 14:16).

When Jesus made that request, it changed everything for His disciples—not only for those who gathered at Pentecost in the upper room in Jerusalem, but for every disciple who would ever follow in their footsteps. When He said, "Father, send them the Holy Spirit," and the Father answered, "I will be most happy to do that," nothing was ever the same again. Heaven was poured out on earth...

> And suddenly there came a sound from heaven as of a rushing mighty wind, and it filled all the house where they were sitting. And there appeared unto them cloven tongues like as of fire, and it sat upon each of them. And they were all filled with the Holy Ghost, and began to speak with other tongues, as the Spirit gave them utterance (Acts 2:2-4).

To understand what really happened that day, realize that the noise described in those verses was not literally the sound of wind blowing. It was a sound from heaven that was *like* a rushing, mighty wind.

The writer of Acts compared it to a windstorm because the environment back then wasn't as noisy as ours is today. No one had ever heard the roar of a jet engine, or a gunshot. Children didn't walk around the streets with boomboxes blaring loud enough to rattle the windows. In those days, a violent storm was the noisiest thing around.

What caused that thunderous, Pentecostal sound?

I'm totally convinced it was the roar of God's power filling the

---

[112] Hebrews 9:23-24

atmosphere of this planet. It was the sound of the Holy Spirit arriving from heaven with thousands, upon thousands, upon thousands of angels. It was the sound of THE BLESSING coming on the scene, and you could have heard it anywhere on earth.

If you've never associated angels with the day of Pentecost, let me remind you that in the beginning, God created an entire host of angels to help mankind fulfill their mission of filling the earth with the Garden of Eden. Those angels were part of THE BLESSING. But, when sin turned THE BLESSING into the curse, they were expelled from earth's atmosphere. They had to be recalled to heaven because Satan and the angels who followed him had taken over.

From then on, angels came to earth only on special assignments.[113] God sent them at times to minister to His people, but only on a limited basis. That's why the angels Jacob saw in his dream had to go back and forth from heaven on a spiritual ladder.[114] They didn't have free access to the earth. A way had to be made for them to come.

That's also why the angel who came to deliver a message to the prophet Daniel had to fight for 21 days (and eventually get help from Michael, the archangel, to break through the demonic forces blocking his way. During that three-week battle, Daniel fasted, prayed and waited. He didn't have the Name of Jesus to use like we do. He couldn't overcome the devil with the blood of the Lamb and the word of his testimony. He just continued praying until the angels bringing his answer were able to get to him.[115]

On the day of Pentecost, however, the whole situation changed. The demonic spirits formerly dominating earth's atmosphere had been defeated and put under the feet of Jesus. Sin had been dealt with. There were born-again men and women on the earth who, through faith in Jesus, had inherited THE BLESSING. So when Jesus asked God to activate the power of THE BLESSING by sending the Holy Spirit, the multitude of angels who had been waiting for 4,000 years to go to work, were released to do their job at last.

---

[113] See Joshua 5:13-14; Judges 13:3; 2 Kings 2:12; Daniel 3:25; Luke 1:19, 26-27, 22:43.
[114] Genesis 28:12
[115] See Daniel 10:1-13

They went out of heaven and flooded the earth's atmosphere.

They're still here today to help you and me, standing ready to serve us as ministering spirits, sent forth to minister for them who shall be heirs of salvation.[116]

"If that's true, then why haven't they been doing more for me?"

Angels are not free agents. They are divinely commissioned to respond to The WORD of God. As Psalm 103 says, they "do his commandments, hearkening unto the voice of his WORD" (verse 20). Either you have not been conducting yourself properly in their presence, or you are not giving them anything to work with.

If you are saying things contrary to THE BLESSING and at odds with The WORD of God, your angels just stand there, inactive on your behalf. They won't act on those unbelieving words. The last angel who acted on something other than The WORD of God was Satan, and they aren't about to follow in his footsteps. They know where he will end up, and they are not on his side.

When a believer says things like, "I feel terrible. I believe I'm getting the flu. I get it every year, and I'm in bed with it for a week," angels cannot respond. God's WORD doesn't promise believers the flu. Angels aren't flu bringers. They probably just scratch their heads and say, "I wonder why that guy is making faith confessions about getting the flu. He doesn't seem to enjoy it very much. But he keeps on declaring it over himself, anyway."

If you want your angels to spring into action, however, begin speaking The WORD. Instead of talking sickness, poverty and defeat, confess THE BLESSING over yourself. Say, "I'm BLESSED in the city. I'm BLESSED in the country. My body is BLESSED. My children are BLESSED. Everything I put my hand to prospers." Those are words the angels can go to work on. Those words will keep them busy doing good things for you.

I've never actually seen the angels assigned to me, but sometimes other people have. One of them was a fellow who came to a meeting where I was preaching years ago in southeast Texas.

---

116 Hebrews 1:14

During the meeting, I said something that didn't quite agree with his ideas and he got up and stormed out of the auditorium. It was a small church, so I couldn't help noticing when he left.

Several days later, however, he came back. It didn't look very much like he wanted to be there because he slipped in the back door and took a seat on the back row, closest to the exit. About halfway through the service, his eyes got big, his jaw dropped and he melted down into the pew. He sat that way for an hour or so, and when the service was over he kind of limped out.

*What's the matter with him?* I thought.

A few days later, I found out. He came to me after one of the meetings and said, "Brother Copeland, I have to apologize to you."

"What for?" I asked.

"You made me so mad I could hardly breathe the other night. I swore I would go home, read my Bible and prove you wrong. But, when I started reading, I found out *I* was wrong. The LORD told me to come back here and repent. I didn't want to, but I figured I'd better do it.

"When I got here, I told The LORD that if He didn't do something to prove to me that what you're teaching is of God, I'm never going to another meeting like this again. Sure enough, about halfway through your message, God opened my eyes and I saw something I'd never seen before."

"What was it?" I asked.

"You know the guy on the television commercial named Mr. Clean®? The huge, bald-headed guy who stands there with his arms crossed and a big smile on his face?"

"Yeah."

"I saw a man standing right behind and little to the side of you who looked like that. He was big! The whole time you were preaching, he stuck so close to you that you could hardly see daylight between you."

I don't mind telling you, I was happy to hear it. I knew that angel was there, but I'd never seen him. I didn't know he looked like Mr. Clean®!

The fellow went on to tell me that when I'd start to wind down a little bit in my preaching, the angel would lean over and say something in my ear. When he did, I'd get excited and go at it again like a house on fire.

"I know I must have looked kind of funny while I was watching him," he said. "All I could think was, *Oh, dear heavens, I'm glad I didn't tangle with that guy!*"

It's not only preachers who have angels like that following them around. God has assigned at least one angel (and probably more) to every believer. Jesus said our angels "do always behold the face of my Father which is in heaven."[117] There must have been multiplied millions of those Mr. Clean®-looking angels entering into the atmosphere on the day of Pentecost.

No wonder it sounded like a tornado hit the place!

### Engulfed by the Fire of God

Though that influx of angels was awesome, it wasn't the most thrilling thing that happened that day. The fire that came blazing into the upper room was the featured event. Forget the religious paintings that show little lighter-type flames flickering over the disciples' heads. That fire was the glorious presence of God Himself coming down to envelop His people.

It was the same fiery presence that radiated from God when He stood in the Garden of Eden, spoke into Adam's limp, lifeless body, and said, "Man, be in Our image!" It was the same fire that blazed like a flaming garment from within Adam and Eve, before sin extinguished it. And, it was the same fire that came down on Mount Sinai to meet Moses. The difference was, at Sinai and every other time God appeared in His flaming glory in the Old Testament, He had to cover Himself with a cloud. Otherwise, His power and holiness would have killed everyone instantly. His lightning-like glory would have vaporized sin and sinner together.

But at Pentecost, God didn't have to cover Himself with a cloud. He didn't have to protect the disciples from His glory. They'd been born again. Their spirits had been renewed and were

---

[117] Matthew 18:10

as pure and sinless as God Himself. Through the new birth, they had become Love, just like He is love. They'd become Light, just as He is Light. They'd become one Spirit with Christ.[118]

For the first time since the Garden of Eden, God had the thrilling liberty to embrace His people. And that's exactly what He did. He came into the upper room in the fullness of His glorious Self and sat down on every one of them! He didn't just put little, golden plate-looking halos on their heads. He enveloped them in Himself. He merged Himself with them, lighting them up from the inside out with His own fiery Spirit. They walked out of that room filled to overflowing with His power and glory in the fullness of THE BLESSING of God.

From that day on, the disciples ministered in that BLESSING just as Jesus did. They went out in His Name and brought the conditions of Eden to everyone who would believe and receive. People were born again, healed and had demons cast out of them. Crowds absolutely scrambled to get close to Peter. Sick people were actually laid out on the street—hoping his shadow would fall on them because if it did, they knew they'd be healed.

There was no virtue or power involved in Peter's actual shadow. The shadow is a frame of reference. The effect of the anointing that was on him extended out about a shadow's length from Peter's body. Anyone who got that close to him would run into it and get healed.

Religious tradition will tell you that happened because Peter was some kind of special apostle or because he was the first pope. But that's not the reason. Peter just had a greater revelation of THE BLESSING that belonged to him through the Name of Jesus. He knew when he walked down the street, THE BLESSING was on the scene.

"Brother Copeland, surely you're not saying we, as believers today, could have the kind of power to heal that the Apostle Peter had!"

I don't have to say it. Peter said it himself after he and John healed the crippled man at the temple gate a few days after Pentecost. When

---

[118] 1 Corinthians 6:17

the crowd gathered excitedly around, he said:

> Ye men of Israel, why marvel ye at this? or why look ye so
> earnestly on us, as though by our own power or holiness we
> had made this man to walk? The God of Abraham, and of
> Isaac, and of Jacob, the God of our fathers, hath glorified his
> Son Jesus…whom God hath raised from the dead; whereof
> we are witnesses. And his name through faith in his name
> hath made this man strong, whom ye see and know: yea, the
> faith which is by him hath given him this perfect soundness
> in the presence of you all (Acts 3:12-16).

When you translate that out of the Elizabethan English of the
*King James Version* Bible and into the West Texas version, Peter
said something like this: "Hey, don't look at me like I did this by
my own holiness or some special calling. Don't make a big deal
of me. I was able to make this guy walk because God—the God
of Abraham, Isaac and Jacob, the God of THE BLESSING—has
glorified His Son, Jesus, and given Him the Name above all names.
It's faith in that Name that made this cripple whole!"

Any believer anywhere, anytime, who will put the same kind of
faith in Jesus' Name that Peter did, can do the same kind of thing.
Any one of us who will dare to believe THE BLESSING that was on
the first Adam is the same BLESSING that has come on us through
the last Adam, can minister just like those first disciples did.

By simple faith in the Name of Jesus, we can reach out in the
power of THE BLESSING—the only power on earth that can
touch a sin-crippled, fallen race and make it whole.

# Chapter 10

# A Reborn Race

*Therefore if any man be in Christ, he is a new creature: old things
are passed away; behold, all things are become new.*
2 Corinthians 5:17

T he thought that every born-again believer can operate in
the power of THE BLESSING the same way Jesus or
the early apostles did, amazes many Christians. They struggle to
picture themselves multiplying natural resources (like loaves and
fish), healing the sick or raising the dead. Yet, in the Bible, Jesus
emphatically declared that any person with simple faith in Him
could do all those things and more:

- "Verily, verily, I say unto you, He that believeth on me,
  the works that I do shall he do also; and greater works
  than these shall he do; because I go unto my Father"
  (John 14:12).

- "And whatsoever ye shall ask in my name, that will I do,
  that the Father may be glorified in the Son. If ye shall ask
  any thing in my name, I will do it" (verses 13-14).

- "If ye have faith as a grain of mustard seed, ye shall say unto this mountain, Remove hence to yonder place; and it shall remove; and nothing shall be impossible unto you" (Matthew 17:20).

- "And these signs shall follow them that believe; In my name shall they cast out devils; they shall speak with new tongues; they shall take up serpents; and if they drink any deadly thing, it shall not hurt them; they shall lay hands on the sick, and they shall recover" (Mark 16:17-18).

If you believe those statements to be true, you may wonder, *Why has the Body of Christ as a whole not embraced them? Why aren't the millions of Christians who show up for church every Sunday, rocking their cities for Jesus by preaching the gospel with signs and wonders following all week long?*

I believe there's one, primary reason for it.

Most Christians don't know who they are. They have been brainwashed by the devil into believing they're "just old sinners saved by grace." They've been convinced by religious tradition that they are nothing more than fallen human beings who have been forgiven by a loving God. As a result, they've spent their entire Christian lives identifying more with defeated Adam than with Jesus Christ, their victorious, resurrected Lord.

"But, Brother Copeland, I *am* just an old sinner who has been forgiven and saved by grace."

No, you're not! You're either a sinner or you've been saved by grace, but you can't be both at the same time.

If you're truly a sinner, then receive Jesus as your Lord and get saved. If you're already saved, then stop thinking of yourself as the same person you were before you were born again. Get the phrase "I'm just an old sinner" out of your mind and out of your mouth because spiritual law declares that we have what we say.[119] If you keep calling yourself a sinner, Satan will see to it that your confession

---

[119] Mark 11:23-24; Proverbs 18:21; Romans 4:17

comes to pass. He'll have you acting like a sinner before sundown and, unless you change what you say, he'll keep you acting that way for the rest of your life.

Don't misunderstand. I'm not saying just because you're saved, you're going to live in sinless perfection. You will miss it and sin from time to time. As you walk out the process of renewing your mind to what The WORD of God says, you'll occasionally behave in ways not consistent with who you really are. But that doesn't change the fact that as a born-again child of God, you are not, by nature, an old sinner. On the contrary, the New Testament says:

> If any man be in Christ, he is a new creature: old things are passed away; behold, all things are become new (2 Corinthians 5:17).

The phrase *new creature* doesn't refer to something old that's been refurbished. It doesn't describe a forgiven sinner who's been cleaned up a little. A *new creature* is a freshly created species of being that has never existed before; and that's what you are.

The old sinner you once were has passed away. He died the death of the cross with Jesus when you gave your life to Him. In that instant, you were re-created. You became a brand-new person in Christ.

> For [God] hath made him to be sin for us, who knew no sin; that we might be made the righteousness of God in him (verse 21).

Notice, that verse doesn't say that God has *accounted* righteousness to us. He hasn't just given us credit for a righteousness we don't really possess. That's an Old Covenant concept. That's what He did for people like Abraham before Jesus came to complete the work of redemption. He counted their sin debt paid on the basis of what Jesus would one day do for them. He treated them as righteous despite their fallen condition.

"Isn't that what God does for us?"

Certainly. He has canceled our sin debt as surely as He did theirs. He has recorded in the Lamb's Book of Life that we were crucified on Calvary. It shows that we died, went to hell and suffered the full penalty for our sins. Heaven has it recorded that we were raised from the dead in righteousness and seated on the throne of grace at God's right hand. On earth, we have it recorded that Jesus did those things. But, heaven has it recorded in our name because He was our substitute. Everything He did was for us.

As New Testament believers, however, we have more than just a legal record of righteousness in heaven. We've actually been *made* the righteousness of God in Christ, as spotless and without sin as Jesus Himself.

To do that He had to make us *new creatures*. He couldn't take our old sin nature and make it righteous any more than we could take a beaten-up Volkswagen to the repair shop and get it back a Cadillac. Such a thing would be impossible. A Cadillac has to be manufactured. It's *made* to be a Cadillac.

The same thing is true spiritually. Truly righteous men must be created or manufactured that way. When they are born again, their old, fouled-up, sinful spirits are, by the power of Almighty God, manufactured into the spiritual equivalent of a Rolls Royce—the car of kings!

### Transformed From the Inside Out

"If I'm such a spiritual giant, then why do I still deal with so many of the same struggles I had before I was born again?"

Because the part of you that was re-created is your spirit—or what the Bible calls *the inner man* or *the hidden man of the heart.*[120] Your spirit is the real you. In the Bible, it is often referred to as the *heart* because it is the core of who you are. It's the life and power center of every human being.

Although your spirit has been reborn in the image of God and is absolutely perfect, there is more to you than your spirit. You are

---

[120] 1 Peter 3:4

a three-part being: You are a spirit; you have a soul; and you live in
a physical body. First Thessalonians 5:23 mentions each of those
parts individually:

> And the very God of peace sanctify you wholly; and I pray
> God your whole spirit and soul and body be preserved blame-
> less unto the coming of our Lord Jesus Christ.

Notice, the spirit is listed first, then the soul, and the body last.
There's a reason for this. The power of the new creation works from
the inside out. It starts in your spirit. Then as your mind is renewed
to what has taken place within you, your soul is changed.[121] And, as
you increasingly grasp your true identity in Christ, your thoughts,
words, actions and outward circumstances reflect that identity.

Second Corinthians 3:18 describes the process best. It says that
as we continue "to behold [in The WORD of God] as in a mirror
the glory of The LORD, [we] are constantly being transfigured
into His very own image in ever increasing splendor and from one
degree of glory to another...."[122]

Believers who don't see in the mirror of The WORD of God
who they are in Christ, can live in defeat for years, feeling as much
a loser as they were before they got saved. I know because I did it.
I had no idea I'd become a new creature when I was born again.
Although I loved Jesus with all my heart, I experienced very little
victory because I was dragging my past with me everywhere I
went—and my past was a very heavy load.

As a child, I'd been told by religious people that I'd never
amount to anything. They made me so mad, I wouldn't have anything to do with them or their churches. But, even so, I believed
what they said. I figured if I was such a good-for-nothing, I might
as well live like the devil; and that's what I did for years.

Thanks to my praying mother, my wife, Gloria, and the belated

---

[121] Romans 12:2: "Be not conformed to this world: but be ye transformed by the renewing of your mind,
that ye may prove what is that good, and acceptable, and perfect, will of God."
[122] *The Amplified Bible*

influence of my sixth grade Sunday school teacher, Mrs. Taggart, I
was born again in my 20s. But I didn't find out I'd been made the
righteousness of God until five frustrating years later. At the time, I
was listening to a sermon by Kenneth E. Hagin on an old, reel-to-reel
tape recorder in my car. I got so excited I almost kicked a hole in
the floorboard. For a guy with a past like mine to find out that old
things have passed away, and all things have become new—that's
good news!

Of course, it's not just good news for people like me, it's vital
information every believer needs to know. All who want to operate
in the fullness of THE BLESSING must understand what really
happened to us when we were saved. We need to realize that the
Creator Himself—the Holy Spirit—hovered over us, planted the
seed of God's WORD within us, and we were spiritually reborn.

What happened in us spiritually is much the same thing that happened in the Virgin Mary physically, when she conceived Jesus. Just
as The WORD became the supernatural sperm seed in her body and
brought forth Jesus into the world, The WORD of God implanted
in our human spirits brings forth Jesus in us. We are born again in
His likeness, "not of corruptible seed, but of incorruptible, by The
WORD of God, which liveth and abideth for ever."[123]

One of the best pictures of what happens to our spirits at the new
birth is found in the Genesis account of the creation of Adam, when
God breathed divine life into him by saying, "Man, be in our image,
after our likeness; have dominion over all the earth and everything in
it."[124] When that WORD went into Adam, he lit up with the very life
of God Himself. He was Love just like God is Love. He was Light
just like God is Light. Adam, like God, was a fire from the loins up
and a fire from the loins down (Ezekiel 1:26-27). The very lightning
of God's glory radiated out of him. If you looked at God and Adam
standing together, you wouldn't be able to tell one from the other
because they were both covered in the same fire.

It's thrilling just to think about it. But what's even more

---

[123] 1 Peter 1:23
[124] Genesis 2:7, 1:26

thrilling is the same thing happened to us when we were born again! The very Spirit of Almighty God breathed new life into us. He lit up our inner man with Himself the same way He lit up Adam in the beginning. He activated in our beings the very same words He spoke at the beginning in the Garden: *"Man, be in Our image, and have dominion!"*

If you could look inside yourself at your spirit right now, you'd be absolutely stunned because what you'd see is all the attributes of God. You'd see love, joy, peace, patience, resurrection power and glory. You'd realize that just as you were born naturally with the physical DNA of your parents, you have been born again with the spiritual genetics of God. Those attributes aren't yet fully developed and mature, but they are all there. Much like a baby at birth has all the physical parts—bones, organs and muscles—his parents have, but on a smaller scale, you already have within you everything you need to grow up and become (on the inside and outside) just like Jesus.

Your inner man is Love just as He is Love. Your spirit is ablaze with the fiery light of His glory. You are Light just as He is Light.

"Brother Copeland, surely you're exaggerating."

No, I'm not. The WORD says it very plainly. It tells us that "God is Light,"[125] and those who have been re-created in His image are light, too. The Bible says it over and over again:

- "For you were once darkness, but now you are light in The LORD. Walk as children of light" (Ephesians 5:8, *New King James Version).*

- "Ye are all the children of light…" (1 Thessalonians 5:5).

- "For God, who commanded the light to shine out of darkness, hath shined in our hearts, to give the light of the knowledge of the glory of God in the face of Jesus Christ" (2 Corinthians 4:6).

---

[125] 1 John 1:5

- "We walk in the light, as he is in the light…" (1 John 1:7).

- "…ye shine as lights in the world" (Philippians 2:15).

- "Let us therefore cast off the works of darkness, and let us put on the armour of light" (Romans 13:12).

- "As he [Jesus!] is, so are we in this world" (1 John 4:17).

## Have Some Fun With Your Father

When you start meditating on scriptures like those and let the reality of them saturate your mind, you'll get rid of the sin-tags the devil has used to drag you down. You'll get to the point where you'd feel as if you were using profanity if you said, "I'm just an old sinner saved by grace." You'll develop a righteousness consciousness instead of a sin consciousness, and that's when you'll really start having fun with The LORD!

Yes, you read that right. I said you'll start having *fun* with God. That sounds almost sacrilegious to many Christians, but it's scriptural, nonetheless. According to the Bible, God wants us to have the kind of fellowship with Him that fills us with joy.[126] He wants us to have such confidence toward Him that, even though He is the Most Holy and the Most High, we can come into His presence and relax without one bit of self-consciousness.

He's not offended when we bounce into His throne room full of joy with a smile and say, "Abba, Father! Let's have a good time together, just You and me!" On the contrary, He is thrilled.

Yet, most Christians would never dream of acting that way before God. They think that to show respect they must come to Him with an undeserving attitude and tell Him how unworthy they are to be in His presence. In reality, they're hurting His heart because He paid an awesome price to provide the way for

---

[126] 1 John 1:3-4

them to come boldly to His throne of grace. He poured out His own blood so every born-again believer could be made so perfectly righteous, they could walk into the holy of holies with no sin consciousness whatsoever.

And He has been waiting more than 2,000 years for the Church, as a whole, to do it.

"But Brother Copeland, you just don't know how hard that is for me. I've really messed some things up. I'm not a shining example of a Christian. Spiritually, I'm just a nobody."

You are *not* a nobody! God chose you to be His child before the foundation of the world. It doesn't matter how unworthy you may feel emotionally, don't ever insult Jesus and the blood He shed by demeaning yourself that way.

Sure, you've made mistakes. We all have. But I learned years ago from my spiritual father, Oral Roberts, what to do about that. One day, when I was a student at Oral Roberts University and working for him, we were riding together in his car and he said, "Kenneth, do you know, I've never made a mistake?"

I didn't have a clue what he was talking about, but I certainly wasn't going to argue with him so I said, "Uh…is that right, sir?"

After letting me think about that awhile, he spoke again. "I've done a lot of things that turned out to be mistakes, but I never did get up in the morning and say, 'I believe I'll make some mistakes today.'"

Then, before I could say anything in response, he leaned right up into my face, looked at me with a sparkle in his Cherokee eyes, and said something that has marked me from that day to this. He said, "Once you have committed your life to The LORD Jesus Christ, and are doing your best to follow His WORD and walk uprightly before Him, you may do something that turns out to be a mistake. You may make some slips, but always remember: You have been redeemed! You didn't set out to make a mistake. There is no condemnation to them who are in Christ Jesus, who walk not after the flesh, but after the spirit.[127] Receive your forgiveness and keep going!"

I got happy when I heard that because up to that point I had always felt like *Mr. Mistake.* From then on, I was *Mr. Redeemed.* If you're a born-again believer, so are you!

### Stop Begging and Start Believing

You're not only redeemed from your past sins and failures, you're redeemed back into THE BLESSING. As far as God is concerned, that BLESSING is already on you. Because you are His born-again child and a joint heir with Jesus, He has already BLESSED you with all that heaven has and all that heaven can do.

Think of it! Everything God has, everything He is, every angel and all kinds of other glorious spiritual assets we haven't even heard of yet, are all ours right now in Christ Jesus. They're not going to be given to us one day in the future, reserved for the sweet by-and-by. The Bible says very clearly:

> BLESSED be the God and Father of our Lord Jesus Christ, who hath BLESSED us *[past tense!]* with all spiritual BLESSINGS in heavenly places in Christ: According as he hath chosen us in him before the foundation of the world, that we should be holy and without blame before him in love (Ephesians 1:3-4).

It's time we, as believers, started acting as if those verses are true. It's time we stopped going before The LORD in prayer saying, "Oh God, please bless me!" That is an absolute waste of breath because we are already BLESSED. We are as BLESSED as we can possibly be.

Instead of begging God to bless us, what we ought to be doing is developing our faith in what He has already done for us. We should be meditating on what the Bible says about who we are and THE BLESSING that is on us, so that we become aware of it all the time. We should be thinking about it every day, putting it

---

[127] Romans 8:1

on 3 by 5 cards on the refrigerator and on our bathroom mirrors to remind ourselves of it, and constantly saying to ourselves: "I am as BLESSED as Adam was before the Fall. I am as BLESSED as Abraham was. I am as BLESSED as Jesus is. I am BLESSED!"

Sometimes, people who think of themselves as *gentile believers* hesitate to fully embrace that second statement. Because they were not born Jewish, they think they are somehow less BLESSED than Abraham and his flesh-and-blood descendants. But the New Testament says otherwise:

> Even as Abraham believed God, and it was accounted to him for righteousness.... They which are of faith, the same are the children of Abraham. And the scripture, foreseeing that God would justify the heathen through faith, preached before the gospel unto Abraham, saying, In thee shall all nations be BLESSED. So then they which be of faith are BLESSED with faithful Abraham (Galatians 3:6-9).

According to those verses, all born-again believers on earth— no matter what their physical birth—are just as much heirs of Abraham as if they'd been naturally born into an orthodox Jewish family. We are all as BLESSED as Isaac or Jacob or Joseph because when we were born again, we *were* born into a very orthodox Jewish family. We were spiritually reborn of the Father Himself.

We're no longer gentiles because, by definition, gentiles are people who have no covenant with God. They are "without Christ...strangers from the covenants of promise, having no hope, and without God in the world."[128] That description fit us before we were saved, but not anymore. Now, we are in Christ Jesus. He has delivered us from that godless condition and the curse that goes with it:

> Christ hath redeemed us from the curse of the law, being made a curse for us: for it is written, Cursed is every one

---

[128] Ephesians 2:12

that hangeth on a tree: that THE BLESSING of Abraham might come on the Gentiles through Jesus Christ; that we might receive the promise of the Spirit through faith (Galatians 3:13-14).

You might have been told *the promise of the Spirit* in that passage refers to the Baptism in the Holy Spirit; and that's the only part of THE BLESSING of Abraham that we, as non-Jewish believers, receive.

I realize some people have that idea, but it's incorrect. In this verse, "the promise of the Spirit" is not referring to the Baptism in the Holy Spirit, but to the promise the Holy Spirit made to Abraham that, through him, all the families of the earth would be BLESSED. The restoration of THE BLESSING is the Holy Spirit's promise. Certainly, that BLESSING *includes* the Baptism in the Holy Spirit. It also includes the new birth, healing, financial prosperity, the ministry of angels and everything else we need to be fruitful and have dominion on the earth.

Don't let anyone talk you into settling for just part of your inheritance. Stand steadfastly on the fact that through the plan of redemption, Jesus has restored to you THE BLESSING *in its entirety.* Then put that BLESSING to work by faith. Let it start creating a Garden of Eden in your home, your church, your business and your neighborhood. Let it flow through you, out into the streets to others who need help.

I'm convinced that as the Church learns to live more fully in THE BLESSING, even politicians and others in positions of influence in the world will start reaching out to Christians, trying to get us on their side. They'll figure out, like Potiphar and Pharaoh, when Joseph handled their financial affairs, that whatever these BLESSED people get involved with is sure to prosper.

### The Head and the Body Are One

If you think THE BLESSING could never operate that strongly through you, let me remind you that as the seed of Abraham, you are scripturally qualified to be a BLESSING to the whole world. You are a joint heir with Jesus.[129] Everything He is and possesses belongs to you, including His Name.

As His representative on the earth, you have His authority. He has made you lord over Satan, sickness and poverty. He has given you power over those things and told you to go and get rid of them.

Though your physical body is still on the earth, spiritually, you've been raised up together and made to sit together in heavenly places in Him:[130]

> Far above all principality, and power, and might, and dominion, and every name that is named, not only in this world, but also in that which is to come: and hath put all things under his feet, and gave him to be the head over all things to the church, which is his body, the fulness of him that filleth all in all" (Ephesians 1:21-23).

Notice, you're not just barely above the devil and all his devices, you are *far* above him. You ought to remind him of that now and then. Remind him of what happened at the Cross. Remind him that you're a joint heir with Jesus. Rattle your sword a little. The devil will flee from you just as he does from Jesus because you are part of His Body—and the Head and the Body are one.

That's so important! *The Head and the Body are one!*

In church, people have a hard time believing that, but on the street, everyone knows it's true. When I walk into a room, no one says, "Here comes Brother Copeland and his body." That would be silly. My head isn't the only thing that's included in my name. I'm Kenneth Copeland from head to foot. Without my body, I can't do anything.

The same is true for Jesus. He can't do anything on earth without us because we are His representatives here. We are His fullness, appointed by God to rule in His Name with holiness, goodness and the

---

[129] Romans 8:17
[130] Ephesians 2:6

love of Almighty God that's been shed in our hearts by the Holy Spirit.

In practical terms, that means if you're a mother or a father, you don't have to put up with sickness on your children. When the devil attacks them with it, you can stand at their bedsides and say, "Satan, I command you in the Name of Jesus and by the power of the eternal, Almighty God to get your filthy hands off my children. I am the seed of Abraham. My children are the seed of Abraham and they are BLESSED—spirit, soul and body."

You can lay your hands on your child and say, "Jesus, my children are in Your care. You're The LORD and High Priest of this household, and You are Healer. By faith, I loose Your healing power now in the body of this little one. I call him healed."

You don't have to cry and beg for Jesus to come down from heaven and touch your child. You don't have to cry and moan and say things like, "Oh, Lord, if You'll just let the hem of Your garment brush over my baby, I know he'll be healed."

It's understandable for believers who have no idea who they are in Christ, or what happened to them when they were born again, to pray that way. They don't know any better. Because no one has taught them anything different, they assume they're in the same position as the woman in the New Testament who had the issue of blood and received healing by touching Jesus' clothes. They identify with the hungry multitudes who sat by the Sea of Galilee and ate the loaves and fish that Jesus multiplied.

But that's not what we ought to be doing. As Jesus' disciples, we should be identifying with *Him.* When we read those New Testament stories, we should see ourselves doing His works. Rather than seeing ourselves as the people in need, we should see ourselves as the ones who *meet* those needs because we have inherited Jesus' ministry. We are now the seed of Abraham who carry THE BLESSING.

Galatians 3 says it this way:

To Abraham and his seed were the promises made. He saith not, And to seeds, as of many; but as of one, And to thy seed, which is Christ.... And if ye be Christ's, then are ye Abraham's seed, and heirs according to the promise (verses 16, 29).

The singular nature of the word *seed* is very important here. When used in reference to Jesus, it indicates that every promise of THE BLESSING in the Old Testament was specifically directed toward Him. He was the singular Seed to whom THE BLESSING of Abraham belonged.

But that's not the end of the story. The chapter goes on to say that those who are in Christ are also Abraham's *seed.* Notice, the word *seed* used to refer to us is just as singular as when used in reference to Jesus. That means THE BLESSING is directed as specifically toward us as it is to Him. We have exactly the same right to walk in it as Jesus does.

Remember that the next time you read the Gospel accounts of Jesus' ministry. Practice seeing yourself in your mind's eye, not as a hungry member of the crowd waiting to be fed, but as the one multiplying the loaves. Instead of seeing yourself as the woman pressing through the crowd trying to touch Jesus' garment, become the one wearing the garment.

By faith, put on Jesus' coat of BLESSING because, as His joint heir, that anointed coat belongs to you.

### It's Time to Enter God's Rest

According to God's WORD, this whole planet belongs to you, me and every other believer. "The promise to Abraham and his posterity, that he should inherit the world"[131] [132] is ours as heirs of THE BLESSING. Through Jesus, the last Adam, we have once again been given title deed to the earth. Through Him, mankind has gotten back the Garden.

"But doesn't the Bible call the devil *the god of this world* in 2 Corinthians 4:4?"

Yes, but the Greek word translated *world* there refers to the

---

[131] Romans 4:13, *The Amplified Bible*

[132] W.E. Vine, *Vine's Expository Dictionary of Biblical Words* (Nashville: Thomas Nelson, 1985) G2889 "world" Gr. *kosmos*, p. 685.

demonically dominated, heathen world *system* of this present age.[133] That's the only thing the devil can claim as his own because the earth itself doesn't belong to him anymore. Jesus has all authority in heaven and on earth now, and that authority is ours through Him.

According to God's Garden of Eden timeline, that puts us back on the seventh day. It brings us back to the point described in Genesis 2, where God "rested from all his work."[134]

> For we which have believed do enter into rest, as he said.... And God did rest the seventh day from all his works.... There remaineth therefore a rest to the people of God. For he that is entered into his rest, he also hath ceased from his own works, as God did from his (Hebrews 4:3-4, 9-10).

With THE BLESSING back in operation, we, as believers, don't have to toil, sweat and strain to *make a living* like people who are dependent on the ungodly system of this world. The earth doesn't fight us when we cultivate it, nor does it produce thorns and thistles and curse us every time we put our hand to it. That curse has been lifted from us! Because of what Jesus did, we can enter into God's rest and put THE BLESSING to work for us. We can stop struggling along in our own strength and trust THE BLESSING to empower us to fulfill our original mission.

What is that mission? The same as it's always been: To create the Garden of Eden wherever we go.

We do that first by preaching the gospel. We share the good news that Jesus has come, paid the price for our sin, and gotten back THE BLESSING for all mankind. And, we do it by letting people know that through Him, the Garden of Eden is open again.

When people believe that message and are born again, we help create the conditions of the Garden in *their* lives by teaching them how to walk, talk and live in THE BLESSING, just as Jesus did. That's

---

[133] Ibid. P685, G165 "world" Gr. *aion.*
[134] Genesis 2:3

called "making disciples," and one of the ways we do it is by giving people an example to follow. We walk in THE BLESSING, ourselves, so that they can follow us as we follow Christ. We become living demonstrations of THE BLESSING by bringing the compassion, power and glory of God on the scene wherever we go.

"But, I just don't have what it takes to do that."

Yes, you do!

In fact, you were born to do it. You were born again by The WORD of God and made an heir of THE BLESSING for the express purpose of BLESSING all the families of the earth.[135] You have within you in seed form, the capacity to BLESS the whole world.

That seed may seem small to you right now, but if you'll nurture it with The WORD of God and faith, it will grow inside you just as the seed of Jesus grew inside Mary's womb. Before long, you'll start seeing the manifestation of it. You'll see the evidence of THE BLESSING at work not only in your own life but, through you, in the lives of others.

If you neglect The WORD and feed on the world's junk all the time, though, you'll stay as sick and broke as you ever were. You'll continue to live according to the dictates of this natural world instead of by the power of THE BLESSING. All the while, that little seed will be lying dormant in your spirit, starving for spiritual food, water and light.

### It's Not Just for Preachers

If you give that seed the nourishment it needs, it will spring out of you. There is no way around it. It's an inviolable, spiritual principle: "Keep your heart with all diligence, for out of it spring the issues of life."[136]

Inside us is the image of Jesus, THE BLESSING, the Anointing and the glory of God. We carry within us the Garden of Eden. If we'll give our attention to it and begin to think, talk and act in accordance

---

[135] Genesis 12:3
[136] Proverbs 4:23, *NKJV*

with it, that inner image will be reproduced everywhere we go.

That's why God sometimes sends us to the most difficult, thistle-growing, demon-infested places in the world. The people in those places are in desperate need of the Garden—and when we go there we bring it with us.

I'm not just talking theory here. This has been done. It's been proven in real life in recent times.

Gloria and I saw a report on television, for instance, about a town in Guatemala of 18,000 people, called Almolonga, where 90 percent of the people had been born again. Big signs leading into town declare "Jesus is Lord of Almolonga!"

A few years ago, the area was an arid wasteland. But now, the crops are remarkable. An average of 40 trucks a day leave Almolonga, loaded down with tons of produce during any of their eight annual harvests.[137]

The camera crew that went in there brought back videos to verify it. They showed cabbages so big they wouldn't fit into a 5-gallon bucket, and carrots the size of your forearm. The farmers were driving Mercedes trucks. The last of the jails closed down in 1988. The townspeople turned it into a chapel because they didn't need a jail anymore. A generation ago, there were only four churches, now there are more than 23.[138]

"Oh, I'm going to ask Jesus to do that in my town!" someone might say. "I'm going to pray He'll cast the devil out of it and get everyone saved, healed and prosperous."

Go ahead and pray that if you want to, but it won't do any good. Jesus never said He'd take the gospel to your town. He didn't say He'd cast the devil out of it. He didn't say He'd lay hands on the people around you and heal them. He said, *"You* go into all the world and preach the gospel to every creature. *You* cast out demons. *You* lay hands on the sick and they'll recover. *You* go—and I'll go with you."

That's just another way of saying, "Exercise authority over the

---

[137] *The 700 Club,* The Christian Broadcasting Network, Inc., "Almolonga, Guatemala" (November 20, 2002).
[138] Ibid.

earth. Take dominion and subdue it. Take THE BLESSING around the globe, and fill the whole place with the glory of God."

That commission isn't just for preachers. It's for every member of the Body of Christ. It's for all "them that believe."[139] So, if you're a believer, you ought to be confessing it. You ought to be acting on it. You ought to be saying every day when you get up, "I am BLESSED. THE BLESSING of Abraham is mine. Jesus has put it in me and on me; and that BLESSING is flowing out of my body. Everywhere I go, I am a BLESSING to people."

If you'll keep saying that, THE BLESSING will eventually connect you with other people who are operating in it and you'll become part of a team. Talk about making a world-changing impact! A team of BLESSED believers can do things that are beyond what anyone can imagine.

I know because that's what's happened to Gloria and me. We didn't have a team of Partners in ministry when we first started. We just had each other, our children, a broken-down, old car, and the ugliest rented house you've ever seen. But we found out we were the seed of Abraham and heirs according to the promise, so I began walking around our little bedroom (it wasn't a very long trip) and saying, "Glory to God! THE BLESSING of Abraham is mine. Jesus is my blood Brother. His Anointing is in me and on me."

I kept confessing that, and the next thing you know it began to produce results. Little by little, things began to change. First, we got just enough money to get out of town to go somewhere to preach.

At that time, I was preaching many of the same things I'm preaching now, but that was over 40 years ago, and such things were totally new to most people. They'd sit in the services and just look at me. You could see the unbelief on their faces.

That's why I had to have three-week meetings. It took two weeks to get enough of the unbelief out of people to have a one-week meeting. But THE BLESSING was working and things just kept moving.

---

[139] Mark 16:17

After a while, it opened the way for me and others to preach on radio and then television.

The whole time, God was working to gather people all over the earth and turn them into the biggest, WORD of God-believing, BLESSED group of people this world has ever seen. He has done it, too. The last I heard, of the 2.2 billion Christians worldwide, 648 million are evangelical and Bible-believing.[140]

That's what I call a good team, and every member is a manifestation of THE BLESSING!

---

[140] http://christianity.about.com/od/denominations/p/christiantoday.htm; www.globalchristianity.org (5/5/2011).

# Chapter 11

# The LORD and High Priest of
# THE BLESSING

But this man, because he continueth ever, hath an unchangeable priesthood. Wherefore he is able also to save them
to the uttermost that come unto God by him, seeing
he ever liveth to make intercession for them.
Hebrews 7:24-25

I t's a marvelous thing to have an intercessor.

I first realized this when I was a young boy, standing
behind my father at a West Texas hotel. He'd taken me with him
on a business trip, and we'd stopped there for the night. While he
was checking in, I'd wandered around the place and found some
men playing shuffleboard. I can't tell you to this day why it was,
but for some reason I just had to get my hands on those pucks.
So I stepped right into the middle of the game, reached down and
picked one up.

I didn't think it would be any big deal. But I was wrong. The
next thing I knew, one of the players came rushing toward me, all
red-faced and ranting about how I'd ruined their game. Half his
size, I froze in front of him like a deer in headlights with no idea
what to do.

That's when my dad showed up.

A boxer in his younger days, he stepped in front of me, and looked eye-to-eye at my accuser. Then he settled the situation with one sentence. "If you have anything to say to my boy, you'll say it to me!"

Instantly, the shuffleboarder backed off and started apologizing. As he did, a marvelous change came over me. Safe behind my dad, I was transformed from a shivering kid to a confident little man with an attitude. I didn't say anything out loud, but inside I was John Wayne. *Yeah, mister, you want a piece of me? My dad and I can whip you with one hand tied behind our backs!*

That's what happens when you have the right intercessor.

You take on a whole new dimension of boldness, because an intercessor isn't just someone who prays for you. An intercessor is someone who stands with you and takes your side. It's someone who backs you up in challenging situations.

When you're facing trouble, an effective intercessor can make a lot of difference.

When that intercessor is Jesus, the Anointed One—the conquering Lord of all, the King of kings to whom all authority has been given both in heaven and on earth—it changes everything.

The sad fact is, however, many Christians don't know that. Though they've read in the Bible that Jesus is the great High Priest, who ever lives to make intercession for them, they've never learned how to take full advantage of that part of His ministry. They've never been taught how to connect with His high priestly ministry by faith.

That's a major problem, because to live in THE BLESSING the way God intends, every believer has to make that connection. We must all learn how to trust Jesus, not only as our Savior and Lord, but as "the Apostle and High Priest of our profession."[141]

## What's a High Priest?

To do that, the first thing we need to understand is what a priest

---

[141] Hebrews 3:1

actually does. Instead of thinking of him simply as a religious person who wears special robes and collars, we must realize that a true priest is a *minister,* someone who is legally appointed as an agent, or an authorized person who administers a service, aid or some kind of care.

A minister is someone who has been given charge over something and is responsible to execute or carry it into effect. The word *administrator* is derived from the word minister. Descriptors include: manage, conduct, furnish, supply, dispense, distribute, direct, control, superintend, furnish help or to be of service.

Some nations use the term *minister* to refer to positions of governmental authority. The person in charge of the treasury, for instance, might be called the minister of finance, or someone responsible for overseeing relationships with other countries might be called the minister of foreign affairs.

Jesus, as our High Priest, is the Minister of THE BLESSING. He is the Chief Administrator in charge of supplying, managing, dispensing, directing and furnishing THE BLESSING by the grace of God to the Body of Christ.

One aspect of THE BLESSING He ministers, for example, is forgiveness and cleansing. Most of us learned to connect with that part of His ministry to some degree when we were first saved. We were born again by believing that Jesus, as our Intercessor, paid the price for sin on our behalf and made us right with God.

That, however, is not the end of the story. Jesus didn't just procure a pardon for us from our past transgressions or merely release us from the penalty of sin. He defeated the whole sin system.

He released the law of the Spirit of life in us and made us free from the law of sin and death,[142] completely destroying the power of sin and the devil, so neither one would ever have any authority over us again. He then ascended to the right hand of God, where He ever lives to make intercession for us as "a merciful and faithful high priest in things pertaining to God, to

---

[142] Romans 8:2

make reconciliation for the sins of the people."[143]

Because Jesus serves today as our High Priest, we can go to Him anytime we sin. He will set us free from both the sin and the sense of unrighteousness that comes with it, ministering the law of the Spirit of life to us and wiping out that sin as if it never existed. We don't have to wallow around feeling condemned and unworthy because:

> If we confess our sins, he is faithful and just to forgive us our sins, and to cleanse us from all unrighteousness (1 John 1:9).

One time when The LORD was showing me just how completely He rids us of the sins we commit, He reminded me of the cabin Gloria and I bought years ago in the Rocky Mountains. We owned that place for about 16 years, and our family had many memorable times there.

*Can you describe that cabin for Me?* He asked.

"Oh, yeah," I answered. "Even though we sold it years ago, I remember everything about it."

*Take Me through it step by step,* He said.

So, I did. I told Him out loud about the little bridge we crossed when we were driving up to it. I told Him about the steep driveway and the garage Gloria and I built, where I kept my motorcycle. I took Him through the front door and showed Him the little mudroom at the entrance and then the living room and kitchen. I took Him downstairs where we kept our skis and showed Him the mountain you could see out the window as you looked across the highway.

I had a great time taking The LORD through that little cabin.

Then The LORD said, *Kenneth, do you know that house doesn't exist anywhere except in your mind?*

*Sure enough, it doesn't!* I thought. *The people we sold it to bulldozed it to the ground. They completely wiped it out and built another house there.*

---

[143] Hebrews 2:17

Then, it hit me. The same thing is true about my sins. Everything I've ever done wrong was wiped out completely when I confessed it to Jesus. He has bulldozed every sin I've ever committed, dumped them all into Blood River and washed them away in the crimson tide.

When I saw that, my spiritual confidence shot up to a whole new level. I was able to release my faith in Jesus' high priestly ministry of forgiveness and cleansing. I was able to put every past sin and the guilt associated with it out of my mind once and for all.

Why should I remember those sins if Jesus doesn't? Why should I waste my time thinking about something that doesn't even exist?

I shouldn't...and neither should you!

Remember that the next time the devil tries to rob you of your confidence before God by reminding you of some sin you've already repented of. Don't let him trap you with that. When he starts accusing you of being a sinner, don't just tell him your sin is forgiven and covered by the blood. *It's not covered!* It's been wiped out, eradicated and completely obliterated, so open your mouth with boldness and tell the devil exactly that.

Tell him that old sin doesn't exist anymore. It's 100 percent gone. It's been dealt with once and for all by your Intercessor who has destroyed your sin and given you THE BLESSING.

"I don't know, Brother Copeland. I think I'd feel silly saying things like that."

It doesn't matter whether you feel silly or not, you need to say them because your words of faith are what activate Jesus' ministry as High Priest in your life. He is, quite literally, the Apostle and High Priest of your profession.[144]

The word *profession* can also be translated *confession.* The Greek word means, "to say the same thing."[145] That word is used in connection with Jesus' high priestly ministry because when we say the same thing God says, speaking in line with THE BLESSING, our High Priest backs up our words. He sees to it that they come to

---

[144] Hebrews 3:1
[145] Rick Renner, *Sparkling Gems From the Greek,* (Tulsa: Teach All Nations, 2003) p. 313.

pass. If we say nothing at all, or if we make confessions contrary to God's WORD, we give Him nothing to administer.

That's why it doesn't do any good to cry, "Oh, Jesus! Don't You know how sick I am? Don't You know how much I'm hurting? Won't You just come and put Your hand on my fevered brow?"

We're not partaking of Jesus' high priestly ministry when we say those kinds of things. He's not appointed to bring to pass confessions like, "I'm sick," "I'm hurting" or "I have a fever." Those conditions are part of the curse, and Jesus has done all He is going to do about the curse. He bore every bit of it for us on the Cross and defeated it completely through His death and resurrection. He has already delivered us from it.

What He stands ready to do now as our High Priest is enforce THE BLESSING in our lives, and He does that in response to our confession of faith. When we declare THE BLESSING, He backs us up. When we say, "Praise God, I am healed by the stripes of Jesus. I am free from the curse of sickness. Every cell of my body is BLESSED!" He administers all the divine power necessary to make those confessions (which are already true in the realm of the spirit) a reality in this natural world.

### Making the Distinction Between High Priest and Lord

"But what am I supposed to do if I make those confessions and the symptoms of sickness don't leave me?"

That's a great question because in that situation, we must connect by faith with another aspect of Jesus' present-day ministry: His ministry as *Lord*. I realize it may sound as if I'm splitting hairs but, the New Testament makes a clear distinction between Jesus' lordship and His high priesthood. Speaking of His post-resurrection exaltation, it says, "God hath made that same Jesus...*both Lord and Christ*."[146]

The term *Christ,* which in Greek means "the Anointed One

---

[146] Acts 2:36

and His Anointing,"[147] refers to Jesus' ministry as High Priest and Administrator of THE BLESSING. The term *Lord* refers to His position as Victor, Champion and Conquering King who put death under His feet. He is the One with the Name above all names at the sound of which, every knee bows and every tongue confesses in heaven, earth and under the earth, that He is Lord, to the glory of God the Father.

Jesus is High Priest of THE BLESSING and over the law of the Spirit of life. He is High Priest over the gifts of the Holy Spirit, healing, and prosperity. Jesus is Lord over the law of sin and death and the curse. He is Lord over sickness, poverty and everything in this world system that attempts to steal any portion of THE BLESSING from us. And, because we have been raised up and seated together with Him in heavenly places, we have both the right and responsibility to stand on that lordship by faith and resist the devil until he flees from us.

That's what the Apostle Paul was telling us to do when he wrote in Ephesians 6:

> Finally, my brethren, be strong in The LORD, and in the power of his might. Put on the whole armour of God, that ye may be able to stand against the wiles of the devil. For we wrestle not against flesh and blood, but against principalities, against powers, against the rulers of the darkness of this world, against spiritual wickedness in high places. Wherefore take unto you the whole armour of God, that ye may be able to withstand in the evil day, and having done all, to stand (verses 10-13).

Notice, that passage doesn't say that Jesus is going to come and wrestle the devil for us. He doesn't have to! He has already defeated Satan's entire crew. The resurrected Lord Jesus Christ is the undisputed King of kings, and Lord of lords, but He is not going to

---

[147] *Vine's Expository Dictionary of Biblical Words,* W.E. Vine, Merrill F. Unger, William White, Jr., editors (Nashville: Thomas Nelson Inc., 1985) "To Anoint," p. 5.

come down out of heaven and personally enforce that lordship over every demonic spirit that gives us trouble.

He delegated that responsibility to us by making *us* "kings and priests,"[148] and gave us the job of reminding the devil that he is a defeated foe. He equipped us to do it in the *power of His might,* making available to us His own armor—His war clothes—to protect us. He also provided His WORD and prayer so we could strengthen and build ourselves up to the point that instead of His armor hanging on us like an oversized suit, we fill out the uniform.

He did it all for us because He expected us to stand in faith on His lordship and put the devil under our feet where he belongs!

"But Brother Copeland, the devil isn't really my problem. It's my employer who's giving me fits. It's my mother-in-law and my mean neighbor across the street and all those gossips down at the church who are messing up my life."

It seems that way sometimes, but according to the Bible, our problem is not with flesh and blood. People are not our enemy. Sure, they do ugly, evil things but that's because the devil is using them. He is operating through them, trying to do us harm.

When we recognize the devil as the source of our trouble, we can deal with him properly. We can't cast him out of someone who doesn't want him cast out, but we can take authority over the demonic spirits working behind the scenes and stop them from bothering us and our families. It doesn't matter whom they are possessing, those spirits have no authority over us.

We are children of God and joint heirs with Jesus. We are kings and lords. So when we resist the devil, he has to flee.

"But I resisted him and he didn't leave!"

To believe that statement, I'd have to conclude that The WORD of God recorded in James 4:7 is a lie, because it's perfectly clear about that. It says, "Submit yourselves therefore to God. Resist the devil, and he *will flee* from you." When your stand against the devil seems to be unsuccessful, instead of claiming The WORD didn't

---

[148] Revelation 1:6

work, ask God where you're missing it.

That's what I do. I say, "Lord, there's something here I don't understand. I need to know what's going on. I know Your WORD is true, so the problem must be with me. I'm willing to make any corrections necessary in my conduct, attitude or thinking. So, show me what's wrong."

Every time I've asked God to do that, He's given me the wisdom I need, liberally, without criticizing me for missing it. If you'll ask Him in faith, He'll do the same for you.

### Swing Your Sword and Stand

Once you know you're properly resisting the devil on the basis of God's WORD, all you have to do to enforce the devil's defeat and run him out of any situation, is to maintain your stand of faith.

Stand therefore, having your loins girt about with truth, and having on the breastplate of righteousness; and your feet shod with the preparation of the gospel of peace; above all, taking the shield of faith, wherewith ye shall be able to quench all the fiery darts of the wicked. And take the helmet of salvation, and the sword of the Spirit, which is The WORD of God: praying always with all prayer and supplication in the Spirit... (Ephesians 6:14-18).

"But sometimes I get tired when I have to stand a long time."

You won't get tired at all if you do what those verses tell you to do. If you'll keep *praying always...in the spirit,* you'll get stronger by the minute because you're building yourself up on your most holy faith.[149] You'll be able to swing the sword of The WORD with power and say with authority, "Satan, I remind you that I am backed by The LORD Jesus Christ Himself, the Conqueror who whipped you and turned you into a big zero 2,000 years ago at His resurrection. Now, I adjure you in His Name to flee, and I declare

---

[149] Jude 20

as of now, that you have fled. I refuse your every attempt to come back. You are gone."

Once you've done that, even if you don't see immediate change, you can keep praying in the spirit and watching over the situation. Keep declaring THE BLESSING over it. Loose ministering angels to go forth and garrison around the situation. Continue to praise and thank God for the fulfillment of His WORD and stay with it until the lordship of Jesus has been fully enforced and THE BLESSING is flowing in the situation again.

When you take that kind of stand on the victorious power and authority of The LORD Jesus, no devil on earth, no principality, power, ruler of the darkness of this world or wicked spirit in heavenly places can oppose you. They'll all bow their knees to you just as they would to Jesus Himself because you are operating in His Name.

I know this from experience because I've done it in some seriously demonic situations. There was one time years ago, for example, when I got a call from a preacher friend of mine telling me that his wife had fallen down in an epileptic seizure in front of their house. Someone passing by had seen her, called the local officials, and they'd taken her to the mental ward of the county hospital. "Brother Copeland, what are we going to do?" he asked. "How are we going to get her out of there?"

I got in the car and headed over there to help him, all the while saying, "Greater is He that is in me than he that is in the world.... Greater is He that is in me than he that is in the Section 8 mental ward.... Greater is He that is in me than the one who has her trapped in there. The Greater One lives within me. The authority of God is residing inside me. I have the Name that's above every name, and in the Name of Jesus, Satan, I bind you now."

The place where they were keeping that little lady looked like a jail, complete with bars, locked doors and an officer standing guard. But by the time I got there, the revelation of my authority was working in me so that didn't bother me. I just looked at the guard and said, "Open the door!" He didn't know who I was and didn't ask. He just unlocked the door and let me walk in.

When I did, every devil in the place went wild. They all knew I was there. One of them was occupying the body of the biggest man I'd ever seen. Wearing nothing but a pair of overalls, that giant of a man stepped in front of me, bristled up and started to growl.

I didn't say a word to him. I just kept walking, and he got out of the way.

Down the hall, I found the pastor's wife in a room. She was so frightened that she had curled herself up into a ball trying to hide from the horror of the place. She almost cried with relief when she saw me. "Oh, Brother Copeland!" she said…and then she started having another seizure.

"No, you don't, Satan!" I yelled. "You don't have any right to that woman's body. Her body is the temple of the Holy Ghost, and in the Name of the Most High, I command you to come out of her and leave her alone, right now!"

Instantly, the seizure stopped and she returned to normal. "Oh, Brother Copeland, please get me out of here," she said.

As we headed out of the room and down the hall, another little woman called out. "Mister! Mister! Can you do for me what you did for her?"

"Sure," I said.

After I took authority over the devil and drove him off her, I prayed the sinner's prayer with her. She received the Baptism in the Holy Spirit and started praying in tongues on the spot. Then I turned back to the pastor's wife and said, "Come on, sweetheart. We're taking you home."

We walked right out the front door the same way I walked in. The same officer opened the door for me both times without any argument.

### Even Death Will Bow Its Knee

Even the spirit of death itself will flee from a believer who is operating in the revelation that Jesus is Lord over it. I've seen it happen—not just in official times of ministry but in my personal life. One of the most memorable was many years ago when my Aunt Eiley was on her deathbed. Gloria and I were staying at my parents' house when my mother got word that if she wanted to see Aunt Eiley before she died, she should get to the hospital right away.

I had just gotten home and was about to eat some eggs when the call came, and Mama went into a state of alarm. "Come on, Kenneth. We have to get down there, now," she said.

Before I could answer, I heard the same words rising up in my spirit that I'd confessed the day I was driving to the mental ward. *Greater is He that is in me than he that is in the world.*

"Mama, I'm going to eat my eggs. Then we'll go," I said.

"Kenneth, get up from that table! We have to go. Eiley is dying. Do you understand?"

I did understand. But I also knew that if I jumped up and let the spirit of death start calling the shots, Aunt Eiley would be dead before we got there. If I wanted to arrest that spirit, I had to speak and act as one who is in authority. I didn't want to eat those eggs. Every bite tasted like shoe leather. But I ate some of them anyway, and then I said, "I'm going to change my shirt, and then we'll go."

Mama didn't have the revelation I did. She was about to jump out of her skin. "Kenneth, will you please hurry up?" she snapped.

She had no idea that my flesh felt like doing the same thing she was doing. If I'd yielded to it, I'd have been rushing around wringing my hands and worrying that Aunt Eiley was going to die before we made it to the hospital. But, I was determined not to yield to my flesh. I'd made up my mind to walk in the spirit and exercise the lordship of Jesus in the situation.

So I walked back to my bedroom as if I had all the time in the world. I changed my shirt slowly—on purpose—praying in the spirit the whole time and saying, "Greater is He who is in me than he who is trying to take Aunt Eiley's life. I will not allow that. You spirit of death, you are arrested in the Name of Jesus."

All the way to the hospital, I kept it up. I kept praying. I kept saying, "I have authority over the spirit of death in the Name of Jesus. I have authority over the rulers of the darkness of this world. I rule them, they don't rule me. I live under the law of the

Spirit of life in Christ Jesus, and I have dominion over the law of sin and death."

When we walked into Aunt Eiley's room, she was already dead. They were just waiting for the doctor to come and sign the death certificate. The minute I saw her, the devil said to me, "See there? You're too late. She's already gone."

"Who asked you?" I answered. "You're not The LORD here. You don't have the power of death anymore. Jesus does and I'm in Him."

Ignoring the family members who had already started crying and grieving over her, I walked over to the bed and said, "Aunt Eiley, I'm going to read from the Bible the verses The LORD told me to read." She just lay there like a corpse as I read the scriptures. Then I said, "In the Name of Jesus, Aunt Eiley, I speak life to you. Now, open your eyes, in Jesus' Name."

Her eyes sprang open and she said, "Glory to God! Kenneth, what are you doing here?"

"I just came down here to minister to you," I said.

My mother pointed out a large lump in the middle of Aunt Eiley's chest that had been choking the life out of her. I reached over, touched it and said, "Get off her. You won't take her life."

In an instant, the thing was gone.

Aunt Eiley was already up in years. She was old enough to die right then, but she didn't have to go that way. What's more, she wasn't quite ready. She wanted to stay around awhile, so she lived two more years in her own home, healthy enough to take care of herself.

After those two years had passed, my mother was driving around town one day and the word of The LORD came to her. *Go by Eiley's house,* He said. *It's time for her to come on home.*

Sure enough, when mother stopped by Aunt Eiley's, she was sitting in her chair, thinking about going to heaven. She told my mother that an angel of The LORD had been there for several hours to escort her home, and she'd decided she was ready to go with him. My mother helped her get into bed, fluffed her pillows for her, and said, "Now, don't be afraid. Just lay your head back and go."

And that's exactly what Aunt Eiley did. She settled back on the pillows, began to speak with other tongues, and then she was gone. She was taken on to glory, not by the spirit of death but by the Spirit of life. She left here for heaven on the arm of an angel of The LORD.

Now that's the way to go!

### It's So Simple, a Child Can Do It

Why don't all believers leave this earth in that kind of peace and triumph?

Because we have let religion rob us of our awesome authority over the devil. We've believed silly funeral clichés like, "The LORD giveth and The LORD taketh away. He's the only One who can give and take life."

God doesn't take away the lives of His children! He's not in the business of killing people. The devil is the one who steals, kills and destroys,[150] and we have authority over him in the Name of Jesus. We exercise the power of life and death with our tongues.[151]

When we use that power in the wrong way, we can set certain spiritual laws in motion that no one can change. I've known of Christians who began to say at an early age they wouldn't live very long. "I don't think I'll live past 50 years old," they'd say. Of course, the devil was right there to accommodate their confession. He started setting up circumstances to bring it to pass and when he did, no one could stop it because that child of God had authorized his own early death with his tongue.

On the other hand, when believers use the authority of their words to agree with Jesus' lordship and His high priestly ministry of THE BLESSING, even a little child can stop death itself in its tracks. My granddaughter Lyndsey is a testimony of that. She was

---

[150] John 10:10
[151] Proverbs 18:21: "Death and life are in the power of the tongue: and they that love it shall eat the fruit thereof."

only 11 years old when a deadly form of meningitis tried to take her life. Gloria and I were out of town when it hit her, and by the time we were able to fly home and get to the hospital, several other children had already died from it.

Of course, our whole family understands the authority that's ours in the Name of Jesus, so none of us was quaking with fear. No, the whole time Lyndsey was lying in the infectious disease ward, fading in and out of consciousness, we were all saying, "Greater is He that's in me…. We won't allow this. We will not allow Lyndsey's life to be taken."

When Gloria and I walked into Lyndsey's hospital room where she was lying unconscious, I already had my assignment from God. I knew what to do and what to say. I just touched her with my index finger and said, "Lyndsey, I speak to the anointing that is on the inside of you. Rise up and remove this burden and destroy this yoke in the Name of Jesus, now!"

Suddenly, her eyes popped open and she yelled, with her teeth gritted in determination, "Paw-Paw, I AM HEALED IN THE NAME OF JESUS!"

When she said that, all of the intense pressure our family had been applying to sickness, disease and death, all the standing and praying and wielding the sword of the Spirit we had done, sent the devil fleeing in terror. Lyndsey's confession of THE BLESSING of healing was backed up and administrated by her High Priest, and by morning she was perfectly all right.

### Making the Covenant Connection

One of my favorite scriptural examples of Jesus' ministry as the Apostle and High Priest of our confession is Psalm 91. It begins with the faith declaration of the psalmist who says:

He that dwelleth in the secret place of the most High shall abide under the shadow of the Almighty. I will say of The LORD, He is my refuge and my fortress: my God; in him will I trust (verses 1-2).

At that point, the voice of the narrative changes. Someone else begins to speak in answer to the psalmist's confession and says to him:

Surely he shall deliver thee from the snare of the fowler, and from the noisome pestilence. He shall cover thee with his feathers, and under his wings shalt thou trust: his truth shall be thy shield and buckler. Thou shalt not be afraid for the terror by night; nor for the arrow that flieth by day (verses 3-5).

Who is the second speaker? It is Jesus, the High Priest! He did for the psalmist exactly what He does for us. When we speak The WORD of The LORD, He declares THE BLESSING over us. He says, "Yes, Kenneth! Yes, Mary! Yes, John! I will administer that confession. I ever live to intercede for you. I ever live to provide you with everything you could ever need or want. I ever live to be your assurance that God will cover you and protect you and keep you from harm. He'll give His angels charge over you and set you on high. He'll show you His salvation in every situation because you are BLESSED."

Can you see what a joy and thrill it is to know we're backed up by Jesus' high priestly ministry? It's an absolutely marvelous thing!

"Yes, but Brother Copeland, for some reason, it just doesn't seem very real to me. Is there anything I can do to get a greater revelation of it?"

Yes, and you can find it in Hebrews. There, the Bible tells us exactly how to connect with Jesus' high priestly ministry. It explains that as "an high priest for ever after the order of Melchisedec,"[152] Jesus does for us what Melchizedek did for Abraham. He ministers to us according to the same pattern.

For this Melchisedec, king of Salem, priest of the most high God, who met Abraham returning from the slaughter of the kings, and BLESSED him; to whom also Abraham gave a tenth part of all... (Hebrews 7:1-2).

---

[152] Hebrews 6:20

We already studied the Genesis account of how Melchizedek, speaking on behalf of God, declared THE BLESSING over Abraham. By saying, "BLESSED be Abram of the most high God, possessor of heaven and earth,"[153] Melchizedek made him joint possessor of heaven and earth and gave to him the dominion God had given to Adam in the beginning.

But, I want you to notice something: Abraham didn't just take that BLESSING and say, "Thank you. I appreciate that," and walk away. Both Genesis and Hebrews tell us he responded to THE BLESSING in a very specific way, just as God had planned for Adam to respond to it in the Garden—by tithing.

This is a vital point, so let it really sink in:

*Abraham connected to THE BLESSING of the high priest through the tithe, and we do it the same way.*

That means we shouldn't just toss checks into a bucket on Sunday morning. We shouldn't give just a few dollars to the church now and then. We ought to make tithing a central part of our fellowship with God. We ought to prayerfully and reverently bring our tithes to Jesus our High Priest and release our faith every time, as a fresh expression of THE BLESSING.

That's right! Tithing is where THE BLESSING is expressed. For "here men that die receive tithes; but there he receiveth them, of whom it is witnessed that he liveth."[154]

"Brother Copeland, surely you're not saying that Jesus actually follows the example of Melchizedek!"

No, I'm saying that Melchizedek's ministry was patterned on the ministry of Jesus. Melchizedek was operating in Jesus' Anointing, standing in the place of the High Priest, ministering the elements of Communion—the bread and wine that symbolize the body and the blood of our Savior. He was administering THE BLESSING on the basis of what Jesus was going to do, not just for Abraham, but for all the families of the earth. According to the Bible, when Abraham gave Melchizedek tithes of all, he was actually bringing his tithe to

---

[153] Genesis 14:19
[154] Hebrews 7:8

Jesus because that's who Melchizedek represented. [155]

Abraham understood far better than many Christians today just how significant that covenant interaction was. He knew the Communion elements, representing blood covenant, meant that God was pledging His own life to him. He understood that God was swearing an oath to him that would never be broken—He would cease to exist before He'd ever break His covenant with Abraham.

> For men verily swear by the greater: and an oath for confirmation is to them an end of all strife. Wherein God, willing more abundantly to show unto the heirs of promise the immutability of his counsel, confirmed it by an oath: That by two immutable things, in which it was impossible for God to lie, we might have a strong consolation, who have fled for refuge to lay hold upon the hope set before us: Which hope we have as an anchor of the soul, both sure and stedfast, and which entereth into that within the veil; whither the forerunner is for us entered, even Jesus, made an high priest for ever after the order of Melchisedec (Hebrews 6:16-20).

The Communion elements and THE BLESSING Abraham connected with by faith when he tithed, completely anchored Abraham's soul in the reality that his covenant with God was his source. So when the king of Sodom tried to wrangle him into a financial deal, Abraham—overflowing with this revelation—exploded with the words, "I won't take as much as a shoestring from you! Let no man say he made Abraham rich but God!"[156]

As New Testament believers, we ought to have that same attitude! We should connect with THE BLESSING through the tithe, and then turn to Satan and say, "Get away from me, you liar! I don't need anything you have. I have a covenant with Almighty God, and He has made me rich—spirit, soul and body."

That's how God planned it. That's why He gave Jesus to be

---

[155] Hebrews 7:1-8
[156] Genesis 14:21-23

our High Priest. So instead of being led by our emotions, running scared of every lying threat the devil comes up with, our souls could be anchored in THE BLESSING.

God swore an oath to us—not in the blood of bulls and goats but in the blood of His own Son—so we, like Abraham, could become fully persuaded that THE BLESSING is our source of supply. He appointed Jesus to receive our tithes so our minds, wills and emotions could stay rock solid through any storm, and we could rest assured that we have a faithful High Priest who is continually ministering that BLESSING to us.

### The Thrill of Tithing in the Light of THE BLESSING

When I first began to see these things in The WORD years ago, The LORD spoke to me and said, *You and Gloria aren't spending enough time tithing. You've gotten into the habit of just writing out checks, laying hands on them and praying over them a little, and then sending them somewhere. That's not enough. You need to make tithing more of a covenant interaction.*

Ever since then, tithing has been very serious business for us. We take the time to bring our tithe before Jesus as our High Priest. We get on our knees and receive Communion over it. We speak words over it that follow the pattern God gave the Israelites in Deuteronomy 26.

We say things like, "Lord of the tithe, we bring this to You with joy and thanksgiving for all You have done for us. We thank You for those who have fed us spiritually. We thank You for those who have blessed us. We thank You for THE BLESSING of Abraham that is ours in Christ Jesus. We thank You that we are joint heirs with Him, and through Him, heirs of the whole world." Then we wait on Him for a while, and listen to what He has to say to us.

When you tithe like that, the joy is indescribable. You begin to understand why God said to the stingy priests in Malachi 3:10:

Bring ye all the tithes into the storehouse, that there may be meat in mine house, and prove me now herewith, saith

The LORD of hosts, if I will not open you the windows of heaven, and pour you out a BLESSING, that there shall not be room enough to receive it.

Notice, that verse doesn't say God will pour out BLESSINGS (plural), it says a BLESSING (singular). It's referring to THE BLESS-ING that includes all other blessings.

When we bring the tithe to our High Priest, not to fulfill a legalistic, religious requirement like the priests in Malachi's day, but in an attitude of faith in THE BLESSING, the stingy spirit that sometimes tries to get on us disappears and we become cheerful givers. Tithing becomes a privilege and a thrill because we're doing it in response to the fact that God Almighty has BLESSED us with everything He is and everything He has. Instead of begrudging Him the 10 percent that's His, we bring it to Him with joy, know-ing He has made us heirs of the whole world.

When we tithe with that attitude, it hits us that this BLESSING is so big, we can't contain it! That's when it starts pouring out of us into the lives of others, expanding the Garden of Eden wherever we go.

I'll warn you, though, religion will try to talk you out of the prosperity of THE BLESSING before you get to that point. Reli-gion will tell you it's humble and pleasing to God for you to stay poor. It will brainwash you into saying ridiculous things like, "I really don't need that prosperity message. My family and I can get by on a modest income. We're not looking to get rich."

There's only one word to describe that attitude—*selfish.*

Maybe you and your family can get by on minimum wage, but what about the work of God? What about your pastor? What about the poor and the homeless? Why don't you believe God for about $10,000 a week, take out your modest income, and sow the rest into the kingdom of God?

We all should think seriously about those questions because one thing is sure: If we don't choose to walk in THE BLESSING, we'll have to answer for it when we stand before the judgment seat of Christ. We'll have to explain to Him why we chose to leave our abundant financial harvest in the field to rot when there was a world full of people in need of it. We'll have to give account for why we acted so selfishly and irresponsibly.

That's tough talk, I know, but really not tough enough. God is fed up with poverty mentality among His people. He has had it with lying religion that goes around telling people that God wants them poor while He lives in a big, expensive palace and paves His streets with gold. As we used to say in West Texas, "That ol' dog ain't gonna hunt no more." God has been pouring out revelation from His WORD about prosperity for the past 50 years, and if we don't walk in it, we'll be accountable to Him for it when this age is over.

That's not only true in the realm of finances. It applies to every other aspect of THE BLESSING as well, because there are people all around us who need the benefits of that BLESSING. They need healing and deliverance. They need to experience the peace of God in some area of their lives, and Jesus, the High Priest, has sent us as His priests, to minister those things to them. We are BLESSED by Him so we can take THE BLESSING to them!

### Living Through Him, You're Unlimited

"Well, I just don't see how someone like me could be much of a blessing to anyone. I don't have that much to offer."

On our own, none of us does, but because we've been born into the family of God and made joint heirs of THE BLESSING, we're not on our own anymore. We're not limited to the meager resources of this natural world. We have access to the limitless resources of heaven because we are living through Jesus.

First John 4:9 says it this way:

In this was manifested the love of God toward us…that God sent his only begotten Son into the world, that we might *live through him.*

Exactly, what does it mean to *live through Jesus?*
Imagine a baby who has been abandoned. No one knows who

his parents are. He was just picked up as an orphan off the street. On his own, that baby has no name, no inheritance. He has no status in life at all.

But, then, someone finds him. They take him to the hospital, clean him up and call a loving, wealthy Christian couple that has been wanting a child. The couple takes that baby into their home, legally adopts him and just falls in love with him. They're so thrilled with him they carry him around and show him off to all their friends. "This is our baby!" they say. "Isn't he beautiful? Don't you think he looks like us?"

Suddenly, that child isn't nameless anymore. He isn't poverty-stricken. He has his parents' name. He lives in their house. He's as rich as they are because, as their heir, everything they have is his. That child is no longer bound and limited by the conditions of his natural birth. He no longer has to live in the poverty he was born into. His adoptive parents have given him a whole new life. He is living through them!

The same thing is true of born-again believers. We've been adopted into our Father's family. Even better, we've been *reborn* into it and made heirs and co-possessors of all our Father's power and wealth through Jesus. We are living richly through Him.

Don't ever again entertain the idea that you don't have much to offer. You have everything to offer! You have the wealth of THE BLESSING at your disposal—24 hours a day, seven days a week. You not only have the privilege of enjoying all the benefits of that BLESSING yourself, you've been commissioned by God to pour them out on others.

One minister who caught a glimpse of this fact years ago was Kenneth E. Hagin. Sometimes, when he was preaching and the Anointing of God was on him, he'd just walk through the congregation pointing at people and saying, "Be BLESSED! Be BLESSED!" Often, the power of God would flow out through him with such strength, it would knock down two rows of people.

I didn't really understand it back then, but I liked it and I could tell Kenneth Hagin was trying to get something across to us by doing it. Then, one night as I was watching him, the word of The LORD came to me. He said, *Kenneth, My people don't realize that they have the same power to BLESS that I do.*

When I heard that, it dawned on me: *That's where those old, religious traditions come from! That's why some denominations go through the ritual of blessing people!* The ritual began with believers who understood they were distributors of God's BLESSING. Through the years, the ritual has become, for the most part, a form of godliness that denies the power thereof.[157] But it started with folks who believed they had been commissioned by God to BLESS people by ministering to them His burden-removing, yoke-destroying power.

It's rare to find Christians who believe in and minister THE BLESSING like that today because, for the most part, the devil has talked the Church out of it. He has sold us such a religious song and dance that most people would consider it almost a capital offense, for example, if an ordinary believer said, "I heal this sick body in the Name of Jesus." They can't see how anyone but Jesus Himself could say the words *I heal.*

Yet, that's almost exactly what Peter said when he healed the lame man at the temple gate. He didn't say, "Well now, I'm just nothing. I'm a little nobody so don't pay attention to me. Only Jesus has the power to heal so let's just ask Him to help us." Quite the opposite! When Peter and John began to minister healing to that man:

> Peter, fastening his eyes upon him with John, said, Look on us. And he gave heed unto them, expecting to receive something of them. Then Peter said, Silver and gold have I none; but such as I have give I thee: In the name of Jesus Christ of Nazareth rise up and walk (Acts 3:4-6).

Because of religiously induced fear in people, we have to be cautious about ministering to them that way today. If we say, "I'm going to heal you," they're likely to become so scared, they won't let

---

[157] 2 Timothy 3:5

us touch them. They go away wondering, *Who does he think he is?*

But even if we don't declare it so bluntly that it frightens people away, we can still walk in that kind of authority. We can minister healing to people by faith in the fact that Jesus has already bought and paid for their healing. It is part of THE BLESSING, and as joint heirs of that BLESSING, we've been sent to deliver it.

If that were the foundation of our faith when we prayed for the sick and laid hands on them, things would be much simpler. We wouldn't think we had to pray for three days, cry and beg God to get someone healed. We could just smile, put our hand on them and say, "God BLESS you, man! In the Name of Jesus, be healed."

Most of us don't have any qualms about praying with that kind of simplicity for someone to be born again. We don't think it's strange at all to just say, "Come on, brother. Let me lead you in prayer and you can be saved." Years ago, people would have fainted at that idea. They thought you had to jump through all kinds of religious hoops before God would save someone. But, thank God, we've learned better than that now where ministering the new birth is concerned, and we're beginning to learn the same lesson in the area of healing and deliverance.

## More Fun Than Anything Else on Earth

We need to get this fact established in our thinking: Administering THE BLESSING isn't supposed to be hard. It's what we're born to do! If we'll just dare to believe that, we can have the time of our lives.

I found that out early in my ministry during some meetings in Lubbock, Texas, which turned out to be some of the most fun I've ever had. I'll admit, they didn't start out that way. For the first few days, it looked as if they were going to be a total failure. People were staying away by the thousands because all the pastors in town had gotten together and announced to their congregations that they shouldn't come.

I went to Jesus about it and said, "Lord, what should we do about this situation?"

He answered with a question of His own. *Do you remember I said in My WORD that when you have a feast, you shouldn't just invite your friends and neighbors, but you should go into the highways and byways and call the poor, lame and blind?*

"Yes."

*Do that.*

"OK," I said. I called a real estate agent in that town and asked him to take me to the poorest, most run-down area in the city. He drove me through it so I could see what it looked like. Later, after I'd gone back to my room to pray and exercise my authority as a believer over the area, I called our ministry team together and told them the plan.

"We're going to knock on doors," I said, "but not for the purpose of advertising our meetings. We're just going to ask the people in every house if there's anyone there who is in need of prayer because, if so, we'd like to pray for them. After we pray for them, if they're interested in learning more, we'll tell them about the healing service we're having on Saturday at the fairgrounds."

Jerry Savelle and I went out together as a team. Gloria and another lady went out as another team. The other six or eight people with us broke up into pairs. We all hit the streets and God moved on that whole neighborhood. Talk about a wild time! It was great!

At one house Jerry and I visited, a little lady opened the door just a crack, as if she were afraid of who might be there. After we offered to pray, she said, "Are you boys Pentecostal?"

"Yes, ma'am, we are."

"Come on in," she said, throwing the door wide open. "This old neighborhood has gotten so bad I can't even get out to go to church anymore. But I've been praying for God to send someone to pray for Sister. She has lost her mind. Would y'all pray for Sister?"

We walked across the alley to Sister's house and found her sitting in a chair in the living room with her eyes closed in a kind of trance, completely out of her mind. Jerry stood on one side of her and I stood on the other. We took authority in the Name of Jesus, and began praying in the spirit. As we prayed, The LORD spoke to me about the situation, so I stepped in front of her and did what He'd shown me to do.

"You're done here, Devil," I said. "This woman doesn't belong to you. She belongs to The LORD Jesus Christ. Now, in the Name of Jesus, you leave her!"

At that moment, Sister's eyes popped open and looked over at the lady who'd brought us there to pray. "Who are these boys?" she said.

"Can you see?" the lady asked, astonished.

"Yes, I can see," Sister answered.

As it turned out, in addition to losing her mind, Sister had lost her eyesight through diabetes several years before. She'd been sitting in that chair most of the time ever since, blind as can be, without so much as one sane thought. When we prayed for her and she was healed, she had no idea that two years had gone by.

The other lady was beside herself with joy. "Oh, thank You, Jesus!" she cried. "Thank You, Lord! My, oh my!" Sister, on the other hand, didn't have a clue that an amazing miracle had happened. She just thanked us for our prayers and offered us a soda.

The next Saturday, the parking lot at the fairgrounds was packed with people, and we had a glorious healing service. All the church people missed it, but the ones who showed up got healed and experienced an outpouring of the Holy Spirit. They found out what it was like to be BLESSED, and we found out what it was like to minister THE BLESSING.

And I can tell you, it's more fun than anything else on earth!

# Chapter 12

# Following the Faith of Abraham

Christ hath redeemed us from the curse of the law, being made
a curse for us: for it is written, Cursed is every one that hangeth
on a tree: that the BLESSING of Abraham might come on
the Gentiles through Jesus Christ; that we might receive the
promise of the Spirit through faith.
Galatians 3:13-14

The first question that comes to mind once you grasp the
awesome magnitude of THE BLESSING is this: *How do I
get it to operate in my life?*

That's something we all need to know because, as we've seen,
incorporated in that BLESSING is everything we'll ever need: health
and healing, victory and dominion in every area of life, abundance—
spirit, soul and body, and the power to be a BLESSING to all the
families of the earth.

All those things became ours the moment we were born again
because that's when THE BLESSING of Abraham came on us
through Jesus Christ. That's when we were "BLESSED…with all
spiritual BLESSINGS in heavenly places in Christ."[158]

As joint heirs with Jesus, we are—*right now*—co-possessors
of everything in heaven and earth. Every promise God ever made

---

[158] Ephesians 1:3

to Abraham and his Seed has been fulfilled in Christ Jesus[159] and deposited into our heavenly account. What we must find out is how to exercise our checking privileges and get those promises from heaven to earth.

The Bible explains it to us with one short phrase in Galatians 3:14: We receive the promise of the Spirit *through faith.*

Those two, simple words are the key to THE BLESSING door.

- It's *through faith* we are born again and become the seed of Abraham.

- It's *through faith* we become legal heirs of THE BLESSING.

- It's *through faith* we release its operation in our lives.

The *faith* of Abraham is what originally activated THE BLESS-ING of Abraham, and it still does. That's why God said that "with-out faith it is impossible to please him."[160] It's been His will from the beginning for us to live in THE BLESSING, and because faith is what connects us to it, we can't please Him without it.

"Well, I don't see it that way," someone might say. "I think being blessed has more to do with keeping God's rules than with faith. If you keep His rules, you'll be blessed. If you don't, you won't."

Thinking that way won't get you very far because no matter how hard you try, you'll never be able to work your way into THE BLESSING. It's God's gift to His children, and it can't be earned.

I can understand this to some degree through my relationship with my son, John, and my daughters, Terri and Kellie. They can't earn my BLESSING. They already have it. They have it because

---

[159] 2 Corinthians 1:20: "For all the promises of God in him are yea, and in him Amen, unto the glory of God by us."
[160] Hebrews 11:6

they're my children, and nothing can change that.

I sat down with John one day when he was about 16 years old and told him that straight out. He'd done some things he wasn't too proud of and I'd been put out with him about them. He knew I was aggravated and, as a result, he had misgivings about where he stood with me. When The LORD showed me how he was feeling (and corrected me for being hard on him instead of extending love and mercy to him, as I should have) I went to him and cleared things up.

I said, "Son, you listen to me and never forget what I'm about to say. If you committed the most heinous crime in the history of mankind and they threw you so deep into prison that you couldn't see the light of day, you'd still never get rid of me. If you get yourself into trouble, I'll pray for you and help you in every way I can. I will never leave you nor forsake you even to the end of the world. You'll never get away from me because I'm yours and you're mine. We're not just father and son, we are brothers in Christ."

That kind of relationship isn't something you can earn. It's a blood covenant relationship. It has served us well, too. Today, John and I are the best of friends, and he is head of all the business affairs of Kenneth Copeland Ministries. He's a good man. He's matured in The LORD, works hard and does what's right in his service for the ministry. But he doesn't do those things to earn my BLESSING. He does them knowing he already has it.

As God's children, we ought to be the same way. We should do what's right, do it because it's right and then do it right—but not in an effort to earn our Father's BLESSING. We should do it in joy and love, knowing that we're already BLESSED. That's the way Abraham lived. He walked in THE BLESSING by simple faith, not by keeping a list of religious rules.

> For if Abraham were justified by works, he hath whereof to glory; but not before God. For what saith the scripture? Abraham believed God, and it was counted unto him for righteousness. Now to him that worketh is the reward not reckoned of grace, but of debt. But to him that worketh not,

but believeth on him that justifieth the ungodly, his faith is counted for righteousness.... For the promise, that he should be the heir of the world, was not to Abraham, or to his seed, through the law, but through the righteousness of faith. For if they which are of the law be heirs, faith is made void, and the promise made of none effect (Romans 4:2-5, 13-14).

Although I'm very much in favor of obeying God's commands (more about that later), the fact is, if someone just keeps rules without faith, their rule-keeping doesn't do any good. No one can keep God's commandments without faith, anyway. They might be able to obey a few of them for a while and be nice when everyone is looking, but if they're not living by faith, they'll fail before sundown.

That's why religion doesn't work.

"Why, Brother Copeland, how can you say that? Christianity is a religion!"

No, a religion has been made out of it, but true Christianity is God and His family—a family made up of people who are saved, made righteous and BLESSED *through faith,* that lives, not by a set of religious rules, but by the love of God and the same kind of faith Abraham had.

Galatians 3:8-9, 11 says it this way:

The scripture, foreseeing that God would justify the heathen through faith, preached before the gospel unto Abraham, saying, In thee shall all nations be BLESSED. So then they which be of faith are BLESSED with faithful Abraham.... for, The just shall live by faith.

### Transferring Things From Heaven to Earth

It's safe to assume that if God wants us to live by faith as Abraham did, He will tell us exactly how to do it. For Him not to do so would be unjust. So, it's no surprise that the whole Bible is filled with revelation about faith.

It tells us, for example, that "through faith...the worlds were framed by The WORD of God."[161] That fact alone reveals just how important and powerful faith actually is. The whole physical universe is made from it. Everything that exists was transferred from the realm of the spirit into the realm of the natural by faith. Everything God created—from the grass to the trees to the cotton in your shirt—is faith turned into a material reality.

It's all a manifestation of the faith of God released through His WORD. In Genesis 1, when God said, "Let there be light," He said it by faith. When He said, "Let there be a firmament in the midst of the waters," He said it by faith. When He said, "Man, be created in Our image," He said it by faith.

God's faith-filled WORD is the carrier mechanism that transfers spiritual things from heaven's storehouse and brings them into the earth where we can use them. His WORD of faith is the conveyance. That's why, in the Hebrew language, the word for *thing* and *word* are the same.[162] To God, the *word* is the *thing* because when He speaks, His WORD becomes the thing that was spoken. As John 1 says:

> In the beginning was The WORD, and The WORD was with God, and The WORD was God. He was in the beginning with God. All things were made through Him [The WORD], and without Him nothing was made that was made.... And *The WORD became* flesh and dwelt among us, and we beheld His glory, the glory as of the only begotten of the Father, full of grace and truth (verses 1-3, 14, *New King James Version*).

Look again at the first few words of the last verse. "The WORD became." That phrase is so vital that I want you to imprint it on your mind by saying it out loud right now: *"The WORD became."*

If we want to follow in the footsteps of Abraham and operate in

---

[161] Hebrews 11:3

[162] James Strong, *Strong's Exhaustive Concordance of the Bible* (Nashville: Thomas Nelson Publishers, 1984) H1697.

faith like he did, we must realize that's what God's WORD always does when it is spoken in faith. It *becomes*...and it does so because it actually contains the power to bring itself to pass. God's WORD contains the creative energy of God Himself.

When you speak it by faith, that WORD releases the same force that made the dust of the earth from which Adam's body was formed. The WORD takes things that exist in heaven that are tangible and real in the realm above the light line, and slows them down to the point where they manifest in this natural realm, below the light line.

If you think that sounds too wild and far-out to believe, I have news for you. As a born-again child of God, you've already proven it's true. That's how you got saved! You confessed God's WORD about salvation by faith, that WORD *became* salvation to you, and you were born again. Simply by believing in your heart and speaking with your mouth the lordship of Jesus, you brought heaven's power to earth and became a whole new creature.

Romans 10:6-10 makes that very clear:

> The righteousness which is of faith speaketh on this wise, Say not in thine heart, Who shall ascend into heaven? (that is, to bring Christ down from above:) Or, Who shall descend into the deep? (that is, to bring up Christ again from the dead.) But what saith it? The WORD is nigh thee, even in thy mouth, and in thy heart: that is, the word of faith, which we preach; That if thou shalt confess with thy mouth The LORD Jesus [who is The WORD], and shalt believe in thine heart that God hath raised him from the dead, thou shalt be saved. For with the heart man believeth unto righteousness; and with the mouth confession is made unto salvation.

Or, as 2 Corinthians 5:21 says it: "He made Him who knew no sin to be sin for us, that we might *become* the righteousness of God in Him" *(New King James Version)*.

Your Christian life began the moment you spoke the word of

faith. It began when you released the same action, the same miraculous force that created the universe. When you confessed The WORD by faith and said, "I receive Jesus as my Lord and Savior," that WORD *became* righteousness in you.

As I said before and will say again: That's what The WORD of faith always does—it becomes. The WORD *becomes* healing. The WORD *becomes* deliverance. The WORD *becomes* prosperity. The WORD of BLESSING *becomes* THE BLESSING in our lives.

"But, I thought God is the One who BLESSES us."

He is. And He does it through His WORD!

That's why your Bible should be the most precious thing in your life. It's not just "the Good Book." It is THE BOOK! It is so far above every other book that it can't even be compared. Some have found the Bible to be true even when it is read backward. It contains codes that just stagger the human mind.

It doesn't matter which way you look at it, the Bible is alive! It's not just a book about Somebody. It *is* Somebody. It is God manifesting Himself through His WORD so we can read it, believe it and speak it.

## Your Manufacturer's Handbook: The Final Authority

I have such respect and reverence for The WORD of God, and such absolute faith in it, that some people accuse me of putting *too* much emphasis on it. "Now, Brother Copeland," they say, "what we need is to have faith in God Himself. The Bible takes second place to His sovereignty."

That may sound like a very spiritual perspective, but it's totally unscriptural. The Bible says that God has magnified His WORD *above* His Name.[163] That means He has chosen, *in His sovereignty,* to put Himself under the authority of His own WORD.

What's more, it's impossible to have faith in anyone (God included) without knowing what they've said. That's just common sense.

If someone decided, for example, they would put faith in me to

---

[163] See Psalm 138:2.

pay their rent, it wouldn't matter how many times they confessed, "I have faith that Kenneth is going to pay my rent." If I never promised it, that person has no right to believe I will do it. He has no basis for true faith.

If, on the other hand, I'd drawn up a contract with that person, stating I would pay his rent, his faith would be well-founded. Had I signed that contract and then, in blood-covenant fashion, cut my arm and let my blood drip down on that piece of paper, he'd have absolute assurance that his rent was as good as paid. He'd have every reason to have faith in me and the promise I had made to him.

That's exactly what God has done for us. He has given us His WORD that He will BLESS us. He has given us His blood-sworn oath that through our union with Jesus, everything He promised to Abraham is ours in full. He has entered into covenant with us and guaranteed that every promise in the Bible (all of which were directed toward Jesus) belongs to us because Jesus is our blood Brother.

I don't know if that means as much to you as it does to me, but it absolutely thrills me because I am part American Indian. (I realize the correct term is *Native American* but I prefer to call myself Indian.) Maybe, because it's in my background, I've always had a great respect for blood covenants. Even as a little boy, I wanted a blood brother so badly, I could hardly stand it.

When I found out the Bible is a blood-covenant book, and the New Testament is actually the New Covenant in Jesus' blood, my faith in God skyrocketed. The more I found out what He had said to me in the book of His blood-sworn oath, the more my ability to believe in Him and what He would do for me soared.

That's when I began to experience the truth of Romans 10:17: "Faith cometh by hearing, and hearing by The WORD of God."

"I don't understand that," you might say. "I've read the Bible my whole life and it hasn't inspired that much faith in me."

I had the same experience until I made a quality decision (a decision from which there is no retreat and about which there is no argument) to make The WORD of God final authority in my life. That's the first step to unlocking its power. You must settle in your heart once and for all that you will believe and act on whatever it says.

You must decide that from this point forward, instead of adjusting The WORD to fit your lifestyle, you will adjust your lifestyle to fit The WORD. If you think a certain way, and then find The WORD says something different, your own preferences and opinions don't matter. The WORD is right. It is what you live by.

I attended a flight school some years ago, where the instructor had a better understanding of that principle than most Christians. In the first class at 8 a.m., he held up a big, fat book with the name *Lockheed* written across it. When he did, every student in the room paid attention because we were there to learn how to fly the Lockheed JetStar, and most of us didn't know anything about it. Personally, I hardly knew how to open the door on it. I was starting training on that particular plane from scratch.

So, when the instructor held up that book and identified it as the aircraft flight manual to the Lockheed JetStar, we were all ears. He said, "Any information you receive anywhere, in any form, whether you hear it from me, read it somewhere or hear it in another classroom setting, that doesn't agree with this book—it's wrong. This book is always right. Anything that contradicts it is always wrong."

As believers, we must have the same attitude toward the Bible if we want its power to be released in our lives. We must treat it as the Manufacturer's manual, believe every WORD of it, and operate accordingly. Then—and only then—will our lives begin to take off.

When I realized that, The WORD became my first priority. I literally fell in love with it. That was over 40 years ago, and to this day there's no book that interests me like the Bible. Sometimes, I'll pick up an autobiography or a history book that interests me and think, *I'm going to enjoy reading this*. I'll have fun with it for a while but, inevitably, something in it will make me think of a particular scripture. Before long, I'll have my Bible open, and be digging around in it, having the time of my life.

Why is that? It's because The WORD *is* my life. It's the first thing I think about anywhere I go and whatever I do. It's my salvation and my health. It's my peace of mind. It's my wealth. I am a wealthy man today because of The WORD. My wealth didn't come from people. It didn't come from projects. It didn't come from any natural source.

The WORD is my source! And, I've discovered that the level of activity of WORD in my life is in equal proportion to the amount of reverence I have for it. So, I reverence it. I love it. I believe it. I live by it. I always keep it first place in my life.

### Plant the Seed and It Will Grow!

Once you've made a quality decision to make The WORD your final authority, the next step in the process of faith is to follow the instructions God gives us in Proverbs 4:20-22:

> My son, attend to my words; incline thine ear unto my sayings. Let them not depart from thine eyes; keep them in the midst of thine heart. For they are life unto those that find them, and health to all their flesh.

For The WORD to produce results in your life, you must give it your attention by spending time studying it and meditating on it.

"How much attention do I have to give it, Brother Copeland?"

That depends on the kind of results you want. Ten percent WORD will produce 10 percent results. Fifty percent WORD will give you 50 percent results. One hundred percent WORD will give you 100 percent results.

When I first began learning about faith as a student at Oral Roberts University, I needed major results fast, so I jumped in at the 100 percent level. I used a technique I'd read about that the U.S. government used to train translators during World War II called *total immersion*. At the beginning of the war, there wasn't time for the translators to become fluent at the normal rate. To speed up the process, they were surrounded 100 percent with the language they were learning. Research proved if they didn't hear or speak anything but that language, it literally made new grooves in their brains and they became fluent in six weeks or less.

While I was thinking about that, The LORD spoke to me. He said, *Son, if you'll do that—if you'll totally immerse yourself in The WORD and give yourself to it for just a period of a week, it will change your entire future. It will change the direction of your life. Your faith will rise to a new level and will never go back.*

I decided to put it to the test. I got my Bible, a notebook and the few tapes on faith I had by Kenneth E. Hagin and set up a study hall for myself in our little garage. I told Gloria, "When you call me for a meal, if I'm not there in five minutes, you and the kids go ahead and eat. I'm going to feed on The WORD."

I locked myself in there for seven days. The only time I came inside was to eat every once in a while and to go to sleep at night. When I did come in, the only thing Gloria and I talked about was faith and The WORD. We didn't discuss anything else the whole time.

When I was out there listening to a tape and Kenneth Hagin referred to a scripture, I'd stop the tape and read the whole book that contained the verse. Then, I'd turn the tape player back on and start listening again. By the end of that seven-day period, exactly what The LORD had said came to pass. The WORD had become the solid foundation of my life.

In one week, The WORD changed my thinking. It revolutionized the way I saw things. I still didn't know much, but what I did know was embedded so deeply that you couldn't beat it out of me with a bat. From that time , faith became my way of life. I didn't live by faith just now and then when I found myself in a crunch. I did it every day.

Some people think God just gave me the ability to live by faith because I'm a preacher. They say I have some kind of special gift for it. But that's not true. The faith I have came by hearing…and hearing…and hearing The WORD of God.

I like to call the time we spend hearing and meditating on The

WORD *The Buildup*. It builds us up to a place of faith. It gets us ready to step out on that WORD and release its creative power.

During The Buildup time, do everything you can to feed on The WORD. Listen to teaching CDs and watch DVDs with anointed preaching that covers your situation. If you're believing to get out of debt, then get messages on that subject. Get out your concordance and make a list of debt and prosperity scriptures to read and study. Get a recorder of some kind and record those scriptures so you can listen to yourself say them over and over. Turn on the recording when you go to bed at night so you can hear The WORD while you sleep.

"Well, I just don't understand how listening to the same verses over and over again is going to do any good."

You don't have to understand it. All you have to do is believe it and act on it. If you'll do that, The WORD will work whether you understand how it works, or not. Jesus said so in the parable of the sower, where He referred to The WORD of God as *seed:*

> So is the kingdom of God, as if a man should cast seed into the ground; and should sleep, and rise night and day, and the seed should spring and grow up, he knoweth not how.… It is like a grain of mustard seed, which, when it is sown in the earth, is less than all the seeds that be in the earth: But when it is sown, it groweth up, and becometh greater than all herbs, and shooteth out great branches; so that the fowls of the air may lodge under the shadow of it (Mark 4:26-27, 31-32).

The WORD is the seed of faith. If you keep on planting it in your heart (and don't uproot it with words of doubt and unbelief) it will grow. Your job is not to figure out how, but to incline your ear and open your heart to it by saying, "Yes, amen! God promised that, and I believe I receive it. It's mine."

When you do that, you're activating a key principle that Jesus taught His disciples. They asked Him one day to increase their faith, and He told them:

If ye had faith as a grain of mustard seed, ye might say unto this sycamine tree, Be thou plucked up by the root, and be thou planted in the sea; and it should obey you (Luke 17:6).

Jesus made it clear: If you want more faith, don't waste your time praying for it. Instead, take the faith you already have (you can be sure you have some because the Bible says that "God hath dealt to every man the measure of faith"),[164] plant it, and it will grow up and become greater than any challenge in your life because greater is He (The WORD) who is in you than he who is in the world.

If you want to live by faith in THE BLESSING, plant the seed by giving attention to what The WORD says about it and confessing, "I believe I am BLESSED." Even if a life of BLESSING seems beyond your wildest imagination right now, keep saying that…and saying it and saying it…because, as simple as they may seem, such words activate your spirit. They set it in motion so it can do what it was designed to do, which is to believe God's WORD.

Your spirit is created to process God's WORD and generate faith from it in much the same way your digestive system processes food and generates physical energy. When you decide to eat something, your stomach automatically begins working. You can pick up an apple intending to take a bite, and your digestive system automatically kicks into gear. Saliva begins flowing. Enzymes get fired up. You don't have to go flip a lot of switches to get your digestion to work. All you have to do is say, "I believe I'll eat a bite," and the whole thing goes into operation.

Your spirit works the same way. When you read a promise in The WORD of God and say, "I believe I receive that," your spirit goes to work digesting that WORD and producing faith—even while your *mind* is arguing with you about it and saying, "I don't believe that. I can't see it."

---

[164] Romans 12:3

When your mind tries to give you trouble like that, don't worry about it. It can't help itself. It wasn't created to believe anything. It was created to agree and make decisions. Certainly, your mind can accept things, analyze them and produce a natural kind of believing. It can determine, for example, a chair is sturdy enough to hold you up and say to you, *Yes, go ahead and sit down on that. I believe it will be all right.* But that kind of believing isn't true faith.

True faith is when you believe The WORD of God in spite of natural evidence to the contrary. It is believing you're healed even when you still feel sick. It comes from your spirit by the agency of God's WORD and says, "I know I don't feel healed. I know I don't sound healed. I know I don't look healed. But I believe I am healed because The WORD says so."

When your mind balks and says, "I can't believe that!" your spirit should answer, "I know it. You're not equipped to believe it, but I am. So I'm taking ascendancy over you. You'll see the evidence of the healing in a while, but until then, I'm ordering you to keep your unbelieving mouth shut. From this point on, I'm in charge and I'm going to speak only words of faith."

### Keep Talking Faith Until You Hit the Gusher

Speaking The WORD is an essential part of The Buildup because what we say is what comes to pass. Our words produce our future. What we're saying today is what we'll have tomorrow. Like it or not, we can't get around it. We live in a word-based, word-created, word-directed environment.

"Death and life are in the power of the tongue: and they that love it shall eat the fruit thereof" (Proverbs 18:21). Or, as Jesus put it in Mark 11:23:

Whosoever shall say unto this mountain, Be thou removed, and be thou cast into the sea; and shall not doubt in his heart, but shall believe that those things which he saith shall come to pass; he shall have whatsoever he saith.

Although we can't escape the fact that our lives are governed by words, we can choose the words under which we live. We can choose words of faith. We can choose words of BLESSING. If we do, then BLESSING is what we'll have.

Sounds simple, doesn't it?

It is—but there is one catch: "Out of the abundance of the heart the mouth speaketh." [165]

Early in our faith lives, Gloria and I discovered for ourselves just how true that is. When we first made the decision to speak only words of faith, we found it was anything but easy. Because we'd spent years filling our hearts with doubt and unbelief, many times we'd speak contrary to The WORD without even noticing it.

So, we made a pact with one another. When one of us would hear the other saying something connected to the curse instead of THE BLESSING, we'd draw attention to it by saying, "That's your confession and I believe every word of it is coming to pass."

The pact was hardest on me because I have a bigger mouth than Gloria does. I was always getting caught saying something I shouldn't. She was quiet a lot of the time in those days, so she got off pretty lightly on the deal. It irritated me. Sometimes when she corrected me, I wanted to say to The LORD what Adam said, "That woman Thou gavest me!"

In the end, however, I was grateful she did it because it forced me to learn to speak from my spirit instead of my flesh. It helped me train myself to say, "I'm healed," even when I was hurting, and "He meets all of my needs according to His riches in glory," even when my mind was screaming, *You don't have enough money to pay the bills!*

It takes effort to establish the habit of talking like that, but I highly recommend doing it. There comes a time when we all need to get ourselves by the ear, yank ourselves down onto our knees before The WORD of God, and say to our flesh, "Be quiet! I'm not letting you talk that unbelief anymore. It's over!" If we want to live

---

[165] Matthew 12:34

in THE BLESSING, we must discipline our flesh, take authority over every contrary thought and speak God's WORD—whether our minds and bodies like it or not.

When you practice making yourself think and speak The WORD, it eventually gets into your heart in such abundance it starts pouring out of you like a gusher. That's when it works because it's coming out bathed in faith. Until that happens, just stay with The Buildup. Keep putting The WORD before your eyes, in your ears and in your mouth. Keep feeding it into your spirit.

If you'll do that, you can rest assured that one day soon, you'll hit the place where even your mind and body agree with it, and you'll know with every fiber of your being you have what you've been saying.

### Call Things That Are Not as Though They Were

Abraham, the father of our faith, proved that beyond any shadow of a doubt. He kept building his faith until he got to the point where he was *fully persuaded*—despite every circumstance to the contrary—that he and his barren, old wife were going to have a baby. And he did it by walking out the process I just outlined.

He started by making a quality decision to believe God's WORD. Romans 4:3 says, "Abraham believed God, and it was counted unto him for righteousness." He meditated on that word of BLESSING and spoke it…and spoke it…and spoke it, by calling himself *the father of many nations,* until that word of BLESSING absolutely took control of his mind.

Verses 16-21 say it this way:

…Abraham; who is the father of us all…before him whom he believed, even God, who quickeneth the dead, and calleth those things which be not as though they were. Who against hope believed in hope, that he might become the father of many nations, according to that which was spoken, So shall thy seed be. And being not weak in faith, he considered not his own body now dead, when he was about an hundred years old, neither yet the deadness of Sarah's womb: He staggered not at the promise of God through unbelief; but was strong in faith, giving glory to God; and being fully persuaded that, what he had promised, he was able also to perform.

Notice, that to walk in faith, Abraham had to do what God does. He had to call things that be not as though they were.

Who taught him how to do that?

God did.

Abraham didn't have anyone else to teach him. There weren't any word of faith preachers back then. So God Himself instructed Abraham as he went along. He taught him how to think and talk according to THE BLESSING. He told him to get away from his relatives and the rest of the moon worshipers in his hometown and then introduced him to a whole new way of living. God's ways made Abraham look a little strange to everyone else, but in the end, everyone agreed that Abraham's strange ways produced results.

If you live by faith, people will think you're strange too, so you might as well get ready for it. When you start calling things that be not as though they were, they'll make fun of you. If you tell them you're just doing what Abraham did and what God does, they may even get mad at you.

That has happened to me. People actually became angry with me and said, "Who do you think you are, running around acting like a little Jesus?"

If they'd been willing to listen, I could have told them who I am. I'm a follower of Christ, and I'm obeying the instructions in Ephesians 5:1: "Therefore be imitators of God as dear children" *(New King James Version)*.

The word *imitator* used in that verse comes from the Greek word which means "to mimic."[166] We're supposed to mimic God the way children mimic their parents. Therefore, if He calls things that be not as though they were, we should, too. It is part of the

---

[166] James Strong, LL.D, S.T.D, *The New Strong's Exhaustive Concordance of the Bible* (Nashville: Thomas Nelson Publishers, 1984) G3402.

faith process, and if we want to walk in THE BLESSING, we must make it a way of life.

We must also act like Abraham did by not considering the circumstances in our lives that contradict God's promises. One way Gloria and I practice doing that is by saying, "I'm not moved by what I see. I'm not moved by what I feel. I'm moved by what I believe, and I believe The WORD of God."

Abraham must have said that sometimes when he thought about his 100-year-old body and looked at his 90-year-old, barren wife. He must have said, "Old man, you don't count. Old woman, you don't either. We're going to have a baby because God has called me *Abraham,* the father of many nations. He has said that we will have a son!"

By thinking and speaking that way, Abraham eventually got to the point of being fully persuaded. He came to the place where he staggered not at the promise of God.

That ought to be an encouragement to us. We may not be trying to believe for exactly the same things Abraham did, but our faith challenges sometimes seem just as big as his. Naturally speaking, it can be tough to believe for a certain amount of money when we're broke, or to face some killer disease, believing that by His stripes we were healed. Situations like that can look just as impossible as having a baby at 100 years old. But, if we'll follow the example of Abraham and keep building up our faith until we're fully persuaded, we'll end up living in the fulfillment of God's promises, just as he did. We'll end up BLESSED.

### There's a Miracle in Your Mouth

"I just don't know if I can do what Abraham did, Brother Copeland. He was someone special. He was one of a kind."

No, actually, he wasn't. The Bible is filled with accounts of people who walked in that kind of faith. We've already studied several of them—people like Isaac, Jacob and Joseph. Hebrews 11 is a veritable Faith Hall of Fame that lists one person after another who believed God much the same way Abraham did. It's not a comprehensive list, either. There are others written about in the Bible who did amazing things by faith that Hebrews 11 doesn't mention.

One of my favorites is "the Shunammite woman," whose story is recorded in 2 Kings 4. She was a seemingly ordinary person whose only outstanding characteristic was her reverence for The WORD of God. She had such faith and respect for it, she built a room onto her house so when the prophet Elisha came to town to preach, he could stay with her and her husband.

As a result of her faith, THE BLESSING of God came on every area of her life. It prospered her household. It prospered her financially. It even caused Elisha to prophesy over her that, after years of barrenness, she would have a son. Sure enough, the next year, she did.

Everything went smoothly for a while. But a few years after the boy was born, the Shunammite woman faced a situation that could have totally derailed her faith. Her son suffered a sunstroke while in the field with his father, and died.

Had she not known how to operate by faith in THE BLESSING, she might have reacted like any other mother. She could have fallen apart and started screaming, "My baby is dead! My baby is dead!"

Instead, she put on her coat without a word and headed out the door to see Elisha. When her husband asked her why she was going, she simply said, "All is well."

Then she saddled a donkey, and said to her servant, "Drive, and go forward; do not slacken the pace for me unless I tell you." And so she departed, and went to the man of God at Mount Carmel. So it was, when the man of God saw her afar off, that he said to his servant Gehazi, "Look, the Shunammite woman! Please run now to meet her, and say to her, 'Is it well with you? Is it well with your husband? Is it well with the child?'" And she answered, "It is well" (verses 24-26, *New King James Version*).

Think of it. Though her son was lying dead, back at home, that woman refused to say anything contrary to THE BLESSING. The only words she let cross her lips were: "All is well!" That was the phrase people used to communicate that they were BLESSED.

At that moment, the Shunammite's circumstances didn't look BLESSED. Emotionally, she didn't feel BLESSED. But she *believed* she was BLESSED. So she called things that be not as though they were, knelt down, grabbed Elisha's feet and refused to leave him until he agreed to go back with her and minister to her child.

Remember, in those days, the prophet was the carrier of God's WORD. He represented the truth and the power of it. In essence, this dear lady was holding tightly to The WORD of God. She was gripping THE BLESSING by faith and refusing to let it go, despite the contrary circumstances.

When Elisha arrived at her house, he found the little boy lying dead on his bed.

> He went in therefore, shut the door behind the two of them, and prayed to The LORD. And he went up and lay on the child, and put his mouth on his mouth, his eyes on his eyes, and his hands on his hands; and he stretched himself out on the child, and the flesh of the child became warm. He re-turned and walked back and forth in the house, and again went up and stretched himself out on him; then the child sneezed seven times, and the child opened his eyes (verses 33-35, *New King James Version).*

What do you think opened the door for Elisha to bring that boy back to life? Was it the fact that he was a prophet?

No, it was the Shunammite woman's faith in THE BLESSING.

She believed in it and confessed it. She stayed connected to it by faith until the power of it flowed through Elisha and raised her son from the dead.

That woman gave us a perfect picture of how faith in THE

BLESSING responds in a time of crisis. Faith opens its mouth and confesses the truth of God's WORD about the situation. Faith says, "All is well!"

When the devil comes tearing into your life with some kind of curse-spawned circumstance, it's not enough just to sit quietly and try to think BLESSED thoughts. You won't be able to do it. If you try to struggle in silence with the kinds of oppressive, fear-filled thoughts that assail you at times like that, your faith will falter. You'll end up saying foolish things like, "I'm not going to make it through this! It's going to kill me! The WORD just doesn't work for me!"

How can I be so sure of that? Because I've learned from The WORD and experience that you can't fight thoughts with thoughts. It doesn't work. The only way to overcome thoughts is with words. Negative thoughts have no defense against faith-filled words.

Your words are so powerful that, according to Jesus, you'll either be justified or condemned by them; and you'll have to give account for them on the Day of Judgment. That's how serious they are to God.

I'll never forget a particular situation when I began to see the kind of life-or-death, BLESSING-or-cursing kind of power I can release through my words. It was in the very early days of this ministry when finances were a daily challenge, and I was pacing the floor, crying out to God about it.

"Lord, I've hit the wall here. I have no funds with which to continue what You've told me to do. I can see in Your WORD that You said You'd supply my needs, but I need Your wisdom about receiving that supply because I don't know what to do."

The minute I said that, the word of The LORD came to me: *Did you ever notice that My pattern throughout history has been that when My people cry out to me for something, I don't just drop it down out of heaven? I call and appoint a man to minister to them on My behalf.*

*When My people called out to me in Egypt, I sent Moses. When My people cried out to me to deliver them from the oppression of their enemies in the Promised Land, I sent people like Gideon and Barak and Samson. That pattern continued all the way up to and including Jesus. Now, He is your Man.*

I jumped up and said, "Oh, Hallelujah! That must mean You have a man somewhere who is going to help me financially. So I'm calling on him to come."

*No,* said The LORD, *that's not what I'm saying. I'm not telling you there is a man; I'm asking you to be that man. I'm asking you to place yourself in the position of being BLESSED and prospered so that you can go and minister BLESSING to those who are calling out to Me.*

"How on earth am I supposed to put myself in that position?" I asked.

He answered by leading me to Romans 10:8, "The WORD is nigh thee, even in thy mouth, and in thy heart...." *You don't need a man to come from somewhere else to meet your needs,* He said. *What you need is right there in The WORD, and it's so close to you that it's in your heart and in your mouth.*

A few days later, someone handed me a little book written by John Osteen entitled, *There's a Miracle in Your Mouth.*[167] Coupled with what God had just said to me, that title hit me like a freight train. I've never gotten over it and never want to!

I have known from that day that my miracle is right here in my own mouth. I don't have to look anywhere else for it. It's not out there in someone else. It's not in someone else's bank account. It's right there in The WORD, and if I'll put that WORD in my heart and speak it with my mouth, it will produce for me just as surely as it produced for God Himself when He said, "Light be!"

### The Decision, The Buildup and The Delivery

Once The Buildup of meditation and confession of The WORD brings you to the place where you're fully persuaded, you're ready to implement the last element of the operation of

---

[167] John Osteen, *There Is a Miracle in Your Mouth* (Houston: John Osteen Publications, 1972).

faith—the element I call *The Delivery*.

When it's time for The Delivery, something happens in your spirit. On the outside, things may not look any better. The symptoms or circumstances you've been standing against may not have changed one bit. Yet, all of a sudden, almost without thinking about it, the declaration of faith comes roaring out of your mouth with such power that you know you have the victory.

At that moment, what once looked almost impossible to your natural mind looks like the easiest thing in the world.

- That's when you know that the good fight of faith is won.

- That's when you know without a doubt that you are more than a conqueror through Him who loves you.

- That's when the devil bows his knee to the command of the Lion of the Tribe of Judah and gets out of your way.

- That's when the promise you've been standing on begins to manifest.

It excites me when the moment of The Delivery comes.

The first time I ever experienced and understood it, I was working for Oral Roberts in one of his healing meetings. My job was to go to the invalid room after his message, recap the sermon and prepare the people to have hands laid on them for healing.

When I walked into that room, I was shocked at the condition of the people. They had every kind of sickness imaginable. Some were in the very throes of death. I had no idea how to help them, so I just did what I'd been told. I took my notepad and went over Oral Roberts' main points. Then, when he came in, I stepped back, out of the way.

I figured my part was done. But I was wrong. Oral Roberts walked over to where I was standing, grabbed the shoulder of my coat and pulled me over to him. "You're going to do the praying!" he said.

I could feel all the blood drain out of my face. *Pray? I have no idea how to pray for people like this,* I thought. *They're the worst cases in the whole place!*

He knew what I was thinking. "Don't worry," he said. "I'll be right here. If you make a mistake, I'll correct it. But don't touch them until you're ready to release your faith."

*Release my faith? What does that mean?* About all I knew back then was the power of the Name of Jesus, so I decided when I spoke that Name, I'd release my faith the best I knew how.

The first person Oral Roberts directed me toward was a woman lying on an old army cot. She'd been brought in by ambulance and, although she just weighed about 75 pounds, she had a malignant tumor in her stomach that was so big that she looked like she was pregnant. She was so close to death that she couldn't even sit up.

By the time we started to pray for her, I was eager. I didn't have a clue what to do, but I was thrilled at the opportunity to see God work in this kind of situation. I reached my hand out toward her and said, "In the Na…" but before I could finish, I heard Oral Roberts' voice over my shoulder. It sounded like the Lion of the Tribe of Judah roaring right there behind me: "You foul, unclean spirit, taking the life of my sister, take your hands off God's property in the Name of Jesus, whose I am and whom I serve!"

That roar of faith was so full of God's power, it made my hair stand straight up. Right before my eyes, the lady coughed up the tumor that had been killing her. It was as big as a fist and looked like a jellyfish with strings hanging from it. She coughed it right out on the ground and then took off running around the tent.

It was a sight to see. The little lady who couldn't even sit up a few seconds before ran…and ran…and ran.

That, dear friend, is the release. It comes after you've made the quality decision. It comes after you've built yourself up on The WORD of God, confessing it and meditating on it until it gets so big on the inside of you that you can't contain it anymore.

When you're ready for the release, no one will have to tell you what to do. You'll just rise up with words and action, and put things straight in the realm of the spirit. You'll rise up and begin reaping your faith crop because you'll know harvest time is finally here.

### Don't Eat Your Harvest Before It's Ripe

When Jesus talked about the time of harvest in the parable of the sower, He described it this way:

> So is the kingdom of God, as if a man should cast seed into the ground; and should sleep, and rise night and day, and the seed should spring and grow up, he knoweth not how. For the earth bringeth forth fruit of herself; first the blade, then the ear, after that the full corn in the ear. But when the fruit is brought forth, immediately he putteth in the sickle, because the harvest is come (Mark 4:26-29).

Notice, you don't get out your sickle and try to start reaping the moment the first little blade of faith appears. You have to be patient and let The WORD finish its work. You have to wait for your faith crop to ripen.

As you do, you'll begin to see the thing you're believing for more clearly with the eyes of your heart. You'll start getting some confirmations and revelations from The LORD about it. He'll begin to show you where that property is you've been standing in faith for. He'll show you the building...or the house...or whatever else you've been claiming according to His WORD.

When those things start to happen, it's exciting. But it's also a time when you must stay full of faith that THE BLESS-ING is working in your life. You must continue to be patient and keep believing it's working—when you see it and when you don't, when you feel it and when you don't. You have to stay steady and on track because the devil will do everything he can to push you into getting out ahead of God and trying to make something happen too early. He'll work hard to pressure you into eating your crop while it's still green.

A lot of people do that, and it's a serious mistake. That's how people end up in financial trouble. They try to buy the building or the house or the car God promised them before it's time, instead of waiting to find out from Him exactly how He wants to get it to them.

Every one of us has done that at one time or another. We can all remember the bitter taste of green corn. But, personally, I don't want to make a steady diet of it. So I asked The LORD one day, "How can we know for sure when our harvest is ripe?"

*I have put in the heart of every human being an awesome sense of timing,* He said. *They have an innate ability to know when something is right.*

I recognized right away just how true that is. People who have never even been on a farm can go to a grocery store and tell immediately what's ripe and what's not. They won't eat fruit that's been picked before it's ready, unless that's all they have to eat, because it just doesn't taste good.

One way we know something is ripe is when it just falls off the tree. That's true in the natural and the spirit realm. When the time for your faith harvest has come, things just start working. Circumstances fall miraculously into line. People just start doing their best to help you in that area. It becomes obvious: THE BLESSING has done its work, and harvest time is here.

Gloria and I know what that's like. We've been through it again and again. When things came together for us to purchase the 1,520 acres of property that our ministry headquarters stands on today, for example, we had already spent 10 years sowing and believing for it, knowing God had promised it to us, without doing one thing in the natural to try to buy it. Year after year, we just waited and stayed steady in the process of faith until finally, one morning, The LORD said to me, *I want you to go see the man who owns that land and tell him that The LORD has need of it.*

"OK!" I said.

I'd never met the man, but I made an appointment with him,

went over to his house and said exactly as I'd been instructed, "The LORD has need of this property."

Eighty-nine years old and sharp as a tack, he answered by saying, "Well, it's for sale."

I'm no different from anyone else. I was figuring, since God sent me over there, the man was supposed to say, "If The LORD needs it, I'll give it to you." But he didn't. He just told me it was for sale and then sat there looking at me.

Since The LORD hadn't given me anything else to say, I just sat there looking back. Fifteen minutes went by with both of us just sitting, listening to the clock on the mantle—tick-tock, tick-tock, tick-tock. Then, finally, he said again, "It's for sale."

"I don't have any money," I answered. "But The LORD will get it for me."

He sat there in silence a few minutes longer and then said, "You come back and see me." (Here's something to remember: If you'll keep your mouth shut at times like that, THE BLESSING will work on your behalf. But if you open your mouth and start spouting your own wisdom, trying to make it work in your own, natural strength, you'll mess things up.)

A few days later when I went back to see him, we sat down in the same place and, again, after a long time of silence, during which he never once smiled, he pointed at me and said, "I'm gonna see you boys through this."

"Thank you, sir," I said. "But you need to know, I don't borrow money. It isn't right to mortgage something that doesn't belong to me and this ministry doesn't belong to me, it belongs to God."

"Come back and see me," he answered.

The next time I met with him, he had another man with him and we met at a different place at his direction. "You need to be on that property," he said.

"Yes, sir," I answered.

"You got anything against paying rent?"

"No sir, I'm paying rent for the place we're in now."

"All right," he said. "I'll rent the property to you and there will be no interest on your rent payment." (When he told me what that payment was going to be, it was so low that it shocked me.) "You don't owe me a thing. If God speaks to you and tells you to leave, you just let me know and then you can go on and do what God tells you to do. That's all the notice I need. Just call me and tell me you're leaving.

"As The LORD blesses you and you have the money to pay for a quarter of that land, I'll deed a quarter of it to you. All of your rent money will go toward the fourth quarter. Does that sound all right to you?"

"It sounds fine to me," I said. "I really do like that plan."

Turning to the man he'd brought with him, he said, "Write that down just the way I said it."

Once it was written, he handed it to me and I signed it. Then he signed it, handed it back to the other man, and said, "Now, take $1 million off that price because I want to be the first donor." Once that was done, he slapped the contract, smiled real big at me and said, "A cement and gravel company has been contacting me wanting to buy the gravel on that land. There's gravel all over it. But I told them they'd have to talk to you."

I wasn't sure what he meant. "You're talking about after I get part of the land paid for, right?"

"No, son," he said, "I've already given you the mineral rights. Sell some of that gravel and pay for your land."

We ended up selling over a million dollars' worth of gravel.

That's what it looks like when THE BLESSING is working and your harvest is ripe!

### Big Things Start as Small Seeds

Maybe you hear a story like that and you can't imagine such a thing ever happening to you. When you think of a figure like a million dollars, it seems so big you can't see how you could ever be BLESSED with that kind of money. But here's what you have to remember: All the land God gave us for this ministry and every dollar that came in to pay for it started out as a seed of faith no bigger than a mustard seed.

Gloria and I didn't start out in this ministry with million-dollar harvests. We started with simple faith in God's WORD. We planted that WORD in our hearts, spoke it with our mouths, refused to uproot it with unbelief and, over time, The WORD did what it always does: It grew up and became greater. It became greater than our debts and wiped them all out the first year we began believing. It became greater than our need for ministry equipment. It kept becoming greater…and greater and greater until, after more than 40 years, it's gotten so big that it's overtaken not just our needs and desires, but our dreams as well.

I mean that literally. I wake up every morning in a house that's so far above anything I could have asked or thought of that it amazes me. I live in a manifestation of one of Gloria's dreams.

She planted the seed for that dream house many years ago when we were living in a little shack in Tulsa that was so run-down that when we moved there, she refused to unpack for two weeks. Naturally speaking, she had no reason to even hope for a nice house back then. We were head-over-heels in debt, had a tiny income, and had promised God we'd never borrow money. But Gloria had read a book by Oral Roberts that said, "Don't let anybody steal your dreams," and she decided that was wise counsel. She did exactly what the book said and wrote down all her dreams along with scriptural promises to go with them. Right at the top of her dream list, she wrote, "A home for my family and for our ministry."

Gloria has always put her study and meditation of The WORD first in her schedule, but once that was done, she liked to spend her free time working on her dream house. She had a picture file where she kept all her favorite photos and clippings from home decorating magazines. As the years passed, the file expanded to include floor plans, furniture ideas and everything else you can imagine.

For years, one of her favorite pastimes was to get those things out and plan and design. She bought graph paper and drew pictures of rooms. She even learned to do architectural drawings. She'd

have a good time fellowshiping with The LORD over it all and saying, "Thank You, Lord, for our home."

As the years passed, God kept moving us to better and better
houses. We enjoyed each one and were grateful for them. All the
while, though, Gloria kept working on her dream file.

Eventually, she picked out the place on Eagle Mountain Lake
near our ministry headquarters where she wanted that house to
be built. We'd get in the boat sometimes and sit out on the water
across from the site and I'd say, "Gloria, tell me again about the
house." She'd describe it and I'd just say, "My, my...think of that!"
Then we'd just praise The LORD all the way back home.

One day, she said to me, "Kenneth, this house I'm working on
is getting so big that I don't know what to do about it. I can't find
any way to cut it down."

"What do you want to cut it down for, girl?" I said. "It's a
dream. Dream on! Let the plans cover the whole living room floor.
I don't care."

"Do you mean that?" she asked.

"Sure," I said. "Go for it!"

A couple of years later, she talked to me again about it. "We're
going to have to pray about this," she said. "This house is getting
so real inside me, either we're going to have to build it, or I'm going to have to quit messing with it."

So, we pulled aside for a week and spent time in prayer asking for the wisdom of God. The first thing Gloria said to Him was,
"Lord, if You tell me it is not Your will for me to build this house,
You just let me know and I will never bring it up again. I'll not
regret it. That will be the end of it. I'll just go on without it and be
as happy as can be."

That was the ground we started on. During the week, The
LORD gave us several confirmations that it was His will for us to
build it. On the morning when the full revelation of it came, the
anointing and the word of The LORD came to me. He said, *You put
your hands on Gloria and minister that house to her. It is a part of
your overall prosperity and I want her to have it.* Then, He gave

me a definite scripture to read to her.

When I did, she began to weep and said, "That's the very scripture The LORD gave me back there years ago when I first started dreaming about this house. It's been in my heart for 30 years."

She'd never said anything to me about it. But The LORD knew, and He used that verse to tell her that harvest time had come. Her hope had taken on faith where that house was concerned. The faith process was complete, and it was time for The Delivery. That's why she had gotten agitated about the situation. She sensed that house was ready to be born.

"Brother Copeland, you mean it took 30 years for The WORD to become that house?"

Yes, but we didn't mind. God provided very nice places for us to live in the meantime. What's more, we were busy doing other things. We were focused on the work of God. We took care of His house and His affairs first. While we were doing that, God was preparing a house for us beyond anything I'd ever dreamed.

Actually, it kind of stumped me when I first saw it. I'd stayed away from it when it was being built. The LORD told me to keep out of it, and let Gloria take care of it. The day I saw it completely finished, it almost bowled me over. The hair stood up on the back of my neck and my knees went weak. I sat down on the lake bank, began to worship God, and said, "Hallelujah! THE BLESSING has manifested itself, and our Garden of Eden has begun."

That night, I could hardly go to sleep for praising God. I just kept saying, "This is the work of The LORD and it's marvelous in my eyes. THE BLESSING of The LORD maketh rich and He adds no sorrow with it."[168] If we'd tried to get that house on our own, we'd have ended up with a mountain of debt and a lot of other problems. But there's no sorrow with that house because it's a work of God! It was produced by Gloria's faith dream and the power of THE BLESSING.

One night, right after we moved into it, I left our bedroom to

---

[168] Proverbs 10:22

get a drink of water and ended up just wandering through the house for a while rejoicing with The LORD over it. When I got back, Gloria said, "What took you so long? Have you been on some kind of a safari or something?"

"Yeah," I said, "because it's so-fari from the bedroom to the kitchen!"

Then the spirit of laughter hit us both and we laughed and laughed, and we've been laughing ever since, full of joy because like everything else good in our lives, that big house began with the seed of The WORD. It began with these simple verses from Isaiah 54:2-3:

> Enlarge the place of your tent, and let the curtains of your habitations be stretched out; spare not; lengthen your cords and strengthen your stakes, for you will spread abroad to the right hand and to the left... *(The Amplified Bible).*

The WORD grew up and became the home of our dreams.

## Open Your Bible and Get a Dream

The WORD of God will do the same thing for you. As the seed of Abraham in Christ Jesus, you're just as BLESSED as we are. So, get your Bible out and start dreaming. If you've been suffering sickness, dream of strength and health and life in your physical body. If your children have strayed from The LORD, dream of them becoming mighty in the kingdom of God. If you've spent years broke or just getting by, dream of having such an abundance that you have enough to enjoy and plenty to give away.

Create an inner image of God's WORD coming to pass and His BLESSING manifesting in your life. Bathe your imagination in The WORD of God until hope rises up within you and begins to take upon itself faith. It will take some time, but it's worth the effort because as you build your hope and faith, you are building your future—a future filled with the realization of your dreams.

One man I know started working on his dream of financial

BLESSING during the worst time of his life. He'd just lost a lucrative job at an age when it's tough to start over in the corporate world. He had all kinds of debt and no savings in the bank. In one day, he was wiped out, with no clue what he was going to do.

Although he was a good man who loved God and went to church, he didn't know much about THE BLESSING until he got hold of the book, *The Laws of Prosperity*.[169] When he read it, he thought, *Dear heavens, that's what I need. I need faith in God's WORD where my finances are concerned.*

So, he took his Bible and the book down to the local Burger King®, bought a cup of coffee (he couldn't afford a hamburger) and spent day after day studying. After a while, he got some teaching tapes and began listening to them. Somewhere along the way, it hit him that God's WORD is the source of his prosperity—not some corporation or some job, but The WORD.

"I determined right there in that Burger King®," he said, "that I was going to put a million dollars into Kenneth Copeland Ministries one day."

He did it, too. Less than eight years later.

God is no respecter of persons, my friend. His WORD works the same way for everyone who will put faith in it. So, grab your Bible, get into the presence of your heavenly Father, and get yourself a dream.

---

[169] Kenneth Copeland, *The Laws of Prosperity* (Fort Worth: Kenneth Copeland Publications, 1974).

Chapter 13

# Breaking the Fear Connection

Be not afraid, only believe.
Mark 5:36

E veryone who has ever lived by faith in God's WORD and
dared to encourage others to do so, eventually runs into
someone who says, "I tried The WORD and it didn't work!"

One friend of mine has a great answer for people like that. He
says, "No, The WORD tried you, and *you* didn't work."

That might sound harsh, but it's the plain truth. God never
drops the ball. He never fails to keep His WORD. He says in
Jeremiah 1:12, "I will hasten my WORD to perform it;" and that's
what He does. Always. Without fail.

That doesn't mean there won't be times when we foul things
up and slow down the manifestation of what we're believing for. It
means that when things quit working and the faith process seems
to stall, we must learn to ask honestly: *What is keeping me from
receiving? Where is the problem here?*

Clearly, God is not holding out on us. (That's religion's excuse,
and it's a lie from hell.) So, if we're not receiving and enjoying
the manifestation of THE BLESSING in our lives and what The
WORD says belongs to us, somehow we must be short-circuiting
the power of faith. Everyone does that at one time or another; and

we do it without even realizing it.

I've done it myself many times, especially in the early years of my faith life. One of the most memorable was when my son, John, was just 3 or 4 years old and became very sick with scarlet fever. His skin turned purplish-red and became as dry and rough as sandpaper from his neck down, especially on his stomach. Any kind of light on his skin would almost set it on fire with fever and pain.

Gloria and I were traveling at the time, and we always took the children with us. I would preach several times a day, and at night I'd lay hands on him and believe God for his healing. When I did, his skin would start to clear up. I could see it improve right before my eyes. But, the next morning, it would be as red and rough as it had been before I prayed.

That continued for about three days—which was two and a half too many—so, I went before The LORD and said, "Lord, I'm missing it here with John's healing. You can't miss it. You never miss it. When we pray for healing, it always comes. John can't be the one missing it because he's just a little fellow. So, something is off base here, and it's in me. I'm just going to be quiet here and wait for You to show me the problem."

Sure enough, after a while, The LORD gave me the instructions I needed. He said, *You're exercising your faith and laying hands on him. You do well and healing begins to manifest, but then you take him back out of My hands.*

"How am I doing that?" I asked.

*You get up and go in there in the middle of the night to check on him. That would be fine if you were doing it in faith, but you're not. You're doing it because you're afraid your prayer isn't working. When you do that, you take him out of My hands.*

I hadn't learned back then what I know now about how fear contaminates faith. I didn't realize how much even a little fear can mess things up. But, that night when I prayed and laid hands on John, I said, "Lord, this time I'm putting him in Your hands in the Name of Jesus, and leaving him there."

At 2 a.m., I woke up, just as I had the previous nights, and without even thinking, I jumped out of bed to check on John. I took a couple of steps and then stopped. "Forgive me, Lord," I said. "I've rolled all the care of this over on You, and I'm not going to meddle with it. I believe I've received his healing, and I'm standing on it."

As soon as I got the words out of my mouth, the devil started pressuring me. *What kind of parent are you? You'd better go see if he's all right.*

I answered right back. "Listen to me, devil. The most responsible thing I could do, as a parent, is keep my child in God's hands. I can't heal him. I can minister healing. I can believe and receive with him, but the power is God's. He is the One doing the healing, and I trust Him, so I'm not going in there."

Still, the pressure didn't let up. The devil kept badgering me. His voice wasn't audible, but in my mind I heard it clearly: *You'd better go in there and check on John. He has kicked his covers off and you need to cover him back up.*

"If he's kicked his covers off, let the angels put them back on him," I answered. "I'm not going in there."

I closed my eyes and tried to sleep, but the devil kept hounding me, so I grabbed my Bible, went in the other room and closed the door to keep from waking Gloria. "Satan," I said, "I am going to take the sword of the Spirit and cut you up every which way."

Then, I started praying in tongues as hard and fast as I could go. I had a sense of victory, and I knew the devil was leaving, but it was just starting to become fun so I said, "No, you aren't going anywhere yet. You come back here and get under my foot and take this." After spending 45 minutes with my foot on his neck in the Name of The LORD Jesus Christ of Nazareth, declaring the truth of The WORD, I said, "Now, you get out of here!"

If you've never talked to the devil like that, I suggest you get started. As believers, we need to exercise our God-given authority over him. Sometimes, we need to get mad enough to drive him out of our homes and out of our business. We need to stop listening to him and send him packing.

When I went back to bed that night, the pressure was gone. I slept well. The next morning I got up, put on my suit and went over to the meeting to preach. After the service was over, I was closing things up when I felt a tug on my coat and turned around to find it was John. "Daddy…" he said.

I was focused on what I was doing so I said, "John, son, I'm busy here. Let me finish this."

Undeterred, he tugged on my coat again. This time, he was hollering at me, "Daddy! Look at me! I'm healed!"

Looking at him again, I saw that he was right. He'd come over in his bathing suit, so I could see that from neck to belly, he was just as healed as he could be.

I learned a big lesson right then. I saw for myself why the Bible commands us 110 times to "fear not!" Our connection to THE BLESSING depends on it.

### Fear Tolerated Is Faith Contaminated

"But, Brother Copeland, in some situations fear is inevitable, isn't it? Aren't there times when we just can't help being afraid?"

No, there aren't. As born-again believers, we never have to be afraid.

Jesus settled that issue by what He said in Mark 5 to a man named Jairus who came seeking healing for his dying child. If you're a parent, you know there is no situation more potentially terrifying than that. Most parents would rather face death themselves than to see their children die.

Leaving his daughter at home on her deathbed, Jairus went to find Jesus. He shoved his way to the front of the crowd that had gathered on the shore of the lake to await His arrival. The minute Jesus stepped out of the boat, Jairus fell down at His feet, "and besought him greatly, saying, My little daughter lieth at the point of death: I pray thee, come and lay thy hands on her, that she may be healed; and she shall live" (verse 23).

*"She shall live."* That was Jairus' confession of faith. That was what he believed would happen. He had replaced the inner image

of his daughter falling prey to death and replaced it with an inner image of Jesus coming to his house and laying hands on her. Calling things that be not as though they were, he declared, *"She will be healed and live" (New International Version).*

> And Jesus went with him; and much people followed him, and thronged him (verse 24).

For a few minutes, everything looked as if it were going according to Jairus' faith plan. But then someone intervened, and things started to happen that he hadn't envisioned.

> A certain woman, which had an issue of blood twelve years, and had suffered many things of many physicians, and had spent all that she had, and was nothing bettered, but rather grew worse, when she had heard of Jesus, came in the press behind, and touched his garment. For she said, If I may touch but his clothes, I shall be whole. And straightway the fountain of her blood was dried up; and she felt in her body that she was healed of that plague (verses 25-29).

Had Jesus just kept walking when that happened, things might have gone differently for Jairus. But He didn't. He stopped and asked who had touched Him.

> And his disciples said unto him, Thou seest the multitude thronging thee, and sayest thou, Who touched me? And he looked round about to see her that had done this thing. But the woman fearing and trembling, knowing what was done in her, came and fell down before him, and told him all the truth (verses 31-33).

How long do you think it took that woman to tell *all the truth* about her 12-year illness, about all the physicians she'd seen who hadn't been able to help her, and all the money she'd spent in the process? That was quite a story—and it must have taken awhile!

All the time she was talking, Jairus was standing there waiting, knowing his daughter was in critical condition. Every second
mattered. Yet Jesus seemed to be in no hurry. When the woman
finished giving her testimony, He began ministering to her.

> While he yet spake, there came from the ruler of the syna-
> gogue's house certain which said, Thy daughter is dead: why
> troublest thou the Master any further? (verse 35).

At that moment, Jairus heard the worst, most fear-provoking
words any parent can hear. But Jesus didn't even give him time to
react. As soon as He heard the words spoken to Jairus, He said,
"Be not afraid, only believe" (verse 36). Or, as Luke 8:50 records
it, "Fear not: believe only, and she shall be made whole."

That's a stunning statement when you think about it! Most
people would have said just the opposite to Jairus in that situation.
They would have patted him and said, "You just go ahead and cry. I
know you're frightened and sad right now, and it's perfectly understandable. Just express your feelings."

But Jesus knew something most people don't. He knew that
*fear tolerated is faith contaminated.* He knew it's impossible
to be in fear and faith at the same time. And, since the life of
Jairus' daughter depended on his faith connection to Jesus, He
commanded him not to fear.

Had it been impossible for Jairus to obey that command—if he
couldn't help being afraid—Jesus' command would have been unjust. But it wasn't impossible for Jairus, even in that high-pressure
situation. And it's not impossible for us, either. In fact, because
Jesus absolutely conquered the power of fear through His work of
redemption, it's far easier for us as born-again believers than it was
for Jairus to *fear not.*

Yet, even without the benefit of the new birth, he did it. With
Jesus by his side, he found a way to obey. He refused to fear and,
as a result, his story has a happy ending.

Jesus went to Jairus' house, told the people who had already started grieving and making a tumult over the girl, that she wasn't dead, but sleeping.

And they laughed him to scorn. But when he had put them all out, he taketh the father and the mother of the damsel, and them that were with him, and entereth in where the damsel was lying. And he took the damsel by the hand, and said unto her, Talitha cumi; which is, being interpreted, Damsel, I say unto thee, arise. And straightway the damsel arose, and walked; for she was of the age of twelve years. And they were astonished with a great astonishment (Mark 5:40-42).

## Don't Make the Fear Connection

Here's why fear is such serious business: Just as faith is the spirit connector to God and THE BLESSING, fear is the spirit connector to the devil and the curse.

We've already seen throughout the Bible, faith is what activates the operation of THE BLESSING. Faith releases the anointing of God in people's lives. When Jesus ministered on earth, and preached *peace* (*shalom:* which includes healing, deliverance, prosperity, and a life with nothing missing and nothing broken), the people who believed what He preached connected with Him and received that peace. They were healed. They were delivered from demons. They ate their fill of loaves and fish.

Those who didn't believe, didn't make that connection. The people in Nazareth, for example, didn't get much at all from Jesus. He wanted to help them so much that He laid hands on them anyway. He tried His best to get at least a little of THE BLESSING to them. But He couldn't do much for them because instead of making the faith connection, they got mad at Him and tried to kill Him.

What made them so angry? He said some things about their religion that frightened them. He pointed out that during an Old Testament famine when there were many widows in Israel, God didn't send the prophet to them. Instead, He sent the prophet to a gentile widow who would respond to His words in faith.

The idea that just being Jewish wasn't enough to assure favor with God, created fear in them. That fear separated them from Jesus, so He couldn't do any mighty works among them.

Most of the other places He went, however, people believed what He said, and their faith opened the door for Him to go about "doing good, and healing all that were *oppressed* of the devil."[170]

The word *oppressed* is an important scriptural word. The Bible uses it to describe all the manifestations of the curse Satan puts on human beings. Sickness, for example, is satanic oppression. So is poverty. Every manifestation of the curse is a form of the devil's oppression; and Isaiah 54:14 shows us exactly what opens the door to it. In this verse, the Spirit of God, prophesying to the Body of Christ about THE BLESSING that would be ours through Jesus, says:

> In righteousness shalt thou be established: thou shalt be far from oppression; for thou shalt not fear: and from terror; for it shall not come near thee.

Notice, it says, thou shalt be far from oppression; *for* thou shalt not fear. In other words, fear is the spirit connector to oppression. Fear is the connector to sickness and disease. Fear is the connector to poverty and every other manifestation of the curse.

You can also say it this way: Fear connects to the spirit of fear just as faith connects to the Spirit of faith. The spirit of fear is the devil himself. It's the spirit the Apostle John referred to as the spirit of antichrist.[171]

To get the full impact of the term *antichrist,* you have to realize that Christ is not Jesus' last name. It's not His title. *Christ* is a Greek word that means "the anointing,"[172] or "the Anointed One." The anointing on Jesus is the power of the Holy Spirit that came on Him

---

[170] Acts 10:38

[171] 1 John 4:3

[172] James Strong, *The New Strong's Exhaustive Concordance of the Bible* (Nashville: Thomas Nelson Publishers, 1984) G5547.

in the Jordan River. It is the power that gave Him the right to say:

> The Spirit of The LORD is upon me, because he hath anointed me to preach the gospel to the poor; he hath sent me to heal the brokenhearted, to preach deliverance to the captives, and recovering of sight to the blind, to set at liberty them that are bruised, to preach the acceptable year of The LORD (Luke 4:18-19).

According to Isaiah 10:27,[173] the yoke (or oppression) of the devil is *destroyed* by the anointing. So, I call the anointing *the burden-removing, yoke-destroying power of God*. Notice, it's not the yoke-*breaking* power but the yoke-*destroying* power. The Hebrew word translated *destroy* refers to corrosion or rust. Do you know what rust does to steel? It disintegrates it. If you just leave rust alone and let it do its work, there won't be any steel left!

That's what the anointing does to the yoke of oppression. It renders it unfit for Satan's use. If it were just broken, it could be mended. But, the anointing doesn't break it. It explodes it into powder. When the anointing comes on the scene, it leaves the devil standing naked, with nothing left. That's the reason he is the *anti*-Christ. He is against that anointing. It's also the reason he is against us. As born-again believers, we are the *Body* of Christ—the Body of that anointing in the earth!

Just as faith in Jesus connects to the Spirit of the anointing, fear connects to the spirit of the anti-anointing. If you doubt it, think about what happened to Job. He'd spent years connected to THE BLESSING of God, then suddenly, found himself connected to the oppression of the devil. Job was a good man. He loved and reverenced The LORD. But somehow, Satan found a way to put his yoke on Job's neck and destroy everything he had.

Job tells us in his own words how that happened. He said, "The thing which I greatly feared is come upon me, and that which I was

---

[173] Isaiah 10:27: "And it shall come to pass in that day, that his burden shall be taken away from off thy shoulder, and his yoke from off thy neck, and the yoke shall be destroyed because of the anointing."

afraid of is come unto me. I was not in safety, neither had I rest, neither was I quiet; yet trouble came."[174]

Do you see what was happening in his life? He wasn't resting in faith. He wasn't quiet. He was up every night, nursing his fears about his children. He thought maybe it might help to worry about them. He didn't realize that by worrying, he was actually opening the door to trouble.

People do the same thing today. Good, God-loving people try to control their children with fear. Have you ever wondered why there's such a thing as a generational curse? It's because children are raised by their parents, and parents pass along their fears to their children.

I saw the results of it years ago in the life of a minister I know. In middle age, he began to experience heart problems and went to one of my mother's Bible studies to get her to pray for him. When he explained his situation to her, he said, "Sister Copeland, my dad died with heart trouble. My granddad died with heart trouble. Neither of them lived to see their 60th birthday. I have high blood pressure and heart trouble now. My mother always told me that the men in our family die young with heart trouble, and it's starting to look like she was right."

Looking him straight in the eye, my mama said, "Tell me the truth about that."

Puzzled, he answered, "I just told you the truth." Then he started telling her the whole story again.

She interrupted him. "I told you to tell me the truth about that!"

This time he was mad. "Lady," he said, "I just *told* you the truth about it."

Describing the incident to me later he said, "Kenneth, at that point she literally boxed my ears! She slapped her hands on the sides of my head, shook it, and said, 'Have you read Isaiah 53?'"

"Yes, I have."

"Well, then, what does it say?"

"It says by His stripes I am healed."

---

"That's right!" she said, "And that's the truth about the matter."

She told me later that when he walked in the door, she saw the spirit of death on him. She knew she had to get through to him quickly because he was dying. He was killing himself just like his daddy and granddaddy had done. Why? Because of what his mother had been telling him. She'd been feeding him heart-problem fear for years because she was afraid he was going to die, and it almost killed him.

A few years later, I ran into him in a motorcycle shop. When I walked in, he was talking on the phone. After he hung up, he said, "Copeland, sit down here. I want to tell you this story." He talked for a while about how my mother had prayed for him. Then he grinned and said, "I was just now on the phone talking to the doctor who gives me a physical every year. This is my 60th birthday and he said I have the heart of a 16-year-old kid!"

He and I had a good time praising The LORD together because that generational curse of fear and heart disease had been broken. The anointed truth of The WORD of God had destroyed the yoke of the devil and made him free.

### Fear Keeps Bad Company

If that's not enough to convince you to "fear not," here's another fact that should seal the deal: Fear itself is a sin.

"Oh, Brother Copeland, you can't be serious!"

I'm as serious as can be.

Sin is anything that disconnects you from THE BLESSING and connects you with death. Many things people think are sin aren't sin at all. Some people believe with all their hearts that using deodorant is a sin. (Personally, I'm more inclined to believe that it's a sin *not* to use it!) Yet those same people will wallow around in fear for years without realizing they're in direct disobedience to The WORD of God. Apparently, they've never paid much attention to Revelation 21:7-8, which says:

He that overcometh shall inherit all things; and I will be his

God, and he shall be my son. But the fearful, and unbelieving, and the abominable, and murderers, and whoremongers,
and sorcerers, and idolaters, and all liars, shall have their part
in the lake which burneth with fire and brimstone: which is
the second death.

Those verses put fear in very bad company. They list it right
alongside such things as unbelief, murder and whoremongering.
That's why I'm shocked when I hear pastors of churches and
preachers who ought to know better, say, "Well, everyone has to be
afraid of something. A little fear can be a good thing."

Is that right? You really believe a little fear is a good thing?

"Yes, amen. That's the truth."

Well, how about a little unbelief then? That's probably a good
thing too, isn't it? How about a little abomination or murder or lying? How about a little whoring around? You think your wife will
agree that's a good thing?

Fear in any measure is totally unacceptable. Going to a horror movie is no different than looking at pornography. It's wrong.
It will connect you to a spirit that you, as a child of God, have no
business being connected to. It is *not* OK. It is a sin because there
is death in it.

When you get right down to it, fear is actually faith in death. The
fear of a dangerous animal is faith in that animal's ability to hurt or
kill you. Fear of disease is faith in the power of that disease to destroy your body. Fear of death is faith in its power and authority.

Fear's objective is to create unbelief. Its goal is to get you to
believe something other than what God has said about your situation, not just to make you *feel* scared. In fact, it's possible to be full
of fear about something without having any of the jumpy, spine-
chilling sensations we normally associate with being frightened.

How, then, can we recognize fear when it tries to come on us?

According to 1 John 4:18, "Fear hath torment."

If fear is there, so is torment. Worry is torment. Anxiety is torment.
Torment is the element Satan uses to cause you to think that

God is not going to help you this time. Torment gets you thinking: *Yeah, The WORD works* but *it doesn't work for me.* Or, *I know the Bible says by His stripes I was healed,* but *the doctor just called and said my test results are bad.* Or, *Sure, God said He meets all of my needs according to His riches in glory, but what if He doesn't do it this time?*

I want you to notice that every one of those statements contain the word *but* which indicates everything said before is incorrect and wiped out. In statements like the ones above, *but* is the badge of unbelief; and unbelief is completely, totally fear dependent. To get rid of the fear and the torment that goes with it, you must get *but* out of the way.

Did you get what I just said? I didn't say you should *cope* with the fear. I didn't say you should *manage* it. I said get rid of it!

There's a big difference between coping with fear and having no fear. Even unsaved people can cope with fear. A rodeo cowboy, for example, has a very dangerous profession. His job is to get on a big, mad, mean bull and ride the thing without getting hurt or killed. Obviously, to do that he has to manage his fear, and he'll probably do it so well that if you watch him in a rodeo, you'll think he is absolutely fearless.

Yet, that same cowboy will get in his truck and drive to his next performance worrying the whole time about his marriage. He'll be scared silly that his wife is going to leave him. He managed fear in one area, but it is still there.

Anyone can cope with fear if they have enough training. Airplane pilots do it all the time. In flight school, they train in a simulator that sets up emergency conditions specifically designed to test their fear level. If they handle one emergency, the trainer will just keep throwing more at them, stacking one crisis on top of another, until the pilot hits the failure level and crashes the plane.

That's what a simulator is for. It's just exactly like the airplane and it helps pilots develop their skills to the point where their training takes over and they're able to manage fear in emergency situations.

That's not what God wants for us. When He tells New Testament believers to fear not, He isn't telling us to manage our fear. He's telling us to totally eradicate it and flush it completely out of our lives.

How do we do that?

I'm glad you asked.

### Redeemed From the Curse of Fear

First, we must come to the absolute, rock-solid, scriptural conviction that through the power of redemption, Jesus has delivered us once and for all from the bondage of fear.

We may not *feel* like we've been delivered from it, but that doesn't matter, the Bible is clear on the issue. Describing what Jesus did for us through His death, burial and resurrection, it says:

Forasmuch then as the children are partakers of flesh and blood, he also himself likewise took part of the same; that through death he might destroy him that had the power of death, that is, the devil; *and deliver them who through fear of death were all their lifetime subject to bondage* (Hebrews 2:14-15).

Every fear that exists is, in one way or another, based on the fear of death, and according to The WORD of God, we've been delivered from it. Jesus stripped it of its power over us by paying the price for sin, taking on Himself its deadly offspring, the curse. He completely paralyzed and put out of commission the devil, who is the foul author of it. By triumphing over death and becoming our Champion and Lord, Jesus freed us once and for all from every kind of fear.

Galatians 3:13 says it this way: "Christ hath redeemed us from the curse of the law, being made a curse for us: for it is written, Cursed is every one that hangeth on a tree."

Many believers don't realize it, but fear is part of the curse. Deuteronomy 28 says so. Warning the children of Israel about what would happen to them if they disconnected from THE BLESSING and opened the door to the curse, it says:

> Among these nations shalt thou find no ease, neither shall the sole of thy foot have rest: but The LORD shall give thee there a trembling heart, and failing of eyes, and sorrow of mind: And thy life shall hang in doubt before thee; and thou shalt fear day and night, and shalt have none assurance of thy life: In the morning thou shalt say, Would God it were even! and at even thou shalt say, Would God it were morning! for the fear of thine heart wherewith thou shalt fear, and for the sight of thine eyes which thou shalt see (verses 65-67).

That's a perfect description of torment at its worst; and— *thank God!*—at Calvary, Jesus bore it for us. As Isaiah 53:5 says, "He was wounded for our transgressions." The center column reference in the *Authorized King James Version* substitutes the word "tormented" for *wounded.*

Jesus was tormented so that we wouldn't have to be.

Usually, when we think of the torment Jesus suffered, we think of it taking place only on the cross. But the devil started pressuring and tormenting Jesus before then. He put Jesus under such stress in the Garden of Gethsemane that blood came out of His pores. In those final hours, Satan was trying to push Him into disobeying God. He was pressing Jesus to sin. But Jesus resisted and said to the Father, "If it be possible, let this cup pass from me: nevertheless not as I will, but as thou wilt" (Matthew 26:39).

When Jesus was on the cross, it began to look to the devil as if he had actually succeeded because there, Jesus finally yielded to the weight of sin and the curse the devil had been trying to put on Him. But Jesus didn't fall prey to that curse because He sinned. He opened Himself up to it in obedience to God. He did it by faith.

Until then, Jesus had never allowed fear to have any place in Him. He'd never, one time, entertained it. That's why He was able to say the night before He went to the Cross, "The prince of this world cometh, and hath nothing in me."[175]

Because Jesus had no fear in Him, the devil couldn't get any of the rest of the curse into Him, either. He was never able to touch Him with sickness and disease. He couldn't touch Him with death. Jesus lived in such freedom from fear, that when the people at Nazareth tried to throw Him off a cliff, they couldn't do it. He just stayed in the light of God and that light blinded them so completely, they couldn't see Him. He just walked away from them in love and faith.

When He went to the cross, however, for the first time in His life, Jesus received fear into Himself along with all the sin, sickness, torment and death that goes with it. No wonder He said, "My God, isn't there some other way than this?" It was a horrible thing. Yet, He did it for us.

He received fear so that we, by faith, could receive complete, eternal deliverance from it. He allowed it to do its dreadful work and connect Him to the darkness of the devil himself so that you and I would never have to fear anything again. He did it so that we could believe and boldly declare with the New Testament writers:

- "[We] have not received the spirit of bondage again to fear; but…the Spirit of adoption, whereby we cry, Abba, Father" (Romans 8:15).

- "For God hath not given us the spirit of fear; but of power, and of love, and of a sound mind" (2 Timothy 1:7).

- "The LORD is my helper, and I will not fear…" (Hebrews 13:6).

### Flush It Out With Love

Once you understand that Jesus has purchased your complete and absolute deliverance from fear, you're on your way to living fear free. You have a solid, scriptural basis from which to resist

---

[175] John 14:30

it. But that, in itself, won't totally get rid of it. What gets rid of it
is the power of love. In the life of a believer, love starts with the
revelation that we are loved by God.

First John 4 says:

> Herein is love, not that we loved God, but that he loved us,
> and sent his Son to be the propitiation for our sins.... And we
> have known and believed the love that God hath to us. God is
> love; and he that dwelleth in love dwelleth in God, and God
> in him. Herein is our love made perfect, that we may have
> boldness in the day of judgment: because as he is, so are we
> in this world. There is no fear in love; but perfect love casteth
> out fear: because fear hath torment. He that feareth is not
> made perfect in love (verses 10, 16-18).

Most people know the Bible says God loves them. If you ask
them about it, they'll say, "Oh yes. God so loved the world that
He gave His only begotten Son." But, when they start to pray, they
think, *Why would God care about a loser like me?* They have an
intellectual understanding of what the Scriptures say about God's
love, but haven't "known and believed the love" God has for them.

I understand what that's like because I used to be that way. I
went through so much junk before I was born again that I stopped
believing in love at all. I got to the point where I had no emotional
response to anyone. As far as I was concerned, there was no such
thing as real love. I thought it must be just some sort of state of
mind. And, if it were real, then I was incapable of it.

Then, I met Gloria. She blew that idea completely apart in five
seconds. The first time I saw her, my emotional cynicism started
to crumble, and I fell head-over-heels in love with her. After we
married and I gave my life to The LORD, I got a little more revelation about God's love. But I was still a long way from knowing and
believing the whole truth about it.

It wasn't until we moved to Tulsa and I was just getting started
in ministry that the full reality of it first hit me. I was pacing around

our little bedroom, reading my Bible and meditating on the truths I was learning, so thrilled about them I could hardly stand it. On that particular day, I was reading in John 17, the prayer Jesus prayed for His disciples just before He went to the cross. I knew the prayer applied to me because in it, He specifically said He was praying not only for the first 12 apostles, but for all who would believe on Him through their word.[176] I figured that covers every Christian who ever lived—including me.

So, when I got to verses 22-23, I was stunned. There, Jesus said:

The glory which thou gavest me I have given them; that they may be one, even as we are one: I in them, and thou in me, that they may be made perfect in one; and that the world may know that thou hast sent me, *and hast loved them, as thou hast loved me.*

*Dear heavens!* I thought. *That says God loves me just as much as He loves Jesus. Surely, that's not right. I must have misread it.*

I read it again and, sure enough, that's what it said!

I got out two or three other translations to double-check it. All of them said the same thing.

The more I thought about it, the more I realized it must be right. *After all, if God so loved the world that He sent His only begotten Son for me, He must love me just as much as He loves His Son. Since that's the truth, I'm going to start confessing it: God loves me just as much as He loves Jesus!*

The first time I said it, my knees shook. My mind was saying, *Who do you think you are to stand there in front of God Almighty and say that God loves you like He does Jesus?*

But, I answered it right back and said, "I have every right to say these words because they are written here in my Bible in red. Anything that's written in red, I have a right to confess because Jesus is my High Priest."

By then, my knees had stopped shaking, and a new boldness

---

[176] Verse 20

was rising up in me. I started walking around that little room again. I'd take a few steps one way and say, "My heavenly Father loves me just as much as He loves Jesus!" I'd take a few steps the other way and say, "Oh, hallelujah! I believe I receive that. I receive it by faith just like I received salvation. I confess it before God: My heavenly Father loves me just as much as He loves Jesus!"

In the days that followed, I kept at it. I'd get in my car and say, "Oh, Lord, I'm going to drive this car today believing that You love me just as much as You do Jesus. And I know that You're going with me wherever I go. I don't even have to ask You to be with me because You've already promised never to leave or forsake me even to the end of the world."

After I'd done that for a while, The LORD said to me, *Why don't you read the rest of the chapter?* So I got my Bible, opened it to John 17 and started reading at the 24th verse:

> Father, I will that they also, whom thou hast given me, be with me where I am; that they may behold my glory, which thou hast given me: for thou lovedst me before the foundation of the world. O righteous Father, the world hath not known thee: but I have known thee, and these have known that thou hast sent me. And I have declared unto them thy name, and will declare it: that the love wherewith thou hast loved me may be in them, and I in them (verses 24-26).

After I read those verses, The LORD stopped me.

"What do You want me to see, Lord?" I asked. "It seems that those verses are saying the same thing again—that You love me with the same love You have for Jesus."

*No, you're missing it,* He said. *Read it again.*

When I did, the truth of it dawned on me. "My, oh my!" I cried, "Jesus is saying that the same love that You love Him with, the very love that created this universe, the love of Almighty God Himself is in me!"

Suddenly, I thought of Romans 5:5: *"The love of God is shed abroad in our hearts by the Holy Ghost which is given unto us.*"

God's own love equipment is inside me. It's inside you. It's inside every person who has ever made Jesus The LORD of their lives. God has given each of us His own mighty compassion and authorized us to love people with His love.

"That's great, Brother Copeland, but what does it have to do with getting rid of fear?"

It has everything to do with it! When we know and believe the love God has for us, and then extend that love He has put inside us to others—fear can't get a foothold in us. It has to go because "perfect love casteth out fear!"

Love literally flushes fear out of our systems. As we activate love by receiving it from God, loving Him in return, and then loving our neighbor as ourselves, the tide of love keeps rising and rising until it sweeps fear away like a flood. That's the moment you can rebuke it, and it will leave you.

### Preach to Yourself Every Day

"But you just don't understand. You don't know what a horrible person I've been. It's hard for me to feel like God loves me!"

Don't worry about that. Your feelings will eventually come in line. In the meantime, just keep feeding your faith in God's love for you by reading and meditating on what The WORD says about it. Every time you think of Jesus, remind yourself that He said, "As the Father hath loved me, so have I loved you."[177]

Get your concordance and look up verses about God's love and mercy. Look up the phrase, "before the foundation of the world," and read about the fact that God knew you and loved you before the earth was ever created. He knew your name and prophesied your future. He loved you before the devil amounted to anything—before sin ever existed. He loved you before time began, and He never changes.

As you read those glorious truths, say out loud, "I receive that

---

[177] John 15:9

in the Name of Jesus. By faith, I take hold of the love God has for me and I'm not going to turn it loose. His love is not based on my feelings. It's based on God's WORD, and His WORD says He loves me. He always has, and He always will!"

When you make confessions like that, you're actually preaching to yourself. And there's nothing better than good, WORD-based preaching about God's love to build your faith to the point where it casts out fear. Jesus knew that better than anyone. That's why He dealt as He did with the madman of Gadara.

Do you remember what the Bible says about that man? He was so filled with demons, it brought fear to the entire region where he lived. Talk about a man with a horrible past! The devil used him to control people through fear.

Because the man didn't sleep, everyone knew there was something unnatural about him. He screamed night and day. He cut himself and cried. He frightened everyone so badly, they chained him, but he broke the chains. They imprisoned him, but he broke out. Eventually, people were too afraid to go near him. They thought he would kill them—and he would have.

You'd think everyone would have been thrilled when Jesus ministered to the man and cast the demons out of him. You'd think when those 2,000 demon-filled pigs rushed into the sea and that fellow was back in his right mind, the local people would have been grateful and happy. But they were so scared, they weren't thinking straight. (That's what fear does to people.)

Instead of celebrating, they were upset because the devilish god they'd been worshiping had lost its power. They started thinking about the economic impact of losing a couple of thousand pigs. Those hogs represented commerce. So they asked Jesus to leave!

He did. He didn't say, "No, I'm anointed of God and I'm going to do some teaching in this area." He got in His boat with His disciples and left.

But, before He did, He turned to the man who had been delivered and said, "Go home to thy friends, and tell them how great things

The LORD hath done for thee, and hath had compassion on thee."[178]

Jesus sent that man back to his hometown to preach the compassion of God—because perfect love casts out fear!

I'm guessing the townspeople listened to him, too. They probably thought, *We'd better sit still and pay attention to what he has to say, just in case he has a relapse. We don't want him to get angry!*

After that fellow finished preaching compassion in that region, things changed. The next time Jesus went there, they had a great outpouring of the power of God.

### Sleep Like a Baby, by Faith

Once the power of love has flushed fear out of your life, keep it out by rebuking and resisting it whenever it raises its ugly head. Absolutely refuse to give it any place in your mind. The moment you catch a fearful thought trying to work its way in, start "casting down imaginations, and every high thing that exalteth itself against the knowledge of God, and bringing into captivity every thought to the obedience of Christ."[179]

Some people claim they can't help having fearful, anxious thoughts. But I don't believe that because the Bible says:

- "Be anxious for nothing, but in everything by prayer and supplication, with thanksgiving, let your requests be made known to God; and the peace of God, which surpasses all understanding, will guard your hearts and minds through Christ Jesus" (Philippians 4:6-7, *New King James Version).*

- "…whatsoever things are honest, whatsoever things are just, whatsoever things are pure, whatsoever things are lovely, whatsoever things are of good report; if there be any virtue, and if there be any praise, think on these things" (verse 8).

---

[178] Mark 5:19
[179] 2 Corinthians 10:5

If the Bible tells us to do these things, we can do them. We can be selective about what we think. If you'll do this little experiment, I will prove it to you: Begin counting silently right now, from one to 10. While you're counting, say your name out loud. Did you notice what happened when you said your name? Your mind stopped counting to listen to what your mouth had to say.

That's the simple solution to taking authority over your thoughts. When they start going the wrong way, use your mouth to turn them in the right direction. Any negative, fearful thought you have can be subdued and overcome by speaking The WORD. You can leave the devil helpless as a kitten by contradicting him with the words of your mouth and refusing to take his thoughts.

I learned that from my daughter Kellie when she was about 4 years old. Determined to get her to clean up her closet, I'd taken her by the hand, showed her what a disaster zone it was, and told her to clean it up. She looked at it for a moment, slipped her hand out of mine and said very simply, "That's not my thought."

When she said that, it hit me that even though I was more than twice her size, if she refused to take that *thought,* there wasn't a thing in the world I could do about it. As I was pondering the situation, The LORD spoke to me and said, *You need to learn to do that where the devil is concerned.*

I've used that ever since. When the devil tries to put worry on me with something, I say, "That's not my thought, Mr. Devil. I'm not going to touch that with my mind." Then I turn to The LORD, and as 1 Peter 5:7 tells me to do, I cast that care over on Him. I say, "Father, I'm giving this problem to You. You have it now. I'll do anything You tell me to do about it, but I'm not going to walk the floor and wring my hands. I'm not going to worry. I'm going to go to bed and sleep soundly, believing THE BLESSING is at work for me. I'm going to rest on The WORD."

"You don't understand my situation," someone might say. "I can't help but worry about it. It weighs on me so heavily that I can't sleep."

If that's the case, you're in sin and you'd better repent and get straightened out. I know that sounds tough, but worry is an extremely serious manifestation of fear, and fear is sin. So get rid of it. Then go to sleep by faith.

I can tell you from personal experience that it's possible to sleep by faith because I've learned how to do it. My sleep patterns got messed up when I was young and sometimes I'd go three or four days without sleeping. Then, I'd just fall asleep like someone had knocked me out and sleep for hours. But, not anymore!

I found out that Psalm 127:2 says, "It is vain for you to rise up early, to sit up late, to eat the bread of sorrows: for so he giveth his beloved sleep." Now, when I head toward bed at night, I start saying, "Glory to God, He gives His beloved sleep! I roll every care of this day over on My Father who loves me just as much as He does Jesus. I receive His love, and I receive the gift of sleep." Then, I go to bed and sleep like a baby.

Sometimes, I'll wake myself up in the middle of the night, praying out loud, "Thank God, THE BLESSING is working. It's working for me now, preparing my day tomorrow. My God loves me...." Then I just drift back to sleep again.

What a way to live! It will get you through anything!

I heard about a woman who lived in England who slept by faith every night of the bombings during World War II. She never even bothered to go to the bomb shelter.

When her neighbors didn't see her there, they went looking for her because they were afraid she'd been killed. "Why don't you come down there with us?" they asked.

"I don't like those shelters," she answered. "They stink and they're terrible."

"But, aren't you afraid?" they said.

"No. I found in The WORD of God that He never sleeps nor slumbers and I thought there's no use in the both of us being awake. So I decided I'd stay in my own bed and get some sleep. The LORD will take care of me."

Before the war was over, every house on her block was wiped

off the face of the earth by German bombs. Every house, that is, but one. Her little house was left standing while she slept through the whole thing.

## Divine Protection Is for Everyone

That wasn't just an isolated incident, either. Things like that happen all the time in the lives of people who learn to live in the love of God and walk free from fear. I have a friend who can give you dozens of examples. He pastors a church in the old New York Stock Exchange building, across from the site of the World Trade Center. Before the attacks on September 11, 2001, his church staff commuted through the World Trade Center every day.

He and his wife have been connected with Gloria and me for a long time. We consider them our spiritual children. So, of course, they teach their church members the things they've learned from us.

Most of their church members worked in or near the World Trade Center, but not one was killed or injured when those buildings came down. Almost all were late to work that day. One of the men is a stickler for being on time. His wife says if he's running behind, he won't even stop to kiss her goodbye because he can't stand to be late. But that morning, he just could not get it together, and he was late.

One church member whose office was in the World Trade Center was walking down the street toward it, and in his spirit he heard The LORD just say, *Run!* So he took off running. He dashed into a subway entrance and when he did, the explosion hit. He lived out the reality of Isaiah 54:14. Terror didn't come near him.

That was true for many that day. More people were late to work on the morning of September 11, 2001, than ever before in the history of Wall Street.

"Well, I don't see why God didn't just speak to everybody like He spoke to the members of that church."

He did. He spoke to everyone there.

"Then, why wasn't everyone saved?"

Because there were three classes of people involved. There

were those who wouldn't have known God if He had worn a sign around His neck, walked in the front door and said, "I'm God. Leave now." Because they'd never paid any attention to Him before, those people would have said, "Who is that fool coming in here saying He's God?" and ignored Him.

There were also people who heard God's voice and didn't act on it. They were like the people in the New Testament who heard God speak to Jesus and thought that it thundered. They all just stood there, and did nothing.

The third group was those who heard Him and did what He said. They got out of there.

One woman from my friend's church had left the building and was heading back in because the people in charge had said it was safe. But she heard The LORD say in her heart, *Get out of here and take everyone with you who will follow you.* So, she turned around and called out to them all. "Come on, we need to leave!"

"But they said we could go back," they answered.

"I don't care what they said. God said get out of here and I'm going. You can do what you want." A lot of people followed her out and went home safely that day.

You need to remember, though, you can't be assured of that kind of protection just because you're a good person. You don't connect with it just by being a Christian. You can be as saved and Holy-Spirit baptized as you can be and carry your Bible with you everywhere you go. But if you tolerate fear and talk it like the world talks it, you're walking away from your divine protection.

God has made that protection available to everyone. He has given the promise that "thou shalt be far from oppression; for thou shalt not fear: and from terror; for it shall not come near thee" to anyone who will receive it by faith and live accordingly. Jesus bought and paid for it so that everyone could take advantage of it. The problem is, some people do and others don't.

One of the most outstanding examples I've ever seen of someone who did take full advantage of that protection was a woman of faith (and a Partner with our ministry) who was kidnapped by a serial killer in San Antonio, Texas, some years ago. The man had already killed more than 20 women when he kidnapped her, and the police were after him. He had jumped her in a parking lot, shoved her in the car with him and said, "Shut your mouth, or I'll kill you."

If she'd been full of fear, it would have been over for her right there. But she was full of faith in The WORD. She was full of love. So, instead of screaming in terror, she said, "No, you won't. You're not going to kill the only person in the world who ever loved you."

She had a scripture book with her and she just started speaking The WORD. When he told her again to shut up, she said, "All right. If I can't talk, can I listen to my tape?"

He said, "Lady, I don't care what you listen to if you'll just keep your mouth shut. I'm tired of listening to you."

She started the tape and it turned out to be one of my messages on faith. After a while, he said, "There's something getting on me! What is all this?"

She started telling him about the love of God and he couldn't believe it. "You don't know what I've done," he said.

"You have a little boy, don't you?" she asked.

The question shocked him. "How did you know that?"

"The Holy Spirit told me that you have a 5-year-old boy. Do you love that boy?"

"Yes, I do. I love him very much."

"Would you like for him to turn out like you?" she asked.

"Oh, my God, no! A million times, no!"

"If you had the power to change him and turn him in a better direction, you would do it, right? Well, that's what God has done for you. Through Jesus, He can change you right now." Then she shared with him the plan of salvation.

Stephen Morin gave his life to Jesus right there in that car. He emptied his revolver and gave the woman all the bullets. Afraid the police would kill him on sight, he said, "Do you think Brother Copeland would accept my gun and take me someplace to surrender if I went to him?"

"I suppose he would," she said.

Before they got to me, however, the police caught him. When they did, he just held up his hands and gave himself up. They didn't hurt him at all.

Sometime later, I went to the Bexar County Jail in San Antonio and baptized him in water. I was the last man to visit him before they executed him. We had a glorious time together right before he went home to be with The LORD.

That woman's story would have had a very different ending had she not trained herself to walk in love and to stay free of fear. But, thank God, she was ready when trouble came. She had the love of God on her mind. She had developed her faith to the place where in the midst of a life-threatening situation, she could respond, not with fear, but with The WORD.

### Don't Wait Till the Devil's at the Door

You have the capacity as a born-again believer to do the same thing. You have been delivered from fear by the blood of Jesus and have the love of Almighty God Himself shed abroad in your heart. But, if you're wise, you won't wait until you're looking a serial killer in the face or dealing with a terrorist attack to develop yourself in those things. Don't wait until something bad happens and then start trying to train for it.

That's the wrong time.

Imagine a guy with a big, fat belly lying on the sofa in his undershirt (the one with the holes in it). He has a can of beer in one hand and a cigar in the other, and he's watching a football game. All of a sudden, some big guy breaks down the front door, walks over to him, slaps the beer and the cigar out of his hands, boxes his jaw, and says, "Get your ugly self out of this house. I'm taking it over. I'm taking your wife, your children and everything you have."

It's too late for Mr. Undershirt to start hunting for his barbells, isn't it? It's too late for him to start working out and building his muscles so he can fight back. He should have been in shape before Mr. Big showed up.

Maybe you feel, spiritually, like you've already made that mistake. The devil has kicked your door down and you're not strong enough in faith to deal with him. If that's the case, find some strong believers and get them to pray for you and believe with you. Let them help you get the devil off your back.

Then, get busy. Spend time in The WORD and in prayer. Find a WORD-preaching, faith-building church and get in it. Get strong in The LORD and in the power of His might so the next time the devil barges in on you, you can deal with him yourself.

Make the decision now to get fear out of your life so you can stay connected to THE BLESSING.

# Chapter 14

# The Royal Law of the Kingdom

Love never fails.
1 Corinthians 13:8, *New King James Version*

To walk in THE BLESSING, everything must hang on love. The faith that connects us to it "worketh by love."[180] The fear that disconnects us from it is cast out by love. Walking in love keeps us in the brightness of THE BLESSING and out of the darkness of the curse. For "He that loveth…abideth in the light, and there is none occasion of stumbling in him."[181]

One day when I was praying, I had a vision from The LORD that helped me grasp as never before, just how true that is. In the spirit, I saw a man trying to hang some huge, heavy curtains on a big wall. He was having a miserable time at it. He'd hang one panel, then run over and grab another; but before he could get the second one hung, the first one would fall down on him. He'd put the second one up, turn around to get the first one, and the one he'd just hung would tumble down on him.

The harder he worked, the more tangled in those curtains he became. It was like a comedy routine. "Look at that guy!" I said.

As I chuckled over his predicament, I noticed something. Each

---

[180] Galatians 5:6
[181] 1 John 2:10

curtain had a name on it. One curtain was "faith." Another was "righteousness." Others included "healing," "prosperity" and "the gifts of the Spirit."

After struggling awhile, the job finally got the best of the poor fellow and he collapsed in a pile of curtains on the floor. Then The LORD drew me in, and I heard the cry of the man's heart. It was anything but funny. "What's wrong with my faith?" he cried. "I believe in faith, but my faith isn't working. I believe in healing, and I'm sick. I believe in prosperity and I can't pay my bills." I knew how he felt. I could remember times when I cried the same way.

Suddenly, my vision zoomed in on the pile of curtains and I saw little snakes slithering in and out of it. They were biting the man and nipping at his heels. That made me mad. "Hey, those are the gifts of God!" I said. "What are devils doing in them?"

At that moment, The LORD drew my attention to the corner of the room. There, I saw a massive rod. It was so big, it looked like part of a bridge, and it was solid gold. Written on the side of it was Matthew 22:37-40:

> Thou shalt love The LORD thy God with all thy heart, and with all thy soul, and with all thy mind. This is the first and great commandment. And the second is like unto it, Thou shalt love thy neighbour as thyself. On these two commandments hang all the law and the prophets.

When I saw that rod, I heard the voice of The LORD. He was shouting, *Hang the rod, not the curtains! The curtains are fastened to the rod!*

### Activate the Law of the Spirit of Life

It hit me that day in a whole new way why walking in love is not just a good idea. It's not just a suggestion. Love is THE commandment of God because love is THE law that governs the operation of THE BLESSING.

To fully understand what that means, you must remember that the word *law* can be defined in two ways. First, there are irrefutable laws such as the laws of nature. Those laws are truth. They cannot be changed, and they work every time they are put to work. The laws of physics fall into that category. So do the laws of mathematics.

It doesn't matter what government is in power or what kind of rules men might come up with, irrefutable laws can't be altered. Congress could pass a law declaring two plus two is five but that wouldn't make it so. The Supreme Court could declare that the law of gravity has been canceled, but it wouldn't matter. Things will still hit the floor when you drop them because gravity always works, and no government on earth can change that.

Although most people think irrefutable laws apply only to the natural realm, the realm of the spirit is also governed by such laws. The spiritual world is not a place where just anything goes. Its laws are even more exact than natural, physical laws. That's not surprising because God, who is a Spirit, created all earthly matter. He patterned the physical world after the spiritual.

One spiritual law we've already discussed is: *"Faith cometh by hearing, and hearing by The WORD of God."* Romans 3:27 calls that "the law of faith." It goes into operation when two elements come together—a hearer and The WORD of God. And it always produces the same thing: faith. It doesn't matter who you are, who your parents are, whether you are a man or woman, or what color your skin is, the law of faith works the same way for everyone, all the time.

"I don't know about that, Brother Copeland. I think faith sometimes comes from drastic circumstances and horrible experiences."

If that were the case, everyone on earth would be a faith giant. But they aren't because faith comes by hearing The WORD. People who use that faith when trouble comes, will get through it better and stronger. People who don't, won't.

A law that works right alongside *the law of faith* is found in Galatians 5:6: *"faith...worketh by love."* That is a practical, unalterable truth. There's nothing religious or abstract about it. Faith works by love like a car works by gasoline. No gas, no go. No love, no faith. No faith, no receiving. Like the law of gravity, *faith worketh by love* is an irrefutable, spiritual law.

The second type of law that exists both in the natural and the spiritual realms is governmental law. Governmental laws are commands put into effect and enforced by the legal authorities of the land. It is possible to break them, but you will experience the consequences. If you run a red light, you'll get a ticket. Steal a car and you'll go to jail.

God's governmental laws are called *commandments.* People can and do break them; and when they do, it's called *sin.* As I've said before, there have been great and absurd debates about what is and is not sin. But the real definition is simple. Sin is violating the established laws of God.

The devil tries to sell the idea that God established those laws because He is mad at us and doesn't want us to have any fun. But, that's a lie. God gave them to us to keep us from killing ourselves. He put them in place to protect us because He knows, even if we don't, that "the wages of sin is death."[182]

People can argue about it all they want to. They can mock the dangers of sin and say there's nothing wrong with it. But that won't change the consequences. Sin always does just what God said it will do. It sets in motion "the law of sin and death."[183]

Sin always leads to death because death is what it produces in the spirit. Adultery, for example, kills. It works death in a family. There's something that happens in the human spirit, soul and body when a person honors Satan by giving him reign in that area. People convince themselves they can contain the damage caused by it. But in reality, opening the door to that one sin gives the devil access to their entire lives.

He'll take advantage of that access, too. That's the way he is. If you let him in the back seat, before long, he is going to be

---

[182] Romans 6:23
[183] Romans 8:2

in the front seat, driving. Once he's there, he'll kill you because that's his goal.

"What are we to do, then?" you might ask. "Do we have to live our lives constantly trying to avoid every, little sin?"

No, thank God, we don't! Instead of concentrating on all the *thou shalts* and *thou shalt nots* of Old Covenant law, we can just focus on walking in love.

> For this, Thou shalt not commit adultery, Thou shalt not kill, Thou shalt not steal, Thou shalt not bear false witness, Thou shalt not covet; and if there be any other commandment, it is briefly comprehended in this saying, namely, Thou shalt love thy neighbour as thyself. Love worketh no ill to his neighbour: therefore love is the fulfilling of the law (Romans 13:9-10).

The law of love is the one law of the New Covenant. The Apostle James called it "the royal law" of God's kingdom.[184] Love is the law of the Spirit of life, and "the law of the Spirit of life in Christ Jesus hath made me free from the law of sin and death."[185]

### Don't Stumble Around—Turn On the Light!

The reason love and life are so closely connected is because God, the author and generator of all life, is Love. Since God is Love, the first few verses of John 1 can actually be rephrased as follows:

> In the beginning was The WORD, and The WORD was with Love, and The WORD was Love. The same was in the beginning with Love. All things were made by Love; and without Love was not any thing made that was made (verses 1-3).

Every cell of your physical body, every molecule in this physical, material universe, every handful of dirt, every bird that

---

[184] James 2:8
[185] Romans 8:2

flies, every fish in the sea and the sea itself—all were made by Love's WORD. Love created you. Love breathed life into you. Therefore, everything that is contrary to Love goes against your very substance. Every word of disharmony violates the way you were made. Unloving words, thoughts and actions do violence to the very nerves and cells in your physical body. (That's why Proverbs 14:30 describes envy as "the rottenness of the bones.") No wonder Jesus said that love is the greatest commandment! No wonder He made it a *command* to love The LORD thy God with all your heart, all your soul, all your mind and all your strength, and your neighbor as yourself!

When we strive and fuss with others, we become our own worst enemy. We actually begin to self-destruct. When we walk in love, however, we not only BLESS others, we edify ourselves.

Ephesians 6:8 says, "Whatsoever good thing any man doeth, the same shall he receive of The LORD." In other words, every act of love, every word of kindness, every loving gesture, enlivens us. The cells in our bodies respond to it. Our minds respond to it. Our spirits expand on the inside of us, strengthening and preparing us to walk in the anointing we were born to carry.

When we take a step outside of love, we step out into darkness. That's where the curse is, and it's not where we, as believers, belong. We belong in the light. We are born of Light because we are born of God; and just as God is Love, God is Light.[186]

> For ye were sometimes darkness, but now are ye light in The LORD: walk as children of light (Ephesians 5:8).

That's not just theology, it's academic fact. Science has proven that light is the ultimate power of the universe. All matter has light at the center of its molecular structure. (The first thing God said at Creation was, "Light be!" That's why your physical body is electrically operated, and its battery runs on light.

Since Light is the source of our physical power, every act of

---

[186] 1 John 1:5

darkness dims that power. Every step outside Love, who is Light, instantly affects every cell of our being. So, every discouraging word, every curse word, every unloving word that comes out of someone's mouth affects his or her body in a negative way. The Bible says, "Where envying and strife is, there is confusion and every evil work."[187] Strife is darkness, and darkness throws our whole system—spirit, soul and body—into confusion.

One day, when The LORD was talking to me about this, He reminded me of 1 John 2:10, "He that loveth his brother abideth in the light, and there is none occasion of stumbling in him."

*Kenneth, what kind of a fool walks into a room, turns out the light, and then stumbles over everything in there?* He asked.

"One like me, maybe?" I answered.

*Yes, you're the one I'm talking to. You have My light inside you, but you keep turning it off and then stumbling around all the time. You could be walking in the light as Jesus is in the light.*

After He said that to me, I got to thinking about how light keeps us aware of what's really going on around us. Light stops us from getting into fear and makes us confident and sure-footed. Satan has a hard time putting anything over on us when we're in the light.

I remembered times when I'd stayed up studying into the wee hours of the morning, when it was dark and everyone was asleep. It would be so quiet, you could practically hear the silence. Then, somewhere outside, I'd hear a noise. *Boom!*

I'd think, *What was that?!* But I wasn't all that quick to jump up and check it out. After all, it was dark outside. Who wants to go poking around in the dark? Why, anything might happen!

The funny thing is, had I been studying in broad daylight, and heard the same noise, I wouldn't have paid any attention to it. If I had, I'd just look outside to see what was going on. Then I'd go back to what I was doing.

That's the difference between darkness and light. Fear abides in

---

[187] James 3:16

darkness. Things that seem scary in the dark don't bother us at all in the daylight. So, the key to living fear free is: Stay in the light. Keep walking in love.

That's what Jesus did. He not only lived a fear-free life but a sin-free life by continually keeping the command of love. At the end of His earthly ministry, He said to His disciples:

> As the Father hath loved me, so have I loved you: continue ye in my love. If ye keep my commandments, ye shall abide in my love; even as I have kept my Father's commandments, and abide in his love. These things have I spoken unto you, that my joy might remain in you, and that your joy might be full. This is my commandment, That ye love one another, as I have loved you (John 15:9-12).

I like to paraphrase it this way: "Now boys, let Me make it easy for you. I know there are a lot of commandments but I'm going to give you just one. You walk in love and THE BLESSING will work."

### Obey Your General Orders, No Matter What

Jesus' command of love is nonnegotiable. You might compare it to the general orders of the Army I learned back in 1957, when I went into military service. My mother was so upset about my being drafted that she decided to cook all my favorite foods. It would have been nice if I'd had better sense than to eat it all, but I didn't. So I gained a lot of weight before I went in.

My very first day in uniform, I was standing in line with the other GIs and saw the training commander coming toward me. He was the "baddest" looking dude I'd ever seen in my life. He stopped in front of me, grinned, poked me in the belly and said, "Ha! We're going to let the wind out of you! Welcome to the United States Army!"

He wasn't lying, either. From that day on, I became his project. Everything about me started to change. The Army changed the way I looked. They started with my hair. Once that was gone, they took my old clothes away and gave me new ones. They changed my food—they changed my entire life.

One of the first things they taught me was there were certain orders that everyone, regardless of rank, had to obey. Anyone who didn't obey those general orders would go to jail. It didn't matter who they were.

In addition to those orders, there were the orders of the superior officer. (To me, that meant everyone because I was the bottom link on the chain of command.) Then, there were the orders of the day. Those were the orders that addressed what uniform you were supposed to wear that day, what the training exercises would be, etc. If you didn't obey the general orders, you could forget about the orders of a superior, as well as the orders of the day, because your orders of the day would be given in jail. That's how important the general orders are.

Can you imagine what a mess it would be if people in the military just ignored their general orders...or made up their own? If for example, the Army sent some GI out to Fort Huachuca in Arizona for his basic training, and he didn't like it there, what if he said, "Whew! This is miserable! It's 115 degrees in the shade out here, and these barracks don't have any air conditioning. Don't we have a base in Hawaii? I believe I'll move to that one. I can be in the Army there just the same as I can here. This is pitiful!" What if he packed up his duffel bag and headed for Honolulu?

You don't have to be an expert in military law to know when that GI reports for duty in Hawaii, within the hour he's going to be locked up in the stockade. Why? He is absent without leave. He is illegal. He doesn't get to choose where he wants to serve. He's part of a greater operation than that, and the commander is the one who makes those decisions.

The same principle holds true for believers. We're no longer civilians. We're in the army of The LORD. The Bible says we're to "endure hardness, as a good soldier of Jesus Christ."[188] We

---

[188] 2 Timothy 2:3

have been given direct orders from our Commander in Chief. He knows what's best for us and for the entire Body of Christ. He created us. He knows who we are and what we are. He knows where our joy will be maximized, and He has directed us to that place by giving us one set of general orders: *Love The LORD your God with all your heart, soul, mind and strength; and love your neighbor as yourself.*

"Brother Copeland," someone might say, "I love Jesus, and I know those are His orders, but I don't keep them all the time."

Then, you don't really love Him.

"What? I know I do!"

No, you don't. Jesus said so, Himself: "He that hath my commandments, and keepeth them, he it is that loveth me."[189] That's not hard to understand, is it? It's simple and direct. Loving The LORD means keeping the commandment of love. He made it a commandment because He knew we wouldn't keep it if He just offered it as a suggestion. So, He gave us no alternative or excuse for violating the law of love.

I'm not saying we never have reasons to violate it. We do. But we must either fix the reasons or ignore them because Jesus said if we love Him, we're going to obey the command.

That means when our feelings get hurt and we're tempted to step out of love, we must tell our flesh what to do. We have to tell our minds what to think and our mouths what to say. Otherwise, we'll end up giving someone a "piece of our mind." We'll give up our place in the overflowing BLESSING of God because we can't operate in strife and in THE BLESSING at the same time.

That in itself is reason enough to run from strife as if it were a snake crawling into our households. We ought to kill strife before it ever gets started because it isn't worth it, my friend. THE BLESSING is too high a price to pay.

---

[189] John 14:21

## When the Thief Steals Your Coat, Give Him a Pair of Shoes to Go With It.

One reason I know this is because I've yielded to it at times and seen the trouble it caused in my own life. In our early years of ministry, for example, when our children were small, I made the mistake of letting myself become spiritually weak. I was preaching day after day without taking the time to feed my own spirit with The WORD. I was trying to survive spiritually just on what God was giving me to minister.

As a result, I became irritable. I did and said things that were harsh. I'd react to the children and to Gloria and snap at her. Of course, I'd repent over it, but two hours later I'd do it again. I found that every time I got into strife even a little, it slugged my nervous system.

I learned a few years later that it's a medically proven fact. Strife, anger, anxiety and other such emotions cause chemical reactions that, over time, are deadly.[190] The human body is a veritable chemistry plant and any form of strife sends shock waves through it. The body's chemistry can get so out of balance it messes up the brain. When that happens, our perspective becomes skewed, resulting in wrong thinking.

Then, of course, the devil takes advantage of the situation. First thing you know, there's a demonic spirit following you around all the time spewing negative garbage at you. Because your brain is compromised, that garbage actually makes sense to you. If you don't run to The WORD and get yourself straightened out, you'll start believing that devilish junk. That's the way Christians slip into depression and other disorders of the mind.

I was on the road to that and knew it, so I sought The LORD about it. I was determined to find out from Him how to stop reacting in strife because I refuse to have it in my life. One day The LORD said to me, *Stop practicing anger.*

---

[190] Don Colbert, M.D., *Deadly Emotions, Understand the Mind-Body-Spirit Connection That Can Heal or Destroy You* (Nashville: Thomas Nelson Publishers, 2003).

"What do You mean?" I asked.

*You get angry at things,* He said.

The minute He said it, I realized it was true. I hadn't thought about it until then, but I'd become angry sometimes with my car or my tools.

*You're practicing anger so much it is present with you all the time. It goes into operation before you can stop it,* He said. *Reverse that. Begin to practice My love all the time. Bring the conscious-ness of My love to the point where it's ever present and ready to be released. Practice it and think about it continually.*

I found out before long, that's when life gets good. That's when it gets sweet. When you're practicing the love of God, you get to where you don't even notice the bad stuff going on around you. You just plow it underfoot and keep going.

That's what I've learned to do with the ugly things some people say about me. People sometimes ask if I'm bothered by the critical newspaper articles and books that are written about our ministry. I really don't know what those articles and books say because I don't read them. I'm certainly not going to pay money to read those things. I have better sense than that.

What's more, I already have a Book that says all I need to know about me. I carry it with me everywhere I go. If someone says something ugly, I just look in The Book and find something good. After more than 40 years of practicing that, I don't care what they say. I can stand and smile while people are saying negative things about me right to my face. Instead of listening to them, I just think, *Bless their hearts, if they knew me the way God knows me, they would love me!*

"Brother Copeland, are you saying you just ignore your enemies?"

No, I don't ignore them, I love them because that's what Jesus told us to do. He said:

Love your enemies, do good to them which hate you, BLESS them that curse you, and pray for them which despitefully use you. And unto him that smiteth thee on the one cheek offer also the other; and him that taketh away thy cloak forbid not to take thy coat also. Give to every man that asketh of thee; and of him that taketh away thy goods ask them not again. And as ye would that men should do to you, do ye also to them likewise. For if ye love them which love you, what thank have ye? for sinners also love those that love them. And if ye do good to them which do good to you, what thank have ye? for sinners also do even the same. And if ye lend to them of whom ye hope to receive, what thank have ye? for sinners also lend to sinners, to receive as much again. But love ye your enemies, and do good, and lend, hoping for nothing again; and your reward shall be great, and ye shall be the children of the Highest: for he is kind unto the unthankful and to the evil. Be ye therefore merciful, as your Father also is merciful (Luke 6:27-36).

According to that passage, there are only two ways to think about our enemies. We will either love them or hate them. We will either do good to them or try to retaliate against them. So, we must decide which we will choose. We can't be wishy-washy about it. We can't just get up in the morning and say, "Well, I'll try my best to be nice to everyone today." We won't make it until noon with that kind of attitude. We'll be in a fuss with someone in traffic before we get to work.

What we must do is make a firm commitment to walk in love no matter what because that's God's command. Backing up that commitment, must be the assurance that God is our source, provider and protector. He is our BLESSER, and His BLESSING will turn every situation to our good.

Once we set our faith firmly on the fact that THE BLESSING has come on us through Christ Jesus and it is our source, it won't make any difference to us what our enemies do. When they say something mean or come against us in some way, we will refuse to retaliate because we'll be ever aware of the fact that THE BLESSING is more important than revenge. We'll say to ourselves, "They can't hurt

me unless I am willing to let go of THE BLESSING, and I'm not
about to do that. I'm going to keep the command of love. I'm not
going to get in the cursing business with them. I'm just going to
rest in the fact that what God has BLESSED, none can curse!"

When you take that attitude, you begin to realize it's no big
deal if some thief steals your coat or your goods. THE BLESSING
will replace whatever he steals. What's more, in the eyes of God,
the thief is of far greater value than coats and goods. God has His
heart set on that thief. He loves him and wants to save him, but He
has no connection with him. That's why it's so vital to God that
*you* love him. You're God's connection to him!

You're not seeing things from His perspective if you're thinking, *How do I protect what I have? If he steals something from
me, I'll hire a good lawyer, sue him and get it back.* God sees you
as His connection to the person who's been talking ugly about
you. You're His connection to the man. You're His connection to
those people who've been trying to pick a fight with you and get
you into strife.

That's why in the above verses Jesus used the phrase "what
thank have ye?" He wanted us to know that when we open the door
of God's love to such people, when we pray for them and BLESS
them, God says, "Thank you! I've been trying to reach those
people. I've been trying to reveal My love to that man. His mama
has been praying for him. I want you to know, I really appreciate
your attitude. When he tried to steal your coat and you gave him
that nice pair of shoes to go with it, that opened the door for Me to
move on his heart. Thank you!"

God's expression of appreciation doesn't stop with a pat on
the back, either. Jesus went on to tell us that if we'd walk in that
kind of love, the rewards of it would absolutely overflow in our
lives. He said:

Judge not, and ye shall not be judged: condemn not, and ye
shall not be condemned: forgive, and ye shall be forgiven:
Give, and it shall be given unto you; good measure, pressed

down, and shaken together, and running over, shall men give into your bosom. For with the same measure that ye mete withal it shall be measured to you again (verses 37-38).

When you get the revelation of this, you'll have the time of your life loving people who used to aggravate you to no end. You'll start praying for and BLESSING the person who cuts in front of you on the freeway instead of griping at him.

There was a fellow who was offended with me one day when I was riding my motorcycle. I pulled into the driveway of a service station and he drove up behind me and just started hollering at me. Red-faced and angry, he let me know at a high decibel what I did that upset him.

I smiled at him real big and said, "Yeah, but you'll forgive me, won't you?"

The first time I said it, he didn't even hear me. He just kept cursing at me. Well, I wasn't about to curse him back. There was a time when I would have. There was a time, years ago, when we probably would have been in a fistfight before we were through. But I know better now, so I just kept grinning and said again, "Yeah, but you'll forgive me, won't you?"

He kept hollering.

"Yeah, but you'll forgive me," I said. "Jesus has forgiven me and I sincerely apologize for upsetting you. That certainly wasn't my intention."

He kept on talking but the fellows who were in the car with him started laughing. One of them turned to him and said, "Why don't you shut up and listen to what the man is saying?"

"Come on," said another, "why don't you just forgive him like he's asking you to do?"

I had to chuckle at that. They were the friends of the man who was hollering at me, but they were on my side!

All the while, I was easing my motorcycle back out of the driveway, getting ready to go. Finally, the man said, "Oh, hell!"

"No...heaven!" I said. "Hallelujah! I forgive you, man. I love you and God loves you." Then I started my bike and rode down the highway, praising God with my BLESSING still intact, having sown the seed of God's love and forgiveness into the lives of that fellow and his friends, and believing the seed of The WORD never returns void. I was thanking God, He was thanking me; and we were both having a glorious time.

What a great way to live!

## Why Love Goes to War

When it comes to loving your enemies, one more thing must be said. God's command to love doesn't mean He never calls on Christians to go to war. He does. He not only calls some believers to military service, He anoints them to be a "minister of God…for good…. a revenger to execute wrath upon him that doeth evil."[191]

Shocking as it may sound, God believes in war. There comes a time in the course of human events when hateful, ungodly, murderous people oppress others to the point that local law enforcement can no longer handle it. At those times, the Prince of Peace becomes a man of war in order to put a stop to it.[192] He not only condones war under those conditions, He teaches His people how to fight;[193] and those who conduct war the way He says to do it will win.

Remember what happened when Chedorlaomer kidnapped Abraham's nephew, Lot? Abraham heard about it and came after him. He gathered up 318 of his trained, armed servants and defeated Ched's massive, mighty forces so completely that the Bible refers to it as a "slaughter." We saw in chapter 5 that it was THE BLESSING that taught Abraham's servants to fight like that. It was THE BLESSING in operation that taught them military tactics and strategies. They had operational technology that Ched's mob didn't have because God Himself taught them to war.

"But I thought THE BLESSING is all about love!" someone might say.

---

[191] Romans 13:4
[192] Exodus 15:3: "The LORD is a man of war: The LORD is his name."
[193] Psalm 144:1: "BLESSED be The LORD my strength, which teacheth my hands to war, and my fingers to fight."

It is, and love fights to protect its covenant partners.

The love of God in me, for example, would cause me to fight anyone who might try to hurt Gloria. I would love them but would do whatever necessary to protect her because I'm in covenant with her. I've promised before God to watch over her.

God loves everyone. He even loves terrorists like Osama bin Laden as much as He does you and me, but He's not in covenant with them. He is in covenant with us through the blood of Jesus, and because of it, He is responsible for our protection. If bin Laden would have accepted Jesus as his Lord and Savior, he could have enjoyed the same kind of covenant protection. He could have come into the family of God and been our brother. If he had, of course, he would have stopped acting as he had been acting and become a man of love instead of a terrorist.

Any believer who walks in God's military anointing, whether as a police officer, fireman, investigative officer or soldier, must learn to conduct himself in combat and stay in love at the same time. Those who go into combat and hate their enemy put themselves into a dangerous position because they're taking themselves out of the biblical exemption for killing.

"What?! There can't be a biblical exemption for killing. The Bible says, 'Thou shalt not kill!'"

No, it doesn't. It says in the Hebrew, "Thou shalt not murder."[194] It also says that if a man goes to war under God's direction, he is innocent of other men's blood that must be shed in battle.[195] He is not held responsible for it because he is acting as the servant of God. If he begins to hate the enemy, however, he takes himself out of that exemption. He becomes a killer, not a protector.

A Christian soldier must never do that. He must kill in times of war for only one reason: because wickedness and violence has run rampant among men, and it has to be stopped so people can live in

---

[194] James Strong, *The New Strong's Exhaustive Concordance of the Bible* (Nashville: Thomas Nelson Publishers, 1984) H7523.

[195] Numbers 32:20-22: "...if ye will go armed before The LORD to war, and will go all of you armed over Jordan before The LORD, until he hath driven out his enemies from before him, and the land be subdued before The LORD: then afterward ye shall return, and be guiltless before The LORD...."

peace. God will take care of the military men and women who are called to help with that task. According to the 91st Psalm, God's warriors (as well as those who serve under their authority) can walk in such divine protection that 11,000 can fall at their feet and they'll never be harmed. If they'll walk in love they'll become an army that cannot be defeated.

### Clean Out the Pipe and Get the Glory Flowing

To stay out of strife, we must learn not only to deal with enemies in love when they come against us, we must also learn to deal with our Christian brothers and sisters when they do us wrong. Jesus addressed that issue directly. Referring to our relationships with others who have confessed Him as Lord of their lives, He said:

> If thy brother shall trespass against thee, go and tell him his fault between thee and him alone: if he shall hear thee, thou hast gained thy brother. But if he will not hear thee, then take with thee one or two more, that in the mouth of two or three witnesses every word may be established. And if he shall neglect to hear them, tell it unto the church: but if he neglect to hear the church, let him be unto thee as an heathen man and a publican (Matthew 18:15-17).

In other words, if there's something amiss between you and another believer, you make the first move. Don't sit around waiting for him to apologize to you. It doesn't make any difference who's right and who's wrong. What matters is getting the problem solved so THE BLESSING can function freely on you and between you. If you go to him and he won't listen to you because he has a root of bitterness and won't let it go, then take another brother in The LORD with you. Do your best to make peace and put things right.

In a case where that doesn't work, then take it to the church. That doesn't mean get up in front of the congregation and tell the whole, miserable story. That's not what Jesus was talking about at all. Bring the situation to the pastor or the leader assigned to help with this kind of thing. Say, "I need your assistance with this. I've done what The WORD says, and I still can't get this issue resolved."

The pastor can then let the brother know that even though he is loved, the church can't afford to sit by and let this strife business interrupt the prayer agreement and THE BLESSING that comes on a body of unified believers. If the offended brother still insists on being in strife, then the church must relate to him differently. That doesn't mean he should be kicked out of the church. Jesus didn't say get rid of him altogether. He said, "Don't be in strife with him and get him out of your prayer life. Get that disagreement out of the way so it doesn't destroy the operations of THE BLESSING."

That's what strife in the Church does! It hinders the corporate BLESSING. If the devil can get us—not just as individuals but as a Body—to step off the love line and get into fighting with each other, he can get us over into his territory. He can have a heyday with us just as he does with the heathen, and get away with it. He can drag sickness into our midst, start siphoning off our finances, shut down our faith and contaminate the gifts of the Spirit to the point where, if they're functioning at all, it's at such a low level that they're totally ineffective.

It never occurs to some believers that love has anything to do with the manifestations of the gifts of the Spirit—or the lack of them. But the New Testament is clear about the connection. It says:

> Earnestly desire the best gifts. And yet I show you a more excellent way. Though I speak with the tongues of men and of angels, but have not love, I have become sounding brass or a clanging cymbal. And though I have the gift of prophecy, and understand all mysteries and all knowledge, and though I have all faith, so that I could remove mountains, but have not love, I am nothing. And though I bestow all my goods to feed the poor, and though I give my body to be burned, but have not love, it profits me nothing. Love suffers long and is kind; love does not envy; love does not parade itself, is not puffed up; does not behave rudely, does not seek its own, is

not provoked, thinks no evil; does not rejoice in iniquity, but rejoices in the truth; bears all things, believes all things, hopes all things, endures all things. Love never fails... (1 Corinthians 12:31-13:8, *New King James Version).*

Love and the gifts of the Spirit are tied together because the gifts are part of THE BLESSING. The more we walk in love, the more they will operate in our lives—not just when we're in church, but all the time. If we try to function in the gifts, however, with unrepented violations of the love commandment outstanding in our lives, our tongue-talking will be worthless. Our prophesying will be empty. Our giving will not cause us to prosper.

Why? Because none of those things work without the love of God. Love is the powerhouse. It never fails.

But whether there are prophecies, they will fail; whether there are tongues, they will cease; whether there is knowledge, it will vanish away. For we know in part and we prophesy in part. But when that which is perfect has come, then that which is in part will be done away (verses 8-10, *New King James Version).*

Religion has misinterpreted the last portion of that passage and taught people that we're in a new dispensation and don't really need prophecy anymore. But that's ridiculous! The Scripture says prophecy is for edification, exhortation and comfort. Obviously, we still need those things. So those verses must be saying something else.

Insert the phrase "in other words" and you'll see what it is. After telling us in verses 1-8 how the lack of love robs the gifts of their true power, and describing to us the behavior of love, the passage goes on to say: "In other words, if you try to prophesy without the love of God, your prophecy will fall useless to the ground. It will fail. Even if it's true, it won't help the people who hear it because there's no love manifest in it. There's no power there. It's just dead. Without love, you'll get to the point where you won't even bother speaking in tongues anymore. Tongues will cease. The gifts of the Spirit will just dry up and you won't have them anymore."

The LORD showed me exactly how that happens, one day when He was dealing with me about some things in my own life. It was about 20 years ago. I was preparing to preach at a meeting, sitting in the middle of the bed in my hotel room, praying and praising The LORD. I had my message all laid out. I knew what The LORD wanted me to minister that night.

Suddenly, I saw in my spirit as clearly as I've ever seen anything, a vision of a piece of pipe about 7 inches in diameter and 4 feet long. It was hanging in the air about an arm's length from me. A torrential flow that looked like water was coming into that pipe from one end, and I knew by the Spirit, it was the glory of God coming out of heaven.

The glory was gushing down, hitting the end of that pipe and splattering in every direction. Yet, coming out from the other end of the pipe was just a tiny stream that spewed out and hit me in the face. I felt like someone was shooting me in the nose with a squirt gun. It was irritating.

"Lord, what's happening here?" I asked.

*The pipe is dirty,* He said. *It's full of silt.*

Silt is very fine dirt that washes into a river or lake. It will suspend in the water and gradually sink to the bottom. Over a period of years, if you don't do something about it, it will fill up the lake and you'll end up with little more than a mudhole.

"What does the pipe represent?" I asked.

*It's your spirit,* He answered. *It's full of spiritual dirt that's slipped in there one grain at a time. It's become so plugged up that My glory can't flow through it.* (Although I didn't know it then, I know now that the glory of God represents THE BLESSING.)

Speechless, I sat there and stared at the pipe. "What kind of dirt is in there?" I asked.

*Unrepented violations of the law of love,* He answered. *You've paid no attention to them and they've built up over the years until they've finally clogged up your spirit. If you don't clean them out, your ministry and anointing will be in trouble. You'll also be in financial trouble because with all that junk in the way, I can't do for you what I want to do financially in your life and ministry.*

"Lord, what kind of violations are You talking about?" I asked. "Show me what I've done so I can repent of them!"

Something that had happened just the day before quickly flashed across my mind. It played out in front of me like a movie on a screen.

Gloria had come home with a paper bag full of cantaloupes she had bought from a street vendor. Pleased with her purchase, she set the bag on the table to show it to me. "This man had the nicest looking cantaloupes!" she said.

Sure enough, the top cantaloupe was beautiful, but as she pulled out the ones underneath, we saw that every one of them was rotten.

"Gloria, what kind of crook did you buy those from?" I asked.

"I don't know how he did that!" she said. "They didn't look like that when he put them in the sack!"

Fuming, I grabbed the bag of cantaloupes and headed for the door.

"Where are you going?" Gloria asked.

"I'm going to feed these rotten cantaloupes to the crook who sold them to you. I'll be back in a little bit either with some better cantaloupes or some of the hair from his head—one of the two!"

Throwing the bag in the car, I headed out to find the man. Of course, when I got to the place he'd been, he was gone, so I huffed all the way back home. I had to settle for taking my anger out on the cantaloupes. I pitched them all into the trash.

*Did you repent of that?* asked The LORD.

"No, Sir. I didn't."

*That's your problem. Your spirit is full of that kind of trash. You don't care enough about the commandment of love to do anything about it.*

That's when the word *commandment* struck me right between the eyes. I realized what a serious thing it is and started repenting right away. I told The LORD if He would bring to my mind everything I needed to repent about, I'd do it. By the time He was finished, I realized there were phone calls and apologies that would have to be made to people. There were notes of repentance that had to be written. I got the pipe cleaned out and, sure enough, the glory of God manifested in the meeting that night.

Things have been on the upswing ever since!

## Don't Drink the Poison

I want to be clear about this. When I say I repented, I don't mean I beat myself up and wallowed around in regret over what I'd done. I didn't bawl and squall and say, "Oh, Jesus, I'm so sorry. I'm such a dog. I'm just no good. I'm so unworthy." That's not repentance, it's self condemnation and doesn't do anyone any good. Not you. Not God. Not the person you've wronged. So, don't ever approach repentance that way.

Instead, follow the instructions God gave us in 1 John 1:9:

If we confess our sins, he is faithful and just to forgive us our sins, and to cleanse us from all unrighteousness.

Simply say, "Lord, I confess this sin to You in full confidence that as my Advocate and High Priest before the Father, You forgive me and cleanse me of all unrighteousness. I know You love me, Lord Jesus. I know my heavenly Father loves me and I believe that, right now, Your blood is washing me from the crown of my head to the soles of my feet. I will never claim that sin again. It's not mine anymore. It's gone, and I am forgiven."

You may still feel guilty. Your emotions may feel like a hammer was dropped on them. But don't be moved by that. Just believe The WORD. Command those symptoms of condemnation to leave you, and go on your way rejoicing in Jesus. Every time the thought of that sin comes back to you, put it down by faith. After a while, your consciousness and emotions will be purged of it. You'll find that faith in the truth of God's forgiveness has made you free.

Don't wait, like I did, until the silt starts to pile up in your spirit before you start repenting. The minute you step out of love, repent right then. Don't put it off until you can get away and take time to pray about it. Stop immediately and say, "God, forgive me. I repent. I refuse to go that way. I receive Your forgiveness and get right back on the path of love right now."

If you said or did something that affected another person, fix it right away. It doesn't make any difference what anyone says or thinks about you. That's beside the point. What's important is that you flush the poison out of your spirit, soul and body. Get rid of that spiritual toxin before it can go to work on you.

"Well, I don't mind repenting to someone for what I did wrong," you might say, "but it irritates me when people who've done me wrong won't do the same thing in return."

If you're going to walk in love, you'll have to get over that. You'll have to forgive those people whether they ask you to do so or not. Refusing to forgive is a breach of the command of love. It's also one of the most ignorant things you can do. Holding on to an offense against someone is like drinking poison and hoping it kills them. That's an insane thought, but apart from love, that's the way people think.

Exercising forgiveness, on the other hand, releases health and life. It's one of the most powerful things you can do to get the love and power of God flowing freely through you again. So take time often to do it.

Get off by yourself every once in a while and ask The LORD to remind you of anyone you need to forgive. Picture the person in your mind and purposely begin to think loving thoughts about him. Say, "Lord, I know You love that person just as much as You love me, so I'm exercising forgiveness over him. I'm changing my attitude toward him. Lord Jesus, I see You wrapping Your big, loving arms around him. I see You forgiving him and letting him know how much You love him. I don't care what he thinks about me. I'm just loving him through You."

If you see that person three or four days later and find the old, offended feelings rising up in you again, don't let that knock you off your stand of faith. Those feelings are just in your flesh, not your spirit. So take authority over them. Say, "No, I'm not yielding to that junk. I have forgiven that person in the Name of Jesus, and I love him."

Then, go out of your way to walk over there to him and say, "Hey, I love you, man!"

He may turn his back and walk away but that doesn't have anything to do with you. As long as you keep on forgiving and loving, you're strengthening the operation of THE BLESSING in your life. Good things start happening for you when you forgive, as a sacrifice, people who treat you badly. When they come around and you just smile and love on them and say, "BLESS you, brother!" you become more than a conqueror through Him who loves you.

The longer you live like that, the stronger the power of love and faith becomes in you. Eventually, it gets to the point where it's bigger than you can contain. It begins to flow out of you and control the atmosphere around you. Some people won't be able to stand it when you walk through the door. They'll grab your hand and say, "Pray for me! You convict me of my sin!"

That actually happened to me a few years ago. Gloria and I were invited to someone's house for dinner in a Midwest city where we were preaching a meeting. When we arrived, we met one of the other guests, the pastor of a large church, who had been openly critical of our ministry. I'd never met him, but knew he'd said some pretty rough things about us.

Instead of letting it bother me, I just loved him and was nice to him. I didn't necessarily feel any gushy emotional warmth for him, I just operated in the love of God toward him by faith. (I figured that was better than kicking his shins under the table!) During the dinner conversation, he said some things that had barbs on them, but I didn't let them get to me. I just let them pass.

When the evening was over, the six of us—our hosts, the pastor and his wife, and Gloria and I—were walking to the door, getting ready to leave when, suddenly, the pastor literally dropped to the floor on his knees. He grabbed my hand, put it on his head and said, "Pray for me, man! I have tried to build my church with hard work instead of prayer, and I am dried up spiritually."

I no more expected him to do that than I expected to fly to the moon. But the love of God got to him, and when that happens, you find out how lovely people really are. In his case, it became clear that he was a good man who'd just been under a lot of pressure. The bigger his church had grown, the heavier his load had become because he was trying to manage it with natural strength. When he realized that, he was so eager to straighten things out that he was willing to ask for prayer from the very person he'd once criticized.

Love never fails! If you'll put it to work by faith, it will produce marvelous things.

One word of caution, though. Don't ever try to use love on someone in an effort to change them. Changing them is not your job. The LORD made that clear to me in a way I'll never forget one night when I made the mistake of griping to myself about something Gloria said. I'd just arrived home from a long series of meetings and was really tired. She was in another room and yelled something to me. Rather than getting up and going in there to see what she wanted, I mumbled to myself, "Oh, she doesn't care anything about me, anyway."

I didn't say it loud enough for her to hear me, but The LORD heard and He jerked the slack out of me. He said, *It's none of your business whether she cares about you or not. It's none of your business whether anyone cares about you or not. It's your business to care about them.*

"Yes, Sir," I answered. "You'll never have to talk to me about that again."

I learned right then I had no business trying to change other people. If they need to change, that's between them and God. Don't waste your time praying, "Oh Lord, change my husband!" Or, "Change my wife." Just stay busy doing what God has commanded *you* to do. Occupy yourself with loving them.

It's amazing what happens when you do that. Your perspective starts to shift. It doesn't take months and years, either. It happens more quickly than you would expect. Suddenly, what other people think of you doesn't mean anything to you anymore. You're so wrapped up in the love of God, so thrilled over the fact that He loves you just as much as He loves Jesus, and so busy expressing His love to others, nothing else makes any difference.

The power of love catches you up out of the muck of the world that's driving everyone else, and elevates you to a higher place. It lifts you up so you can begin to minister to those who are truly suffering. Before long, love is flowing through you in such measure that you're always looking for someone to BLESS. Instead of thinking about what others can do for you, you'll be saying, "Hey, man. Is there any way I can help you? Is there anything I can do for you?"

Before I was born again, that kind of thinking was the furthest thing from my mind. Love was totally opposite to my natural lifestyle. I was mad at everyone in the whole world except Gloria. So, not long after I got saved, The LORD had to set me straight on that score. One day when I was praying and fellowshiping with Him, He said, *Kenneth, I love you but I don't like you very much.*

"Why, Lord?" I asked.

*You do and say things that are crosswise of My desires. When you get irritated and snap at people, I can't join in on that. I can't be a part of it. I have to withdraw from a part of your life and I don't like being locked out of any part of your life. I want to be part of the whole thing. I want to BLESS everything you do, everything you say, and everywhere you go. I will manifest Myself at all times, if you'll learn to walk in love.*

After more than 40 years now, I can tell you He has kept that promise. The more I've learned to walk in love, the more He has manifested Himself in my life—everywhere, all the time. My life today is better than I ever dreamed it could be—all because of love.

## Stir Up Your Mind to Remember

"But Brother Copeland, I come from a rough background. I just don't think I have the capacity to walk in that kind of love."

Yes, you do! As a born-again child of God, you've been born of the Spirit of Compassion. You have been re-created in the likeness of Love Himself. You're not just an old, forgiven sinner. You're a new species of being. Your old background has passed away, and all things have become new. Everything in you is made of love. All God's mercy, goodness, kindness, love, joy, peace and meekness have been invested into your spirit.

You have the same capacity to love that God has because His own love has been shed abroad in your heart by the Holy Ghost. What you must do is activate that capacity by making love the priority of your life. You must decide that, first and foremost, you are a keeper of the commandment of love.

You may be a husband, wife, father or mother. You may be a preacher or a businessman. As important as those roles are in your life, job No. 1 is to watch over that command and guard it. Keep it in your mouth, your eyes and your ears. Keep it ever before your face so you can be the husband, wife, father, mother, preacher or businessman you should be before God.

It's surprising, but most people in the Body of Christ don't do that. I used to wonder why. I knew it couldn't be because they don't know about it. You can ask a thousand born-again Christians anywhere, at any time of the day if we're supposed to love one another, and every one will say, "Yes." Not one will say, "I don't know. I've never heard anything about that."

God's command of love is so basic, everyone knows it. Yet, the vast majority of Christians do not practice it. We are not famous for the way we love each other. We are known for our squabbles. Why is that?

It's because we don't keep love in the forefront of our thinking. We forget about it!

The LORD knew that was going to be a problem for us. That's

why He inspired the Apostle Peter to write:

> This second epistle, beloved, I now write unto you; in both which I stir up your pure minds by way of remembrance: that ye may be mindful of the words which were spoken before by the holy prophets, and of the commandment of us the apostles of The LORD and Saviour (2 Peter 3:1-2).

All too often, we let the Savior's love command slip simply because we haven't ingrained it into our memories. How do we change that? By surrounding ourselves with reminders of that command. By thinking about it first thing in the morning and all day long. By confessing scriptures like those in 1 Corinthians 13 and saying:

> The love of God is in me so I am patient and kind. The love of God is in me so I do not envy and I'm not puffed up. The love of God is in me so I don't behave rudely or selfishly. The love of God is in me so I am not provoked and I think no evil. By the love of God that abides in me, I bear all things, believe all things, hope all things, endure all things. God's love in me never fails.

If you're committed to keeping the command of love, you should be making those kinds of confessions all the time. Drive down the street with one hand on the steering wheel and the other pointed at heaven saying, "I love my neighbor as myself because that's pleasing to my Father. He loves me as much as He loves Jesus, and I walk in the power of His love." Then, if someone pulls out in front of you, you won't hit the horn and try to blow their back tires out—and then have to repent for it later. You'll respond in love instead of offense. You'll say, "Oh God, BLESS that person," because you're already in motion. You're already a BLESSING going somewhere to happen.

When love becomes ingrained in you like that, you'll be able to walk in it in any circumstance. No matter what kind of meanness or aggravation you encounter, you'll be able to take authority over your flesh and your mind, and operate by your spirit in the love of God.

To maintain that kind of spiritual strength, however, you must spend time with The LORD. Spend time in His WORD and keep yourself filled with it. One church service a week will not do it. Your fellowship with The LORD must be a daily thing because some days, your flesh will get up on the wrong side of the bed. It won't want to love anyone or anything. You'll feel like you've been pulled under the door—lowdown, doggy, depressed, down and out.

The best way I know to overcome those feelings is by ministering to The LORD. First thing every morning, tell Him how much you love Him. Tell Him how much you appreciate His love for you and how thrilled you are about all He has done in your life. Let Him know you're not only willing but eager to do His will all day long. Follow the instructions in Ephesians 5:19-20:

> Speaking to yourselves in psalms and hymns and spiritual songs, singing and making melody in your heart to The LORD; giving thanks always for all things unto God and the Father in the name of our Lord Jesus Christ.

That will prime your pump and get the love flowing. Then you'll be ready to go out and release it to others by "speaking the truth in love."[196] You'll be ready to do what the Bible says to do:

> Let all bitterness, and wrath, and anger, and clamour, and evil speaking, be put away from you, with all malice: And be ye kind one to another, tenderhearted, forgiving one another, even as God for Christ's sake hath forgiven you. Be ye therefore followers of God, as dear children; and walk in love, as Christ also hath loved us, and hath given himself for us an offering and a sacrifice to God for a sweetsmelling savour (Ephesians 4:31-5:2).

---

[196] Ephesians 4:15

## Live Where the Wicked One Can't Touch You

When you live like that, THE BLESSING is continually working for you. You don't have to strive and sweat to make things turn out for yourself. You don't have to worry about a thing. All you have to do is keep the command of love and stand on the covenant. Love, believe, obey…and you'll be BLESSED.

Through the years, I've learned to live that way more and more. When God says, "Give," I give. When He says, "Go," I go. He's the Boss. I do what He says, and I expect to be BLESSED at every turn. I expect to be BLESSED when I leave, and I expect to be BLESSED on the way back. It doesn't matter whether people treat me right or not. I'm BLESSED wherever I go.

I don't mind telling you, I enjoy it. But the best part of it all is the more established I become in love, the better I comprehend my heavenly Father and the more I understand His heart, purposes and plans.

"Brother Copeland, no one can really understand God! He's beyond comprehension."

That's not what the Bible says. It tells us we *can* comprehend Him if we become rooted and grounded in love. In fact, the Apostle Paul prayed that the Church would do that very thing:

> For this cause I bow my knees unto the Father of our Lord Jesus Christ, of whom the whole family in heaven and earth is named, that he would grant you, according to the riches of his glory, to be strengthened with might by his Spirit in the inner man; that Christ may dwell in your hearts by faith; that ye, being rooted and grounded in love, may be able to comprehend with all saints what is the breadth, and length, and depth, and height; and to know the love of Christ, which passeth knowledge, that ye might be filled with all the fulness of God (Ephesians 3:14-19).

Comprehension is greater than understanding. To comprehend

is to have a working knowledge of something. You can understand, for example, that if you buy a ticket and get on an airplane, it will take you somewhere. But that understanding doesn't qualify you to fly the plane. To do that, you must be a trained pilot with a higher level of comprehension of principles and laws of flight, and a working knowledge of the airplane that qualifies you on an entirely different level.

That's what walking in love does for us as believers. It takes us to a higher level of comprehension in God. It gives us a working knowledge of who He is and how He operates, so instead of being bound to the beggarly elements of this natural realm, we can soar with Him. It lifts us to the place where we are so wrapped up in His love and light and so free from fear that the wicked one touches us not.[197]

That's what happened to the Apostles John and Paul. They got to the point where they were so far beyond the devil's reach, no one could kill them without their permission.

"I thought Paul was beheaded!"

Yes, but not before he said, "I am ready to be offered." He laid down his life on purpose. He had finished his race and chose martyrdom because he wanted a higher class of resurrection. Study it out for yourself. Paul had already whipped death at every turn. He'd been delivered out of shipwrecks and dungeons and all kinds of other perilous situations. He'd even been stoned to death once. But God brought him back to life and he got up, dusted himself off and went back to work.[198]

The Apostle John had the same kind of testimony. His opponents tried every way you can imagine to kill him. History tells us they boiled him in oil and he still wouldn't die. So they threw him away. They took him out to the Isle of Patmos, hoping to shut him up, and he wrote the book of Revelation while he was there.

Another early disciple who walked in that kind of death-defying

---

love was Stephen. He had such a revelation of it that while people were stoning him, he said, "Lord, forgive them. Don't charge them with this sin."

Most people think the stoning killed Stephen, but they're mistaken. While they were stoning him the heavens opened up, he saw Jesus standing at the right hand of Almighty God ready to receive him, and he "fell asleep."[199] Jesus withdrew him from his body while they were throwing rocks at him. He said, "Come on home, boy!" and Stephen popped out of his body. He went to be with The LORD, and his flesh just fell down dead. They didn't kill him with the rocks. You can't kill a man who is already dead.

The place where the wicked one touches us not—that's where THE BLESSING is taking us! We may not be there yet, but we're on the way. With every step of love we take, we're getting closer, and THE BLESSING is overtaking us more and more.

What happens as it overtakes us? It begins to change things in our lives into a replica of the Garden of Eden. It turns sickness into health and poverty into wealth. All THE BLESSINGS of God come on us, and we begin to have "days of heaven upon the earth."[200]

The farther down THE BLESSING road we go together, the wilder and more glorious it will be. I know because I've seen what happens when believers walk that road with one another. It beats all you've ever seen.

A few years ago, for example, a fellow believer came to Gloria and me and asked if he could buy a small, single-engine airplane we owned. "How much do you want for it?" he asked. When I told him the price, he said, "I don't want to pay that for it."

Of course, that was no surprise. I'd heard that before and so have you.

But then things took a different turn. He did something no one had ever done to me before. He upped the price $15,000!

"No," I said. "That's too much."

"Well, that's my deal," he answered. "That's what I want to pay."

---

[199] Acts 7:60
[200] Deuteronomy 11:21

After we argued about it awhile, I had to laugh. It was the wildest conversation I'd ever heard! But here's the explanation: We both understand and operate in THE BLESSING. I was trying to BLESS him by selling him the plane for less than I would normally ask for it. He was trying to BLESS me by paying more for it than I wanted. "The rest of the world would never believe this conversation," I said.

In the end, he won. I let him pay me the extra money. That was a few years ago, and today he is flying a jet worth far more than that little plane he first bought from Gloria and me—and it is fully paid for by THE BLESSING.

There is nothing the world has to offer that even compares with this kind of living. I not only have The WORD of God, but four decades of personal experience to prove it. Gloria and I have lived in THE BLESSING so long now, we absolutely trust it. We don't let things rattle us anymore and you shouldn't either. Whatever comes against us—whether it's pain in our bodies, someone talking ugly about us, or anything else—we just keep walking in love and trusting THE BLESSING.

We don't do it just when we're preaching. We do it in the ordinary events of life, and it's fun!

We were on a motorcycle trip one time, stopped in at a restaurant, and got stuck with the meanest waitress you've ever seen. We'd been looking forward to eating there, but could see right away that she was going to do all she could to hinder our enjoyment. She was storming around, getting irritated because one of us didn't want ice in our water, and other minor things.

I gave her a little while to settle down but when she didn't, I said, "Hey, you've had a hard day today, haven't you?"

That's all it took. She unloaded the whole story on me. She told me what her sister-in-law had done…and that they were about to have a wedding…and how everything was going wrong. The whole time she was talking, I was praying for her in the spirit. (I wasn't listening to what she was saying. Her story would have upset me, too! So I just let it go in one ear and out the other.)

When she finished her story, I grabbed her by the hand and said, "Let's pray."

"Uh...OK...I guess that would be all right," she answered.

Our whole group prayed with her and after that she got happy. She practically danced around the table waiting on everyone. She forgot about her sister-in-law and when we left, she heartily thanked us and told us to be sure and come back.

That's what we as believers are called to do. We're called to walk in love—in big ways and small—and take THE BLESSING wherever we go. We're called to bring the conditions of Eden into our homes and workplaces, into restaurants and neighborhoods. It's not hard to do because through Jesus THE BLESSING is already on us. It's in every cell of our bodies and every step we take. It is with us, in us and flowing through us.

The more we love God and love other people, the more it will work. If we stay with it, it will spread...and spread...and spread, until it affects the whole world. People will come in to the kingdom of God because of THE BLESSING coming out of us.

That's when we'll truly be living the good life because that's what we were born to do.

# Chapter 15

# Come Sit With Me

But God, who is rich in mercy, for his great love wherewith he loved
us, even when we were dead in sins, hath quickened us together with
Christ, (by grace ye are saved;) and hath raised us up together, and
made us sit together in heavenly *places in Christ Jesus.*
Ephesians 2:4-6

When I was a little boy, it seemed I was always getting into some kind of trouble. Mama usually caught me at it and made me regret it by giving me the most dreaded warning of my young life: "You just wait until your daddy gets home."

I felt like my whole world turned upside down when she said that because I lived looking forward to my dad's homecomings. His business kept him traveling most weekdays so he was gone the majority of the time. He came back on Friday afternoons, and that was a happy day for me…unless I knew that the first thing he'd hear from Mama was what I'd done wrong.

Even then, however, my dad had a reassuring way about him. Instead of jumping on me, he'd just say, "Come on over here, boy. Sit down here next to your daddy." I'd ease up next to him and he'd put his big arm around me. "Son, everything is going to be all right," he'd say. "We're going to work through this thing. Daddy is going to help you, now."

At those words, my world would turn right side up again.

Not long ago, during a time of prayer, I heard those same words in my spirit. I had run to the throne of grace to find help in a time of turmoil and very plainly heard my Lord and Savior say, *Come on up here, Kenneth, and sit down here on the throne with Me. Everything is going to be all right. My angels are at work on your behalf. My power is in operation. THE BLESSING is working for you, Son. So just sit down here and rest. Everything is in good shape.*

That's what The LORD would say to all His children in every situation if we'd just draw near and settle down long enough to hear Him. But all too often, we haven't done it. We've paced the floor instead, worrying about seemingly insurmountable problems. We've tossed and turned all night wondering what we're going to do. We've run in circles until we're exhausted, trying—and failing—to find the solution.

If we would pay attention to what The WORD says, however, we'd never have to do those things again. We would do something entirely different when problems arose and troubles threatened to overwhelm us. We would do something scriptural—something that would actually do some good.

We would simply sit down.

*Sit down.* Amazing as it seems, that is exactly what God has instructed us as born-again believers to do. He has issued us an invitation that enables us to triumph over every test and trial the devil sends our way. He has said to us: "Sit thou at my right hand, until I make thine enemies thy footstool."[201]

"But Brother Copeland, I thought God said that to Jesus."

He did. But it applies to us just as surely as it does to our resurrected Lord Himself because Jesus isn't sitting alone at God's right hand. We are seated there with Him. It's astounding, but true. God has not only quickened us together with Jesus, He has raised us up and made us sit together in heavenly places with Him!

No one sits in the presence of Almighty God except His family.

---

[201] Psalm 110:1

Angels don't come into the throne room and sit down. They're not allowed to sit, but we are. We have been invited by The LORD Himself to "come boldly unto the throne of grace, that we may obtain mercy, and find grace to help in time of need."[202] We have been given the scriptural right not just to come before that throne but to sit down on it with Him. We are the overcomers[203] about whom Jesus said, "To him that overcometh will I grant to sit with me in my throne, even as I also overcame, and am set down with my Father in his throne."[204]

Why then, do so many believers grovel on the throne-room floor instead? Why do they approach God like beggars and plead for help, or struggle in their own strength to work things out?

It's because the idea of sitting down and trusting God to take care of them seems presumptuous and irresponsible. "I can't just ignore this mess," they say. "It would be asking too much to expect God to take care of everything for me. Surely, God expects me to do something!"

They don't realize that what God expects us to do is sit down and enter His rest, and He is grieved when we don't do it. The book of Hebrews makes that very clear. It says:

> Wherefore (as the Holy Ghost saith, Today if ye will hear his voice, harden not your heart, as in the provocation, in the day of temptation in the wilderness: when your fathers tempted me, proved me, and saw my works forty years. Wherefore I was grieved with that generation, and said, They do always err in their hearts; and they have not known my ways. So I sware in my wrath, They shall not enter into my rest (Hebrews 3:7-11).

Was God grieved with the Israelites because they expected too much from Him? Was He put out with them because instead

---

[202] Hebrews 4:16
[203] 1 John 5:5: "Who is he that overcometh the world, but he that believeth that Jesus is the Son of God?"
[204] Revelation 3:21

of worrying and working hard trying to meet their own needs and fight their own battles, they expected Him to take care of them? Was He aggravated because they wanted too much land?

No. He was grieved because they wouldn't take what He offered. He offered them a life of divine rest in the Promised Land and they kept saying, "We can't do it. There are big giants in that land. We're just little grasshoppers. They'll wipe us out!"

The Israelites hadn't even seen those giants. They'd just believed the bad report the unbelieving spies brought back. God had already said, "I've given you the land." That should have been enough for them. They should have been able to rest in God's promise—giants or no giants. But they hardened their hearts. They refused to believe THE BLESSING of God was powerful enough to give them victory, so they died in the wilderness.

We can learn a valuable lesson from their mistake because God is saying the same thing to us today. He is saying, "You're BLESSED! Rest in that fact and step into the land of victory I have promised you." He is saying:

> Take heed, brethren, lest there be in any of you an evil heart of unbelief, in departing from the living God. But exhort one another daily, while it is called Today; lest any of you be hardened through the deceitfulness of sin. For we are made partakers of Christ, if we hold the beginning of our confidence stedfast unto the end; while it is said, Today if ye will hear his voice, harden not your hearts, as in the provocation. For some, when they had heard, did provoke: howbeit not all that came out of Egypt by Moses. But with whom was he grieved forty years? was it not with them that had sinned, whose carcases fell in the wilderness? And to whom sware he that they should not enter into his rest, but to them that believed not? So we see that they could not enter in because of unbelief (verses 12-19).

The kind of unbelief that keeps us out of God's rest creeps up on us through fear-filled, religious words like, "Sometimes God answers prayer, and sometimes He doesn't. You just never know what God is going to do."

That kind of junk doesn't come from the Bible! It comes from people who put more faith in their experiences than in God's WORD. They have failed for some reason to lay hold of His promises in their own lives and, like the Israelite spies, bring back bad reports to discourage the hearts of other people.

If you believe those reports, you're doing the same thing the wilderness-wandering Israelites did—hardening your heart in unbelief. I realize that's not what you mean to do, but you're doing it whether you mean to or not if you don't believe what God says. You're letting unbelief stop you from entering your promised land, and in the eyes of God that's sin.

### Sit Down. The WORD Has Us Covered.

Hebrews 4 warns us not to do that:

Let us therefore fear, lest, a promise being left us of entering into his rest, any of you should seem to come short of it. For unto us was the gospel preached, as well as unto them: but The WORD preached did not profit them, not being mixed with faith in them that heard it. For we which have believed do enter into rest, as he said, As I have sworn in my wrath, if they shall enter into my rest: although the works were finished from the foundation of the world. For he spake in a certain place of the seventh day on this wise, And God did rest the seventh day from all his works. And in this place again, If they shall enter into my rest. Seeing therefore it remaineth that some must enter therein, and they to whom it was first preached entered not in because of unbelief: Again, he limiteth a certain day, saying in David, Today, after so long a time; as it is said, Today if ye will hear his voice, harden not your hearts. For if Jesus had given them rest, then would he not afterward have spoken of another day. There remaineth therefore a rest to the people of God. For he that is entered into his rest, he also hath ceased from his own works, as God did from his. Let us labour therefore to enter into that rest, lest any man fall after the same example of unbelief. For The WORD of God is quick, and powerful, and sharper than any twoedged sword... (1-12).

*Believe God and enter His rest.* Even in the midst of the most dire circumstances, those are God's instructions to us. Even when we're facing our own personal giants, He wants us to cease from our own works, stop running in circles, do what He did on the seventh day of Creation and trust THE BLESSING to take care of things for us. He wants us to get up there, right next to Jesus...and sit down.

How is such a thing possible?

Look again at the last verse of the passage above. It says we can do it FOR (or because) The WORD of God is...

quick, and powerful, and sharper than any twoedged sword, piercing even to the dividing asunder of soul and spirit, and of the joints and marrow, and is a discerner of the thoughts and intents of the heart. Neither is there any creature that is not manifest in his sight: but all things are naked and opened unto the eyes of him with whom we have to do (verses 12-13).

We can sit down because no matter what kind of situation we're facing, no matter how dangerous and confusing it might appear, God's WORD covers it, sees through it and will reveal the answer to its defeat. The living WORD of God will penetrate the darkest difficulties and shed light on the most impossible situations.

We can sit down and relax next to Jesus with The Book of His wisdom in our laps, knowing that everything is open and clear to Him. It doesn't matter if there is war on every side, or everyone is talking doom and gloom, and there's trouble all around us. It doesn't matter if we've just lost our jobs and the economy has gone belly up. We can sit down and shout, "Hallelujah! The WORD has me covered. Everything is going to be all right!"

## Sit Down. God's Wisdom Is on the Way.

"But, what if my situation requires me to take action?" you may ask. "How can I sit down and rest in faith when I don't know what to do?"

Follow the instructions in James 1:2-6. Instead of agonizing over the situation,

> Count it all joy when ye fall into divers temptations; knowing this, that the trying of your faith worketh patience. But let patience have her perfect work, that ye may be perfect and entire, wanting nothing. If any of you lack wisdom, let him ask of God, that giveth to all men liberally, and upbraideth not; and it shall be given him. But let him ask in faith, nothing wavering. For he that wavereth is like a wave of the sea driven with the wind and tossed.

If you knew what to do, it wouldn't be a trial. So count it all joy and sit down in God's rest, believing His wisdom is on the way. Stop wearing yourself out, wracking your brain hour after hour, searching every nook and cranny for the answer.

We need to get off the hamster wheel of human reasoning and stop asking *ourselves* what we should do. Instead, we need to start asking God. He will always tell us if we ask in faith and show us what to do in every test and trial—even those we brought on ourselves by our own foolishness.

The devil, of course, will tell us otherwise. He'll say, "Yeah, you fouled this thing up, and now you'll have to fix it before God will have anything to do with you." But when he tries to pawn that junk off on us, we can just show him the door. We can say, "Get out of my house, you liar! If God withheld His wisdom from us because of our faults, none of us would ever have our faults corrected. God didn't cause this mess I'm in, but He is more than willing to teach me how to get out of it. So, Devil, you just move on down the road. I'm going to sit down here with Jesus and rest in faith because His wisdom is on the way."

Once you say that, stick with it by faith. Don't waver. Don't be double-minded, praying one minute and worrying the next. God can't get anything to us when we're acting that way. So just stay steady. Refuse to be upset. Release patience and keep sitting in peace next to The LORD, expecting to come through this trial perfect and whole, lacking nothing. If the answer you need doesn't come right away, don't get nervous about it. Just keep reminding yourself that Jesus said in John 16:13:

> Howbeit when he, the Spirit of truth, is come, he will guide you into all truth: for he shall not speak of himself; but whatsoever he shall hear, that shall he speak: and he will show you things to come.

Notice, that verse doesn't say the Holy Spirit *might* guide us into all truth, it says, He *will*.

October 8, 2008, during a time of fellowship with The LORD, I was reading that scripture and the words *He will* seemed to jump off the page and attach themselves to my heart. As they did, the word of The LORD came to me. He said: *I am your Lord and I am your Savior; and I am responsible for you before Almighty God like I am the rest of My Body. I am responsible for the daily welfare of anyone who has come to Me and made Me Lord.*

Although I already knew that, I appreciated Him reminding me of it. It's always good to have the assurance that Jesus is taking care of us. But, it's especially thrilling when the whole world is wringing its hands, worrying about going bankrupt. And on that particular morning that's exactly what was about to happen. The stock market was about to take a nose dive. Banks were starting to fail. This world's economy was starting to crumble in a massive way. All the world's "wise men" would soon be saying, "We don't know what to do."

The LORD was getting me ready for that. He didn't want me chiming in with them. He wanted me to be listening, getting my instructions from Him about how to handle what was coming. So, after reminding me that He was responsible for my daily welfare, He directed me back to John 16:13 and the issue of the Holy Spirit's communication with us.

*The Holy Spirit does not have a hearing problem,* He said. *I am speaking all the time, every day.... I speak The WORD. The Holy Spirit hears it. He speaks to you and you're too busy. You don't hear what I'm saying about half the time.*

I don't mind telling you, when I heard that, I jumped up and repented. "Forgive me, Lord," I said. "I'm opening my ears to You, now!"

As The LORD continued speaking to me, He told me some things that were coming and gave me instructions about how to get through them safe and sound. He let me know that the sand under the foundation of the world's economy had given way. Politicians were going to throw more sand at it to try to get it built up, but it wouldn't do any good because it was bloated and coming down. He said:

> *Don't pay attention to or make any plans based on what the media says or what the politicians say. Stand on My WORD in John 16. I will lead you. I will tell you. I will show you what's to come. All that the Father has is Mine, and I'll give it all to you....*

> *Pay attention to Me. I will lead you through troubled times. I already have THE plan for you and it's very good. Follow it. It will not only get you through, it will place you in a very high place—a rich place—a strong place of victory.*

*You will have to discipline yourself and be diligent to listen to Me. All the other voices will have a plan, a word, an idea for your future and security. Don't listen to Babylon's system. It has fallen apart. My system is stronger than ever. My kingdom is flourishing, and THE BLESSING is the place to be.*

*Keep your eyes on My WORD. Listen to it. It will guide you, and I will perform it. Love Me. Love My people as I have loved you.... Love never fails, and neither does My plan.*

That's not just The LORD'S word to me. It's what He promised in the Bible to all of us, and we can rest on that promise.

"But Brother Copeland," you might say, "what should I do if I'm in a mess and having trouble getting my ears open enough to hear God's voice?"

I can tell you what Gloria and I do in such situations. We take some time, separate ourselves from the normal activities of life, and spend a few days praying about whatever it is we're facing. Sometimes we do it together. Sometimes we do it by ourselves. But we always do it in faith, believing that what Jesus said is true: His sheep hear His voice.[205]

During those seasons of prayer, we set aside our other prayer responsibilities and just fellowship with God over that one specific situation for two or three days. We usually spend a lot of time praying in the spirit because we don't know what to pray about it with our understanding. We need to draw wisdom up from our spirits so we say, "I receive the wisdom of God in this situation..." and then start praying in the Holy Ghost.

I learned how to do that in 1967 while I was a student at Oral Roberts University, and I've been doing it ever since. I've done it over some very serious matters—matters of health, finance, ministry, children and family—and I've never had to pray more than three days to get the answer I needed. Sometimes I've gotten it late

---

[205] John 10:2-4

on the second day, but always by the third day, I will have received the wisdom of The LORD, and I'll be rejoicing and thanking Him for it. From that point on, I'll know what I am supposed to do and say; and it will be a joy to watch God work things out.

## Sit Down and Shed the Cares of This World

I'm not saying that I'm never tempted to worry about the situation again. Particularly if it takes awhile for it to be resolved, there will be times when the devil ratchets up the pressure and tries to push me into fear. But that is not the time to slide off the throne of grace onto the floor and start wailing to God about how bad things are.

It's fine to pray in faith about the situation. It's good to speak The WORD and fellowship with The LORD about it by praying in the spirit. But I've learned, and so should you, that it's not OK to wring your hands, become anxious and abandon the rest of God. Once you've sat down next to Jesus believing The WORD has you covered, you must keep your heavenly seat and obey the instructions He gave us in John 14:1 and 27: "Let not your heart be troubled: ye believe in God, believe also in me.... Peace I leave with you, my peace I give unto you: not as the world giveth, give I unto you. Let not your heart be troubled, neither let it be afraid."

"But you just don't understand what I'm going through!"

That may be true, but I do understand this: Jesus gave us His own peace, and He expects us to use it. He told us not to be troubled or afraid and that means we can do it—in any situation. So, the best thing we can do is stop arguing with Him, and start obeying Him. No matter how riled up our emotions might be, we can get ourselves by the ear and say, "Mouth, you stop contradicting The WORD. Heart, you settle down and receive by faith the peace Jesus has given you. Mind, quit meditating on the circumstances, and start meditating on the truth of God's WORD. I refuse to let myself be troubled. I'm going to be peaceful because Jesus told me to, and I'm going to obey Him."

You may feel awful the whole time you're saying it. You may feel agitated and torn up inside, but we don't base our lives on our feelings. We base them on faith in the eternal WORD of God. So overrule your feelings. Take your place in the rest of God, and notify the devil that he will not come in and disturb you. You are in the secret place of the Most High God, in His throne room behind closed doors.

If you'll do that, the peace of Jesus will immediately go to work on you. Before you know it, all that inner turmoil will just drain out. The agitation that seemed as if it would never leave will evaporate and soon, you'll be standing there with a big smile on your face, giving glory to God. I know because it's happened to me more times than I can count. I'll give one big rip-roaring shout of praise to God and the knot that had threatened to put a permanent kink in my belly will be gone in an instant. I'm left shouting hallelujah and wondering what I was so upset about, anyway!

First Peter 5:5-9 gives us the key to experiencing that kind of breakthrough:

> Be clothed with humility: for God resisteth the proud, and giveth grace to the humble. Humble yourselves therefore under the mighty hand of God, that he may exalt you in due time: casting all your care upon him; for he careth for you. Be sober, be vigilant; because your adversary the devil, as a roaring lion, walketh about, seeking whom he may devour: whom resist stedfast in the faith, knowing that the same afflictions are accomplished in your brethren that are in the world.

Has it ever occurred to you that when we worry about things, we actually put ourselves in opposition to God? We step into a place of pride where we're trying to be our own source and acting like everything depends on us. When we find ourselves in that position, we must change our attitudes and clothe ourselves with humility.

Clothing yourself is a purposeful thing. It doesn't happen automatically. When you get up in the morning, your clothes don't run out of the closet and jump on you. You have to make a decision about what to wear. Then, you must take action, and put the clothes on.

The same is true when it comes to casting your cares on The LORD. You must decide to do it, and then act on that decision. You must shed the cares of this world on purpose, and give them to Jesus. Then, you must leave them in His hands by bringing into captivity every thought to the obedience of Christ.

That isn't always easy, but you can do it if you'll just remember that when you give your cares to Jesus, He receives them. When you put the situation that has concerned you into His hands and say to Him, "Lord, will You take care of this for me?" He says, "Of course I will"![206]

One day, when I was rolling the care of a particular situation over on The LORD, He said it to me this way, *Kenneth, I will take care of it. I will be your Caretaker.* He pointed out to me that if I were to hire someone to be the caretaker of a nice piece of property, landscaped with fine gardens and hedges, I wouldn't hire just anyone with a mower who knows nothing about gardening. I'd find someone trained and equipped to handle the job. I'd go looking for a caretaker who could tend to that property better than I ever could. Once I found him, I'd stop worrying about it and leave the property in his hands.

That's what we do with Jesus. We let Him be our Caretaker because He is well able to do the job. Then we relax and enter into His rest.

"Oh, Brother Copeland, I couldn't possibly relax right now! My family is facing a financial crisis that could absolutely ruin us. It would be irresponsible for me not to be upset about it."

As long as you take that attitude, you're trying to be your own god, and you don't qualify for that position. You're supposed to

---

[206] Luke 5:13, *The Living Bible*

be at peace. You're supposed to have a heart that's not troubled. You're supposed to be free of care because the cares of this world will choke your faith, and without faith it's impossible for you to receive anything from The LORD. Jesus went to great lengths to teach us that in the parable of the sower. He said:

> Now these are the ones sown among thorns; they are the ones who hear The WORD, and the cares of this world, the deceitfulness of riches, and the desires for other things entering in choke The WORD, and it becomes unfruitful (Mark 4:18-19, *New King James Version).*

According to Jesus, cares are spiritual thorns. They can be overwhelming mental burdens and exhausting emotional affairs— or worry. If we let them into our hearts, they'll choke The WORD and make it unfruitful in our lives. I found that out one time when our ministry fell $6 million behind on the television bill. I let the care of that debt get to me. It upset me to think that I was believing God all the time to be debt free and I owed $6 million.

The more I fretted about it, the bigger the debt grew. The pressure of it became so intense that I went to The LORD and said, "I'm going to start selling off the ministry property to get out from under this."

*Really?* He answered. *What are you going to sell next month?*

I knew He was right. That wasn't the answer to the situation. I was just shooting off my big mouth.

Months passed as the situation kept dragging on and I kept on fuming about it. Finally, I found myself facing a board meeting where I'd have to tell the trustees about the state of the ministry. I dreaded having to get up and admit to those people what a horrible job I'd done. Our executive director had compiled a year-end report from the heads of the various departments that I needed to read before the meeting, but that was the last thing I wanted to do. I figured the whole thing would be a disaster. So, I didn't open it until the night before the board meeting.

About midnight, I dragged it out and forced myself to go over it. With every page, I got more excited. "Gloria, come here and look at this! This has been the best year this ministry has ever had, and I didn't know it. Every department has been in debt-free operation overflow...except the television department."

Right then, the word of The LORD came to me so strongly, it almost knocked me out of my chair. He said, *Yes, every department in this ministry has had the best year ever—all but the one you carried the care of yourself. Your department is failing. You'd better get out from under the care of it and let Me have it.*

"Lord, forgive me!" I exclaimed. "I have sinned, and I repent and receive my forgiveness for it." Then I grabbed Gloria's hand and we started praying. After we finished, I wrote down on a piece of paper: *Lord, in the Name of Jesus I roll the care of this television bill and all the TV finances over on You. I'll never as long as I live write an appeal letter. I don't beg people for money. I sow seed and I believe You, and I'm not carrying the care of this anymore. From this moment on, I refuse it in my thought life.*

I put the time and date on it, then Gloria and I both signed it.

After that, every time the thought of that debt came to mind, I cast it out of my thinking. I opened my mouth and said, "That's not my care. I've given it to Jesus." At the end of two weeks, it only came to mind a couple of times a day. At the end of three weeks, someone had to mention it for me to even remember that $6 million bill.

Three months later, it was paid in full. Why? Because I wasn't carrying the care of it anymore. Jesus had picked it up.

## Two Systems of Finance

"Yeah, but you're a preacher," someone might say. "You have special faith to believe God for money like that. You don't have to get out in the world and work for a living like I do."

I'm no different than anyone else when it comes to believing God for money. I don't have some kind of special faith equipment. I do have a revelation, though, about how God intends for believers to conduct our financial affairs: He doesn't want us going out in the

world and working for a living. It doesn't matter what our voca-
tion is—whether we're called to be a preacher, a pilot, or a public-
school teacher—we don't have any business depending on this
fallen world's system for our support. In the kingdom of God it's
THE BLESSING of The LORD that makes rich, and He adds no
sorrow with it.[207]

There is a vast difference between living by faith in THE
BLESSING (which I call the Eden way) and the world's system of
finance. The world's system is rooted in the curse. It came into being
after Adam turned his back on THE BLESSING and God said to him:

> Cursed is the ground for thy sake; in sorrow shalt thou eat of
> it all the days of thy life; thorns also and thistles shall it bring
> forth to thee; and thou shalt eat the herb of the field; in the
> sweat of thy face shalt thou eat bread… (Genesis 3:17-19).

When Adam heard those words, they came as a heartbreaking shock to him because he wasn't created to spend his life
looking for food. He was created for a much more glorious
purpose. He'd been given the worldwide assignment of BLESS-
ING the whole earth and expanding the Garden of Eden until
it filled the planet. Along with that assignment, God had given
him "every herb bearing seed, which is upon the face of all the
earth, and every tree, in the which is the fruit of a tree yielding
seed; to…be for meat."[208]

Adam didn't have to worry about going hungry. Food was all
around him. THE BLESSING had created a garden full of it. He
didn't have to earn it. He just received it and enjoyed it. When he
lost THE BLESSING through sin, however, that changed. Adam
had to forget his worldwide mission for God and focus on his own
provision. He never got out of his own backyard because he spent
his life trying to keep food on the table and clothes on his back. He
had to toil and sweat for a living because he was under the curse.

---

[207] Proverbs 10:22
[208] Genesis 1:29

After Adam died, Noah's sons Ham and Japheth came up with their own way of dealing with that curse. Turning their backs on THE BLESSING God had declared over their father after the Flood, they followed in Adam's footsteps and departed from God's way of doing things. Instead of obeying Him and trusting THE BLESSING to prosper them, they invented their own system of commerce which became the fend-for-yourself, dog-eat-dog, lie-cheat-and-steal economy we see in the world today.

In that system, people attempt to meet their own needs without God. They believe that to be BLESSED they must be rich, so they spend their lives struggling to make money. According to Psalm 73:12, "These are the ungodly, who prosper in the world; they increase in riches." Notice, that verse says *they* increase in riches. Rather than looking to God to prosper them, they devise ways to increase themselves.

I call that system of commerce the Babylonian system because it made its scriptural debut at the tower of Babel—and it is divinely destined to fail. To find that out, all you have to do is look at the first people who operated in it. Unlike most people today, they actually understood God's way of doing things. They knew His method of creating is to *imagine it, believe it and speak it.* There was just one catch: They figured that method would work with or without God, and they decided to use it without Him.

And they said…let us build us a city and a tower, whose top may reach unto heaven; and let us make us a name, lest we be scattered abroad upon the face of the whole earth. And The LORD came down to see the city and the tower, which the children of men builded. And The LORD said, Behold, the people is one, and they have all one language; and this they begin to do: and now nothing will be restrained from them, which they have imagined to do. Go to, let us go down, and there confound their language, that they may not understand one another's speech. So The LORD scattered them abroad from thence upon the face of all the earth: and they left off to build the city (Genesis 11:4-8).

What God did at Babel went far beyond confusing the tower-builders' speech patterns. He spoke confusion into their godless way of operating. He put a cap on their ability to imagine and convey to others the pictures in their minds. Their communication with one another fell apart to the point where they couldn't figure out what to do anymore, so they had to wander away, leaving a half-built tower as a monument to their failure.

From that day to this, the same thing has happened to every group of ungodly, disobedient people that has tried to use its own human power to create and sustain its earthly kingdoms. These groups have been able only to build their towers, cities, nations and economies to a certain point before confusion has set in and things have started to crumble.

It has happened before and will happen again. Babel is simply set up to fail.

Believers, however, are not. God has delivered us out of that ungodly system. The problem is, historically, the Church hasn't been altogether sure of that. Believers haven't totally trusted THE BLESSING, so they've tried to combine God's way with Babel's way. As a result, they've gotten on the wrong financial path. They have become financially disoriented and confused.

Confusion creates disorder in the mind. It comes into our lives when we try to blend the ways of God with the ways of the world, and the result is disaster! Proverbs 14:12 says it this way: "There is a way which seemeth right unto a man, but the end thereof are the ways of death."

Confused believers make bad decisions. They do things that seem right and logical in the eyes of the world, without realizing those things cut them off from THE BLESSING and open the door to the curse in their lives. When the economy gets tough, for example, they quit tithing. They listen to their worldly friends say, "Tithe? You can't be wasting your money like that right now. You'd better hang on to it. Don't you know you're about to lose everything?"

By mixing the world's perspective into their thinking, they lose sight of the fact that tithing is the best thing anyone can do when money gets tight. Tithing keeps the door open to God's promises of provision. That's why Malachi 3:10-11 says:

> Bring ye all the tithes into the storehouse, that there may be meat in mine house, and prove me now herewith, saith The LORD of hosts, if I will not open you the windows of heaven, and pour you out a BLESSING, that there shall not be room enough to receive it. And I will rebuke the devourer for your sakes, and he shall not destroy the fruits of your ground; neither shall your vine cast her fruit before the time in the field, saith The LORD of hosts.

The tither is the last one to lose his job—and if he does lose it, God always has a better one waiting somewhere else. Talk about financial security. The tither is the only one who truly has it!

Why can't the world see that?

They're confused. They've been confused ever since the tower of Babel because God scrambled their imaginations there. Although that was thousands of years ago, to this day, the unsaved person or the carnally minded Christian cannot control his imagination.

I didn't say they can't *use* their imaginations. They just have difficulty controlling them. They see themselves losing their jobs, their homes, their health and their lives before they're 50 years old. They worry and meditate on those kinds of imaginations until they believe them and then they say it, and say it, and worry, and say it some more, until those imaginations come to pass.

Then they cry, "Why do these kinds of things always happen to me?" Then, once they're finished crying, they get back up and start running after money again, trying somehow to get BLESSED.

Jesus called that system *mammon,* and bluntly said:

> No man can serve two masters: for either he will hate the

one, and love the other; or else he will hold to the one, and despise the other. Ye cannot serve God and mammon (Matthew 6:24).

No true believer would purposely serve the world's god of mammon. Yet, when we worry about finances and struggle to meet our own needs, that's exactly what we're doing. We are binding ourselves to the world's sorrow-ridden system with all its shortcomings. In that system, we work harder...and harder...and still fall behind. If we do find a way to get ahead, we pay a high price for it by sacrificing time in God's WORD, our family relationships or our health. While the figures in our bankbooks tell us we're getting richer, in reality we're becoming poorer.

That's the way the world's economic system works. One way or another, there's always sorrow with it because it's under the curse. As believers, however, we are no longer under that curse! Jesus has redeemed us from it. We don't have to earn a living with our sweat and toil. THE BLESSING makes us rich.

Unlike the world, we aren't BLESSED because we're rich, we are rich because we're BLESSED! We have the glorious privilege of simply trusting God and doing what Jesus tells us to do in verses 26-33:

Behold the fowls of the air: for they sow not, neither do they reap, nor gather into barns; yet your heavenly Father feedeth them. Are ye not much better than they? Which of you by taking thought can add one cubit unto his stature? And why take ye thought for raiment? Consider the lilies of the field, how they grow; they toil not, neither do they spin: And yet I say unto you, That even Solomon in all his glory was not arrayed like one of these. Wherefore, if God so clothe the grass of the field, which today is, and tomorrow is cast into the oven, shall he not much more clothe you, O ye of little faith? Therefore take no thought, saying, What shall we eat? or, What shall we drink? or, Wherewithal shall we be clothed?

(For after all these things do the Gentiles seek:) for your heavenly Father knoweth that ye have need of all these things. But seek ye first the kingdom of God, and his righteousness; and all these things shall be added unto you.

"Brother Copeland, surely you aren't saying because I'm a Christian, I don't have to work anymore!"

No, I'm not saying you don't have to work. I'm saying you don't have to work *for a living.* You don't have any more business sweating and toiling to earn your money than Adam did before the Fall. Making money is not your job. That's the job of THE BLESS-ING. Your job is to seek the kingdom of God. Your job is to report to your heavenly Father every day and say, "Father, I'm here to receive Your assignment. What would You like me to do for You today? I am at Your service."

I can tell you from The WORD and from experience, if you'll do that, God will keep you busy. (He's kept Gloria and me running as fast as we can go for more than 40 years now.) I can also tell you that He will pay you far more than you could ever earn. He'll not only meet your needs, He'll satisfy your wants.[209] He'll make "all grace abound toward you; that ye always having all sufficiency in all things, may abound to every good work."[210]

The fact that God says He'll fulfill our wants and desires scares some people. They're afraid to believe it because they think it will make them materialistic. But materialism isn't defined by having material goods. If it were, God wouldn't have said He gives us richly all *things* to enjoy.[211] Materialism is trying to satisfy spiritual needs with material goods. It's saying, "I just have to have that new car or I won't be happy." That's not only materialistic, it's covetous and wrong.

There is nothing at all wrong, however, with believing God for a new car. He delights in giving us such things. He just wants us to

---

[209] Psalm 23:1: "The LORD is my shepherd; I shall not want."
[210] 2 Corinthians 9:8
[211] 1 Timothy 6:17

go about getting it His way and not the world's way. He wants us to roll the care of it over on Him and say, "Lord, I've sown my seed and I know exactly what the car I'd like to have looks like. I'm trusting You to get it to me in due season. In the meantime, I'm going to wash this BLESSED car I'm driving now and keep thanking You for it. It's been a BLESSING, and I appreciate it."

That's a sweet way to increase! You get up every morning thinking, *What is God going to do for me today?* Every time the phone rings, you think, *This is it! God is about to BLESS me again!* I've been living this way for decades now. It still excites me when the phone rings because I'm always expecting.

### Back to the Eden Way

It's impossible to have that kind of fun when you are working for a living. What's more, no matter how hard you work, you can't earn the kind of wealth THE BLESSING brings. Yet, believers by the millions still try to do it. Despite the clear teaching in God's WORD that He is the One who causes us to prosper, they cling to the conviction that they must earn a living because it is so ingrained in them, it's hard to shake.

I wrestled with it myself for a long time. But The LORD finally freed me from it by directing me to Romans 4:3-4:

> Abraham believed God, and it was counted unto him for righteousness. Now to him that worketh is the reward not reckoned of grace, but of debt.

One day while reading those verses, The LORD pointed out to me that any part of THE BLESSING we try to earn is not by grace. Then He asked me a question: *Kenneth, is it possible to earn the new birth?*

"Of course not," I answered. "We could never work hard enough to earn salvation. Working for it just gets in the way. The new birth can only be received by faith through grace."

*Is it possible to earn healing?* He continued.

"No, divine healing is a gift of grace that was purchased for us by the stripes of Jesus. We can't earn it. Like the new birth, it must be received by simple faith."

*What about the Baptism in the Holy Spirit?*

"The same thing is true there. People struggled and tried to be good enough to earn the Baptism in the Holy Spirit for years and found it didn't work. They discovered that, like every other part of THE BLESSING, it is received by faith through grace."

*Kenneth, if you didn't earn your salvation; and you didn't earn your healing; and you didn't earn the Baptism in the Holy Spirit, why do you think you could earn your prosperity?*

For me, that settled the issue forever. I saw with absolute clarity that just as Jesus was made sin for us so we could be made righteous, just as He bore our sicknesses on the cross so we could be healed, He became poor for our sakes, so we, through His poverty, might be rich.[212] No believer who will put faith in the fullness of what The LORD has done for us will ever have to toil for a living again.

Jesus has restored the Eden way. Because He has given us back THE BLESSING, we can leave the world's stinking mammon-mentality behind and stop trying to meet our own needs. We can get busy with our Garden of Eden assignment and start enjoying THE BLESSING that goes with it. We can spend our lives doing the will of our Father and being a BLESSING everywhere He sends us. If He sends us to a school to work as a janitor, we can do it, not to earn a living, but because God has assigned us to take His kingdom to that place. We can bring the glory and power of God there—and do a first-rate job of sweeping the floors and washing the windows while we're at it.

"But, I couldn't make ends meet on a janitor's salary!" someone might say.

Who said anything about living on a janitor's salary? Don't expect to live on it. Expect to give on it! Act on the instructions in Ephesians 4:28: "Let him that stole steal no more: but rather let

---

[212] 2 Corinthians 8:9

him labour, working with his hands the thing which is good, that he may have to give to him that needeth."

Use the janitorial income to minister financial BLESSED to someone. Invest it in the kingdom of God. The Bible says when you do that, The LORD Jesus, your heavenly High Priest, will multiply and increase the fruits of it until you are "enriched in every thing to all bountifulness."[213] A janitor who is enriched in everything to all bountifulness isn't a poor man. He's a rich man. He can have a jet if he wants one.

"Why would a janitor want a jet?"

It depends on what he does on his weekends! I know a farmer who decided years ago that he wanted an airplane so he could fly all over the place and preach the gospel when he wasn't working his farm. God gave it to him and it enabled him to BLESS so many people that his preaching finally took over his farming. Now he flies around preaching full time.

Even if you're not called to preach, God wants to do the same kind of thing for you. He wants to BLESS you beyond your wildest dreams in every way, including financially. He can get the job done, too, in any economy. He can multiply your resources when every economic indicator says it can't be done. He can bring you supernatural increase in the most unlikely situations.

Jesus proved that one morning on the Sea of Galilee. After preaching from Peter's boat, Jesus told him to, "Launch out into the deep, and let down your nets for a draught."[214] Talk about unlikely conditions for increase! Every good fisherman knows you can't catch fish with a net in the daytime. What's more, Peter and his partners had been fishing all night and caught nothing. There just weren't any fish to be found. So when the sun came up, they gave up, washed their nets (a tough job) and prepared to go home.

Peter was Jewish—the seed of Abraham, heir of THE BLESSING. But he didn't realize what belonged to him and didn't understand that Jesus wanted to BLESS him. He still had a toiling mentality, so

---

[213] 2 Corinthians 9:11
[214] Luke 5:4

he answered Jesus, "Master, we have toiled all the night, and have taken nothing: nevertheless at thy word I will let down the net."[215]

It didn't even occur to Peter that he was about to be BLESSED. Because of his mentality, all he could think about was how much work it would be to wash those nets again and what an exercise in futility it was going to be. But Peter honored Jesus' spiritual status, though to him it was obvious Jesus knew nothing about the fishing business. So, he did his religious duty, but did the least he possibly could. He cast out an old, rotten net, thinking that after he hauled it back in—empty, no doubt—he wouldn't bother washing it again.

Bad choice.

That's the problem with a toiling mindset. It blinds you to God's BLESSING. If you're still living under the work-for-a-living, curse mentality, your BLESSING can be staring you in the face, and you'll miss it. Even when you're trying to be respectful of God's WORD, you will make bad decisions right in Jesus' presence.

That's what Peter did. He went fishing with Jesus, assuming he wasn't going to catch anything, put out one rotten net, and when the fish started piling into it, it broke. He'd left all his good nets on the shore. So he had to call to his partners in the other ship to come and help. "And they came, and filled both the ships, so that they began to sink."[216]

We usually think about that as a miracle. But actually it was just THE BLESSING in operation. Fish run away from toil, but they run toward THE BLESSING! And since THE BLESSING was on Jesus, they jumped into Peter's net even when the sun was shining.

The same BLESSING is on believers today, and it will work for us anytime, anywhere just as it did in Peter's day. THE BLESS-ING doesn't care what the economic conditions are. It doesn't care if the stock market is up, down or sideways or if the prognostica-tors are proclaiming recession or depression. It just keeps on work-ing, making us rich and adding no sorrow with it.

If we'll put faith in that BLESSING and enter God's rest, we can

[215] Verse 5
[216] Verse 7

stop worrying about finances once and for all. We can give up working for a living and just report to our heavenly Father for our assignment every day. We can get up every morning and say, "Praise God, my financial fish are coming in faster than I can string them. I'm on my way to a boat-sinking load of abundance. I am BLESSED!"

### Sit Down...Saying!

We've already discussed the importance of the confession of faith, but it bears repeating. If you want to live in God's rest, you must continually declare The WORD. You can't just sit there and be silent. Faith talks! So hold fast to your confession of faith.

Sit down, saying The WORD of God about your situation and nothing else. Sit down with praise on your lips and declare, "The LORD is my refuge and my fortress, my God, in Him will I trust. I have a Father, and He is God. He is my strength and my overflowing power. He is the sustainer of my life. I don't fear when I walk through the dark valley because my God is with me, and He is the biggest One in the valley. I don't have a care in the world because He cares for me!"

I know it's not always easy to say those things. When bad news of some kind is screaming at you or your body is in pain, the last thing your flesh wants to do is say something good. It would much rather talk about how horrible things are and how sick you feel. But don't yield to it. Instead, sit down in the secret place of the Most High right next to Jesus and keep speaking The WORD.

The LORD helped me do that a few years ago when I was in so much pain I literally couldn't see straight. I'd had degenerative joint disease for some time, without knowing it. When I went to the doctor to find out what the problem was, I hurt so badly that sometimes my vision would blur and go in and out. The MRI they ran on me showed that one disc in my spine had exploded and there were hernias in several of the others. The transverse (crosscut) view of my vertebrae showed a big spot where the bone had degenerated.

Medically, the prognosis was bad. The doctor said there was no way to get rid of the disease and the best I could do was try to control it. I wasn't about to believe that report because it was contrary to The WORD of God. So, right away I began saying, "I am redeemed from the curse."

In the natural, my body didn't feel the least bit redeemed. In fact, a few days after I began making that faith declaration, I was lying on my face feeling as if someone had stabbed me in the back. I've never hurt like that in my life. On the MRI I'd seen where a big chunk of the blown disc had wedged itself down into the nerve canal, so I knew what was causing the pain.

While I was lying there, the word of The LORD came to me. He said, *You will overcome this.* I took Him at His Word and just kept laboring to enter His rest. I went to work increasing my confession of The WORD. I must have said it thousands of times. "THE BLESSING is working in me. THE BLESSING of Abraham has come on me through Christ Jesus. That BLESSING is driving this curse out of my body."

I said it every morning. I said it all during the day. I'd drive down the highway saying, "I'm BLESSED coming in and I'm BLESSED going out. My bones are fat just like The WORD of God says they are." I said it so much and prayed in the spirit over it so much and shouted about it so much that I learned how to be grateful to God by faith, even in the midst of the pain. I even got to the point where I'd wake myself up at night saying out loud, "THE BLESSING is working in me now. It is purifying my bones and bringing health to them."

After about 18 months, I had another MRI and it showed the once blown-up disc was back in place, standing up like it's supposed to be. There were no hernias in any other discs in my back and no sign of any degenerative joint disease in my body. Every trace of it was gone!

What happened?

I sat down, *saying!* I sat down, speaking THE BLESSING, and that BLESSING released and intensely applied, did its job. It drove that curse out of my body, and I am a healthy man today.

## Sit Down Trusting Your Faithful High Priest

> Wherefore in all things it behooved him to be made like unto his brethren, that he might be a merciful and faithful high priest in things pertaining to God, to make reconciliation for the sins of the people (Hebrews 2:17).

The last thing I have to say about sitting down is this: Do it, trusting that Jesus has done His job as your High Priest. Do it, believing He has reconciled you 100 percent to God, and there is nothing between you and Him but perfect love and perfect peace.

It doesn't matter how many times you may have missed it. It doesn't matter how much you might have messed things up in the past. If you've repented, all that bad stuff has been washed away by the blood of Jesus. God hasn't just forgiven you, He has forgotten every sin you've ever committed. He has wiped it out of His mind forever. You are as innocent in His eyes as a newborn baby.

A friend got hold of that revelation when he was in prison. He was there for good reason. He had committed the crime he was serving time for and as far as the United States legal system was concerned, he was guilty. He admitted it. But when he began to see what Jesus his High Priest had done for him, he began walking around saying, "I'm an innocent man. I'm innocent, and I'm getting out of this place. Innocent people don't belong in prison."

The people around him laughed at him. They said, "Do you realize they'd have to change the state laws for you to be eligible for parole in any less than three years? Even when you are eligible, after what you did, they're not going to let you out. You're going to be in this joint for three years, plus!"

Instead of believing that and getting upset about it, he just sat down with Jesus and trusted His high-priestly ministry. He kept saying, "I'm innocent. I don't belong in here."

Some of the other inmates got so mad about it they wanted to kill him. The officers mocked him. It didn't make any difference to him. He just stuck with The WORD and said, "I plead the blood. I'm an innocent man."

Before long, an article came out in the newspaper. The legislature, during a special session, had changed the law, which made him eligible for parole. In less than a year, he was released as a free man.

One scripture that reveals how completely innocent God's children truly are in His sight is Isaiah 43:25: "I, even I, am he that blotteth out thy transgressions for mine own sake, and will not remember thy sins." One time while meditating on that verse, I began thinking about why it's phrased that way. "Lord," I said, "it seems to me You blotted out our transgression for our sake. Why would You say You did it for Your own sake? What do You get out of it?"

Immediately, His answer came leaping back at me. He said, *Do you want to remember bad things about your children?*

"No," I said.

*Neither do I.*

After He straightened me out about that, I looked at the next verse. It says: "Put me in remembrance: let us plead together: declare thou, that thou mayest be justified."[217]

"Lord, what are we supposed to put You in remembrance of?" I asked.

*Kenneth, I've blotted your transgressions out of My mind,* He said. *They are gone. I am offering you a blank page in My memory. Now, you fill it up with what you want Me to remember about you.*

It didn't take me long to respond. I shouted right away as loud as I could, "I'm BLESSED! I'm BLESSED! Thank You for not forgetting that, Lord!"

That's what you should be saying to Him, too. You don't want to go to the throne of grace, sit down with Jesus, and start reminding Him of all the ways you've missed it over the years. You don't want to say, "Oh, God! I'm just a sorry, no-good failure. I've been trying to do better, but I miss it more often than not. I know You

---

[217] Verse 26

must be ashamed of me. I'm so sorry...."

Why would you want Him to remember that kind of garbage?

"Yeah, but I've sinned and haven't repented about it yet."

Then repent right now and move on, trusting Jesus to be faithful and just.

For Him to not blot out your transgressions from His memory would be unjust. It would be unmerciful. He would have to violate the Scripture and break His promise to God. He would never do that, and you know it. So take Him at His WORD and shed your old religious, unworthy sin mentality. Throw off those old garments of unworthiness, and put on your robe of righteousness. You're not an old sinner anymore. You've been saved by grace. Now you're a king and a priest with a seat next to Royalty Himself.

You can enter unashamedly into the secret place of God's rest because the Scripture says He is not ashamed to call us His brethren.[218] You can sit down next to Him like you belong there. You can trust Him to greet you with a smile on His face, saying, "Come on in. I have your enemies on the run. You just sit here with Me, and I'll make them your footstool."

Take Him up on that invitation! Sit down and enter into the rest of God. Let THE BLESSING go to work in you, on you, around you and through you. Every time you leave the house, go on assignment for God, taking THE BLESSING and the conditions of Eden with you wherever you go.

That's what I do. I may only be going to the grocery store, but I go expecting to bring THE BLESSING. That makes it an adventure as far as I'm concerned.

You'll be amazed at the kind of things that will happen to you if you'll start living that way. Gloria and I were walking across the parking lot of a discount store one day, about to go shopping, when a car roared up next to us and stopped. A lady jumped out of the front seat and shouted, "Brother Copeland! The LORD told me you'd be here. I'm a schoolteacher. Some

---

[218] Hebrews 2:11

businessmen are trying to take my house away from me. I've been believing God to take care of the situation and this morning when I was praying, the Holy Spirit told me that you'd be here and I should ask you to pray for me."

Gloria and I were happy to pray for the lady, but before we did, I asked her to tell more about the situation. She said, "I only owe $9,000 on my home, but somehow they've got me in a legal mess and they are foreclosing on it. I don't owe them anything but they're doing it anyway."

"That doesn't sound right to me," I said. Apparently, it didn't seem right to The LORD either because when we began to talk to Him about it, He said to me, *You handle this for her.*

When I got home, I called the ministry and talked to some people in our legal department. I gave them her name and said, "Pay the $9,000 that's left on that lady's mortgage and get those people out of her way."

That's what I call a fun shopping trip—going to buy things at the discount store and ending up paying off some dear believer's house. That's THE BLESSING in action!

If you're just getting started in this, you may not yet be at the place financially where you can do that, but start where you are. BLESS people with your loving attitude. BLESS them with your smile. Buy someone's lunch.

All the while, just keep putting your faith in THE BLESSING. Keep expecting it to increase you. Meditate on it and act on it until the reality of it revolutionizes your thinking, fuels your faith and sends you soaring into the heights of God's will for your life. Stay with it until, like the true seed of Abraham that you are in Christ Jesus, you become a BLESSING to all the families of the earth!

# Prayer for Salvation and Baptism in the Holy Spirit

*Heavenly Father, I come to You in the Name of Jesus. Your Word says, "Whosoever shall call on the name of the Lord shall be saved" (Acts 2:21). I am calling on You. I pray and ask Jesus to come into my heart and be Lord over my life according to Romans 10:9-10: "If thou shalt confess with thy mouth the Lord Jesus, and shalt believe in thine heart that God hath raised him from the dead, thou shalt be saved. For with the heart man believeth unto righteousness; and with the mouth confession is made unto salvation." I do that now. I confess that Jesus is Lord, and I believe in my heart that God raised Him from the dead.*

*I am now reborn! I am a Christian—a child of Almighty God! I am saved! You also said in Your Word, "If ye then, being evil, know how to give good gifts unto your children: HOW MUCH MORE shall your heavenly Father give the Holy Spirit to them that ask him?" (Luke 11:13). I'm also asking You to fill me with the Holy Spirit. Holy Spirit, rise up within me as I praise God. I fully expect to speak with other tongues as You give me the utterance (Acts 2:4). In Jesus' Name. Amen!*

Begin to praise God for filling you with the Holy Spirit. Speak those words and syllables you receive—not in your own language, but the language given to you by the Holy Spirit. You have to use your own voice. God will not force you to speak. Don't be concerned with how it sounds. It is a heavenly language!

Continue with the blessing God has given you and pray in the spirit every day.

You are a born-again, Spirit-filled believer. You'll never be the same!

Find a good church that boldly preaches God's Word and obeys it. Become part of a church family who will love and care for you as you love and care for them.

We need to be connected to each other. It increases our strength in God. It's God's plan for us.

Make it a habit to watch the *Believer's Voice of Victory* television broadcast and become a doer of the Word, who is blessed in his doing (James 1:22-25).

# THE
# BLESSING
## OF THE LORD

MAKES RICH AND HE ADDS NO SORROW WITH IT
PROVERBS 10:22

KENNETH COPELAND

# THE
# BLESSING
## OF THE
# LORD

MAKES RICH
AND HE ADDS
NO SORROW
WITH IT

PROVERBS 10:22

# STUDY GUIDE

Living in THE BLESSING is God's will for you!

In this companion study guide, you're sure to gain a clear understanding of this revelation and experience everything God has for you.

Discover God's original plan for your life as you complete the detailed questions and meditate on the discussion topics taken from THE BLESSING book, chapter by chapter. Plus, there's plenty of room to write what God is speaking directly to *you*—allowing you to create an action plan for taking hold of THE BLESSING in your life.

This study guide is ideal for pastors, Bible study leaders, families or individuals who desire to experience the fullness of THE BLESSING.

Your blessed life of peace and joy awaits…*success is guaranteed!*

## World Offices
## Kenneth Copeland Ministries

For more information about KCM and our products, please write to the office nearest you:

### Kenneth Copeland Ministries
Fort Worth, TX  76192-0001

**Kenneth Copeland**
Locked Bag 2600
Mansfield Delivery Centre
QUEENSLAND 4122
AUSTRALIA

**Kenneth Copeland**
Private Bag X 909
FONTAINEBLEAU
2032
REPUBLIC OF SOUTH AFRICA

**Kenneth Copeland Ministries**
Post Office Box 84
L'VIV  79000
UKRAINE

**Kenneth Copeland**
Post Office Box 15
BATH
BA1  3XN
U.K.

**Kenneth Copeland**
PO Box 3111 STN LCD 1
Langley BC  V3A 4R3
CANADA

**Kenneth Copeland Ministries**
**Singapore Ltd.**
Rochor Post Office
Locked Bag Service No. 1
Singapore  911884

# We're Here for You!

Join Kenneth and Gloria Copeland and the *Believer's Voice of Victory* broadcasts Monday through Friday and on Sunday each week, and learn how faith in God's Word can take your life from ordinary to extraordinary.

You can catch the *Believer's Voice of Victory* broadcast on your local, cable or satellite channels.* And it's also available 24 hours a day by webcast at BVOV.TV.

Enjoy inspired teaching and encouragement from Kenneth and Gloria Copeland and guest ministers each month in the *Believer's Voice of Victory* magazine. Also included are real-life testimonies of God's miraculous power and divine intervention in the lives of people just like you!

To receive a FREE subscription to
*Believer's Voice of Victory,* write to:
Kenneth Copeland Ministries
Fort Worth, TX 76192-0001
Or call: 800-600-7395
Or visit: **www.kcm.org**

If you are writing from outside the U.S., please contact the KCM office nearest you. Addresses for all Kenneth Copeland Ministries offices are listed on the previous page.

* Check your local listings for times and stations in your area.